P9-DFG-044

World Tapestry

World Tapestry

From Its Origins to the Present

by

Madeleine Jarry

G.P. Putnam's Sons • New York

Cover:

The Triumphs of Petrarch • THE TRIUMPH OF LOVE • Early sixteenth century. Vienna. Kunsthistorisches Museum. Photo E. Meyer.

Iconographic documentation: Dominique Bergès and Marie-Thérèse May.

Layout: Martin Altenburger and Brigitte Luriau.

Originally published in France 1968 under the title *La Tapisserie*.

 Published on the same day in the Dominion of Canada by Longmans Canada Limited, Toronto.

Library of Congress Catalog Card Number: 68-22257.

Printed in France.

Contents

	Tapestry as an important art	7
I	The origins of tapestry	9
II	Europe in the fourteenth century	29
III	The Arras and Tournai workshops in the fifteenth century	51
IV	Tapestry at the dawn of the Renaissance	95
V	The sixteenth century : tapestry during the Renaissance	137
VI	The seventeenth century : from Rubens to Le Brun	185
VII	French workshops in the eighteenth century	227
VIII	Tapestry outside of France in the seventeenth and eighteenth centuries	253
IX	Tapestry in the nineteenth and twentieth centuries : decline and revival	299
	Technique	343
	Bibliography	349
	Catalogue of tapestries reproduced	355

Tapestry as an important art

apestry is one of the simplest and oldest techniques of textile art. Known since antiquity not only in Egypt but also in Asia and Pre-Columbian America, it developed independently in each of these areas. The purpose of this book is not to linger over the tapestry remnants that have come down to us, those pieces of garments or of wall hangings that have survived the ravages of time, but rather to present tapestry as an important creative expression and to show the great achievements which, during the course of centuries, have made it a major art form throughout the world.

We shall examine the different factories and their productions, as well as the achievements of the weavers, many of whose names are familiar although their history is still incomplete. We will emphasize the problems of "tapestry style" often by comparing the art of tapestry with the inseparable art of painting. The distance between them, however, is considerable, for there is a basic difference between tapestry, which is a manual craft subject to a model, and painting, which enjoys complete creative freedom. Tapestry, one might say, loses a certain spontaneity, yet other characteristics which distinguish it from painting contribute to its richness and provide it with immense artistic resources.

Tapestry is a collective art and can be compared to the performance of a symphony, the composer being the cartoon painter and the weavers the musicians. Thus, in transposing a painted cartoon into a woven work, the weaver, who is both artisan and artist, must call upon all his skill, his years of training and even his own personality to capture every nuance of the tapestry design as first created by the painter of the cartoon.

During the Middle Ages tapestry was a "useful art." Hangings not only adorned the walls of royal and princely residences but also those of churches; "chambers of tapestries" were effective insulation against draughts. But the fundamental purpose of tapestry was to cover a large surface and offer the possibility of monumental decoration. This force of expression which set mural tapestry on the level of great art was understood by every prince enamored of beauty. In 1377, for example, the Duc d'Anjou ordered Nicolas Bataille to execute the Angers APOCALYPSE *to illustrate the text of the revelation of St. John. Ten years later Philip the Bold, desiring to commemorate the victory of his father-in-law Louis de Mâle over the rebellious Flemings, commissioned Michel Bernard of Arras to create the huge tapestry of* THE BATTLE OF ROOSEBEKE. *Since then the looms of Europe have produced innumerable tapestries to celebrate great deeds and conquests. Only one outstanding example among many is* THE STORY OF THE KING *which was woven at the Gobelins factory after the cartoons of Charles Le Brun on order of Louis XIV.*

Even in the early nineteenth century, when the fine art of tapestry almost ceased to be understood, Napoleon ordered the Gobelins to begin a HISTORY OF THE EMPIRE. *Thus we see that in every period tapestry was considered a work of sumptuous and original art.*

During the last century tapestry lost its role of major importance, but today, after an eclipse of more than a hundred years, thanks to the joint efforts of cartoon painters and weavers it has once again become a "total art."

Tapestry, however, is a slow art, requiring infinite patience. As a result, when compared to such rapid arts as painting, its style often tends to lag behind current artistic modes by several years.

I The origins of tapestry

Antiquity. - Coptic tapestries - Peruvian tapestries. - Chinese silk tapestry: the "k'o-ssu." - Relations between East and West during antiquity and the High Middle Ages. - The development of tapestry in the West before the fourteenth century.

APESTRY was known on the banks of the Nile almost two thousand years before the Christian era, although it is likely that the art had been practiced in other adjoining civilizations before then. At a later date tapestry was made in Western Asia and Greece and was also produced in Pre-Columbian Peru as well as in China during the T'ang period. Our information about tapestry in those remote times is based largely on written descriptions or on paintings and sculptures depicting the art, for actual textile fragments are rare although some Egyptian specimens, from royal tombs, date from 1483 B.C. Coptic and Peruvian tapestries which have survived are small in size. The most ancient large-scale mural tapestry decorated with figures is probably a Chinese tapestry dating from the eighth century, which is now in the Taïmadera Temple in Japan. The hanging from the church of St. Gereon at Cologne, probably made in that city at the close of the eleventh century, is no doubt the oldest example of tapestry woven in Europe in the Middle Ages.

Antiquity

At the dawn of history the Egyptians practiced the art of decorating fabrics either by means of embroidery or by weaving. Wall paintings preserved in burial vaults depict looms which are similar to those later used in the West. More concrete evidence is at hand in the pieces of fabric found in the tombs of Amenophis II and of Tutankhamen which prove that the technique of tapestry was known as early as the XVIII Dynasty.

Tapestry was also very popular among the Babylonians for many centuries before the Christian era. We have no documentary evidence of this

PRAYING FIGURES AND CROSS. Fragment of a Coptic Tapestry. 0.75 × 1.06 m. Egypt, 11th century.

This fragment represents the corner of a large tapestry with a green background. A band at right angles, in the upper section, is adorned with Nereids on a yellow background. Above this band, wearing loincloths, are dancers who alternate with horsemen. In the center, two praying figures, wearing dalmatic dress, frame the upper part of a cross, itself surmounted by a Coptic cross.

Paris. Collection Ch. Ratton. Photo Hachette.

FISH. Fragment of a Coptic tapestry. 0.33 × 0.44 m. Egypt, 2nd or 3rd century.
This fragment, found at Antinoë in the excavations made by A. Gayet (1898-1906), *shows fish swimming against a green background. Their shadows are represented as in certain Roman paintings or mosaics. The Lyons Musée historique des tissus contains a fragment of a similar tapestry.*
Paris. Louvre. Photo Hachette.

period, but ancient writers were unanimous in their praise of the superb quality of tapestries woven at both Babylon and Nineveh. In fact, the words for Babylonian tapestry, *babylonica peristremata*, were often used by Latin poets, who mentioned them with great praise.

Numerous texts indicate that tapestry was commonly used in Greece. Although these references were often beautifully worded, the descriptions lack precision, and we are therefore uncertain whether this was true tapestry woven on a loom, or embroidery. Among the most famous of these references in Greek poetry of the Heroic Age is to the loom on which Penelope, besieged by suitors as she awaited the return of Ulysses, wove a shroud during the day only to unravel her work each night.

In Rome tapestry had certain characteristics indicating foreign importation and almost all the terms applied to the technique were of Greek origin. During the Imperial period, tapestries were frequently used not only in public edifices but also in palaces and private villas. In his *Metamorphoses* Ovid related the competition between Minerva and Arachne and gave a precise description of their looms which are similar to those of the present day: "Both set up their looms and stretched the warp upon them. Then they went to work... The goddess in a fury of anger slit the web from top to bottom and beat the girl on the head with her shuttle.

"Arachne... mortified and furiously angry, hanged herself."

Coptic tapestries

The Coptic weavers, whose tapestries have often been called the "Gobelins of Egypt," produced outstanding work, examples of which are among the oldest tapestries to have survived. Coptic art lies between that of Pharaonic Egypt and Muslim Egypt, between the third and seventh centuries A.D., although this date has been extended by some authorities to the twelfth century, since the Arab conquest of Egypt in 640 did not check the progress of the Coptic tradition in tapestry. The Arabs used the word "Copht" or "Copt" merely to designate the inhabitants along the Nile, but the history of the Copts can be identified with that of Christianity in Egypt.

About the middle of the third century a revolution occurred in the manners and mores of Romanized Egyptian society. Many innovations were introduced, among them the mummification and the burial of the dead in garments richly decorated with woven bands or squares. Alongside such garments there have also been discovered in the tombs at Saqqara, Achim and Antinoe hangings and cushion fragments executed in a technique similar to that of the Gobelins. The method for producing tapestry might have been based on an ancient Egyptian tradition, yet the use of wool for the weft dates only from the Hellenistic period of Egyptian art. There is a difference of thickness between the warp of linen and the weft of wool, the thicker warp of linen disappearing beneath the wool with its fine, tight threads. The invention of this technique is attributed to the Syrians, who were past masters in the art of dyeing woolen threads in various colors and especially famous for their purple dyes. The lack of documentation makes it difficult to give precise dates for the duration of this Coptic preeminence in tapestry, and archæologists often fail to agree. However, the researches made during recent years by Père du Bourguet revealed the main features of the stylistic development from the art of Hellenistic spirit dating from the third and fourth centuries down to the introduction of Islamic forms beginning with the Arab conquest of Egypt and lasting until the twelfth century.

The Coptic tapestries that appear to be the most ancient are decorated squares (Hermitage, Leningrad) representing the god Nile and the goddess Gea treated in a very naturalistic style similar to that of the mosaic portraits at Antioch. To achieve a modeling effect, gradation and hatching techniques were used. The same comments might be applied to the pieces of the Fish which are divided between the Louvre and the Musée des Tissus at Lyons. These were followed by other tapestries in which the naturalistic elements were replaced by an increased stylization of the motifs inspired both by Byzantine

Medallion with Horsemen. Coptic work. 0.18 × 0.20 m. Egypt, 5th-6th century.
Two horsemen turning in their saddles and shooting an arrow are represented on a scarlet background. They are designed above superimposed animals, also placed back to back. The influence of the Sassanian style is obvious.
Lyons. Musée historique des Tissus. Photo Photographic Archives.

SQUARE WITH NEREIDS. Coptic work. 0.30 × 0.30 m. Egypt, 6th century.
This piece of tapestry was found at Antinoë during the Clédat excavations, 1909-1910. *In the center is the portrait of a woman with a crowned head set in a nimbus. The rest of the decorations consist of Nereids and fish.* Paris. Louvre. Photo Hachette.

art and that of Persia. From Greece the Copts borrowed such subjects as famous dancers, musicians and naiads from the Dyonisiac mysteries, often weaving them in purple wool that approached violet brown in shade so that they stand out vividly against the background of the warp. Such purple tapestries were an attempt to imitate those works woven with gold threads, *vestes pictae aurum intextae*, mentioned in texts by Pliny, a rare example of which is now in the National Museum at Budapest. The VIMINACIUM TAPESTRY has been the subject of a study by Mme. Agnès Geijer who has dated it as from the third century.

Although the Copts borrowed freely from the Greeks, it is to Sassanian Persia that we are indebted for the heraldic stylization of certain themes such as knights confronting each other which are represented in very rich colors. This development of style follows the introduction of a special technique: the use of several shuttles of weft threads in addition to the first to delineate clearly the outlines of the subjects represented and to limit them in relation to one another. The hatching method was eliminated. In these tapestries there was no attempt at modeling. The weaver juxtaposed flat surfaces of color.

The second half of the tenth century witnessed the efflorescence of a style that permitted an even greater stylization of the subject. The figures were treated more heavily, and their attitudes and features took on a stiffness that finally became stereotyped. As one critic wrote, they look as though they had been "eaten by the large eyes which tend to form a square." The colors in these tapestries blaze forth and are distributed in such a way as to obtain mass effects, the background and subject put into sharp contrast by the use of two or more totally unrelated colors.

The Muslim conquest cut off relations with Byzantium, which was the great source of Christian art. Despite the severe Islamic law against the use of images, Coptic art continued under the Tulunid dynasty (868-905) and that of the Fatimids (968-1171). The Titaz looms specialized in narrow silk bands often representing inscriptions woven in linen fabrics. At Fayum the weavers showed greater freedom in scenes with figures and animals. Nevertheless, art developed towards pure decoration which was more important for the arrangement of the masses of color than for the subjects represented. The rich chromatic quality of these tapestries is in fact often surprising.

Most of the works which have survived are generally small, consisting of narrow and large bands and square patches woven on robes. But in addition we have pieces of mural tapestry executed in the Gobelins technique, in kinked fabrics or even in embroidery. A large piece dating from the fourth or fifth centuries (Textile Museum, Washington, D. C.) is decorated with two superimposed columns of a pediment on which two birds are perched, while within the frame, in a regular pattern of checks to create the illusion of a garden trellis, we see other birds and grapes. The large tapestries in the Musées royaux d'Art et d'Histoire of Brussels and the Abegg-Stiflung of Berne, woven after the Arab Conquest, depict stiff figures in hieratic attitudes; the colors are still glowing and warm. Other tapestries are decorated with a series of large pink flowers often alternating with parrots to create a distinct decorative effect. The PRAYING FIGURES AND CROSS in the Ratton Collection, a late example dating from the eleventh century, is decorated in the center with a band at right angles, foreshadowing the concept of a border to enclose the central subject. The figures—dancers and knights—are grossly distorted in a way curiously reminiscent of those in Peruvian fabrics. These Coptic tapestries are of exceptional interest for the history of Western tapestry since they offer tangible examples of a richly conceived and executed art that forms a link between ancient and Western medieval art. There is no doubt that the technique of the Coptic weavers left its mark on the Christian West.

PERUVIAN TAPESTRY. Fragment detail. Dimensions of the fragment, 0.405 × 0.30 m. End of the Chimu period (900-1400).

The major part of the design consists of zigzag stripes of two colors each, decorated with "T" motifs. The colors are dark brown, white, olive green, purple, blackish brown, yellow and dark pink.

Boston Museum of Fine Arts. Museum photo.

Peruvian tapestries

Of all the peoples who inhabited America before the arrival of Columbus, the ancient Peruvians were the most skillful weavers. Along the hundreds of miles of sand that form the Peruvian coast, fabrics in remarkably good condition have been discovered in moisture-free tombs where several generations had buried their dead. Owing to this exceptionally dry climate, comparable to that of Egypt, the garments in which the dead were buried have been preserved in excellent condition. Ancient chronicles and scenes painted on vases reveal that weaving and spinning were generally done by women, whose great manual skill compensated for the crudeness of their tools. Their looms consisted of scarcely more than the two parallel slats between which they warped. One of these slats was held by a cord to a beam or rafter, while the other was connected to the weaver by a strap which passed at the level of her back in such a way that a mere movement of the body, forward or backward, was enough to diminish or increase the tension of the warp threads. This elementary loom had neither rollers nor pedals, yet the weavers were so expert

PERUVIAN TAPESTRY. Fragment. 0.715 × 0.41 m. End of the Chimu period (900-1400).
The yellow background is decorated with stylized birds of various colors, arranged in parallel rows. The border is adorned with animals which are probably monkeys.
Boston Museum of Fine Arts. Museum photo.

PERUVIAN TAPESTRY. Fragment detail from Pachacamac.
This detail represents stylized pumas.
Collection d'Harcourt. Photo by courtesy of Editions Morancé, Paris.

that they developed a great number of techniques, especially what is generally referred to as the "Gobelins" process. The textile material was excellent. In addition to cotton and plant fibers, Peruvian weavers used the silklike wool of the domesticated llama and alpaca as well as the even finer wool of the wild vicuña and guanaco. These woolen and cotton threads consisting of one or several strands, often double, were given a strong torsion and dyed in colors that arouse admiration for their vibrant beauty.

Archæologists agree on the existence of a great artistic culture in the regions of Nazca and the Paracas Peninsula in the south and of Chimu in the north, the origins of which date from about the Christian era. The flowering of this culture began in about the sixth century. From that time, the increasing influence of a civilization arising in the Tiahuanaco region, south of Lake Titicaca, appears to have spread to the far north, from the coast to Quito. After the decline of this style, the old Nazca and Chimu styles enjoyed a renascence until the establishment of the Incan domination (eleventh to sixteenth centuries). Peruvian tapestries are extremely fine, certain pieces having sixty to a hundred *duites* to the centimeter. The motifs represented have lively patterns which create a characteristic angular decoration far removed from the rounded forms found in Coptic works. Tapestry was used either for narrow bands to decorate the lower part of the garment or to cover the entire surface of an *uncu*, the Indian shirt consisting of a piece of rectangular fabric with an opening in the center for the head. Other pieces are from tapestries used to decorate the walls of dwellings. After the Spanish Conquest, the art of tapestry enjoyed a new efflorescence.

In the coastal region (Lima, the necropolises of Ancon, Chancay, Pachacamo and Cajamarquilla), we find many representations of animals. Birds, cats and foxes as well as tribal chiefs wearing rich garments with opulent headdresses and warriors carrying arms are all treated with a strong sense of realism. Farther south at Pisco, Paracas, Ica and

Nazca, we find scenes with symbolical subjects, usually groups of fantastic beings represented with emphasized stylization. These decorative motifs often acquired strange forms which are reduced to an abstraction similar to that found in contemporary art.

K'o-ssu. Fragment. Width 0.178 m. China, Southern Sung period (1127-1279). Silk.

This k'o-ssu *comes from the cover of the painting entitled* The Instructions of the Adviser to the Ladies of the Palace, *which is attributed to the painter Ku-Kai-tche (Tang or early Sung period). We cannot determine the date when this* k'o-ssu *was attached to the painting. This tapestry represents peonies and snowballs on a blue background.* British Museum. Museum photo.

◀ Tapestry Braid or K'o-ssu. Detail. Dimension of the fragment, 0.46 × 0.026 m. The height of the medallion in the shape of a flower is 0.034 m. China, about the 9th century. Woven in silk.

This braid was part of fabrics found by Pelliot in the early 20th century during excavation at Touen-Houang. The white background is decorated with yellow, green, red, orange, mauve, pink and blue ornaments.

Paris. Musée Guiment. Photo Hachette.

Chinese silk tapestry : the k'o-ssu

The art of growing silkworms and weaving silken fabrics originated in China. Tapestry technique dates from a very remote period, but various specialists in the Occident and China believe that silk tapestry or *k'o-ssu* developed during the T'ang period (seventh to tenth centuries). In his commentary on a *k'o-ssu* decorated with peonies, the scholar Chang Hi-tche, who lived during the Ming period (fourteenth to seventeenth centuries), wrote that this art was in great favor during the reigns of T'sitong and Ming-Huang. In the region of the oasis of Turkestan in Central Asia, Van le Coq discovered the remains of silk tapestries dating from the eighth century. Stein and Peillot believe that the *k'o-ssu* pieces which they found in the grottoes of the Thousand Buddhas at Touen-houang date from the close of the T'ang period. But Schuyler Camman is of the opinion that they were woven by the Ouigdurs who occupied this region from 847 to 1031.

It appears very probable, however, that the Chinese were familiar with tapestry well before the eighth century. Pauline Simmons points out that the most ancient Chinese mural tapestry is the one now in Japan, in the Taimadera Temple near Nara. This large work measures more than four square yards; it was woven in silk in one stretch and dates from the eighth century. It has been restored and heightened by painting a number of times. The subject is taken from the story told by Shan Tao (631-681), a priest who lived during the T'ang period, and represents in the center of the composition the Buddha Amida in the decoration of the Palace of Paradise. The perfection of the weaving shows that the *k'o-ssu* technique had been practiced for a very long time.

The word *k'o-ssu* was written in various ways. Today it means "broken threads," indicating the interruption of the weft where one color changes to another. In fact, these threads end at the edge of the colored spaces instead of running over the entire width of the fabric; openings or slits known in the Gobelins technique as *relais* appear between the colors. Thus the Gobelins and Chinese weaving methods are quite similar except that the Chinese executed tapestries whose warp and weft were entirely of silk. The artist used a brush to finish off certain details, but this practice was always considered an expedient scarcely to be recommended.

The delicacy achieved in this work is remarkable. During the Sung period (960-1279) the imperial families encouraged painting and patronized the art of tapestry; an important weaving center flourished at Ting-tcheou (Hopei). The great weaving masters were Tchou K'o-jeou, Tchen Tsoufan, Wou Hiu, Wou To and Tchou Sing-tong. It is often said that their remarkable work exceeded in beauty the paintings they had copied. An ancient text states that Tchou K'o-jeou's skill in manipulating the silk threads was comparable to that of the great painters handling a brush.

Much used to decorate official garments, the *k'o-ssu* was regarded by the Chinese as the most precious fabric. It was also used in purely decorative panels and occasionally to cover artistic or literary documents. In his book on the tapestries of the Sung dynasty, J.-P. Dubosc included the reproduction of five *k'o-ssu* of a special style which he dates from the northern Sung period (early twelfth century). All include bird motifs (ducks, peacocks, barnacle geese, parrots, phoenixes) against a flower background usually consisting of peonies. The colors used are purple, green, yellow, two different tones of blue and two of white. As Dubosc points out, the general effect recalls the incised and molded decorations of the white Tings of the Sung period.

The most important *k'o-ssu* collection in China, other than the one in the palace at Peking, was that of Tchou K'i K'ien, who sold it to the Mukden National Museum. In 1934 he wrote a detailed two-volume catalogue for the museum in which he recorded that for the Sung period alone he owned twenty-one *k'o-ssu* specimens. Two of these include the woven signature of the celebrated Tchou K'o-jeou.

During the Yüan period (1279-1368) a government factory was established at Hangchow. One of the characteristics of Yüan weaving is the frequent use of gold and silver threads.

Relations between East and West during Antiquity and the High Middle Ages

Even during antiquity relations existed between East and West and there was a considerable trade in luxury goods. In fact, China began to export her silk fabrics at a very early date. Excavation work has revealed that these relations existed as early as the third century B.C. with other Asiatic countries and at the beginning of the Christian era with the countries of the Mediterranean area.

The Persian court was one of the principal clients of Chinese merchants and often served as their intermediary. Prior to the fourth century the Persians

THE SAINT GEREON TAPESTRY. Fragment detail. 0.73 × 0.73 m. Cologne, late 11th century.
This tapestry was discovered in the church of Saint Gereon; pieces are now divided between the Musée des tissus at Lyons and the Germanisches National Museum in Nuremberg. The décor, consisting of medallions in which a griffin is fighting an ox, was inspired by a Byzantine or Syrian silk model. The border ornamentation reveals a relationship with illustrations of certain 11th-century German gospel-books.
Nuremberg. Germanisches National Museum. Museum photo.

Christ and the Apostles. Detail representing Christ. Ensemble dimensions 1.20 × 9 m. Lower Saxony, last quarter of the 12th century.

According to tradition, this tapestry was woven in the convent of Quedlimburg by the abbess Agnes. The theme is related to the Last Judgment. Here Christ is represented as Judge of the World, enthroned in a mandorla. The style is linked to that of Ottonian miniatures.

Halberstadt Cathedral. Courtesy of the Domgemeindekirchenrat.

Abraham and the Archangel Michael. 1.10 × 10.26 m. Lower Saxony, mid-12th century.
According to tradition, this tapestry was also woven by the abbess Agnes in the convent of Quedlimburg. The story of the patriarch Abraham is represented in four scenes, in addition to that of the archangel Michael,

who is fighting the dragon. The development of the action is followed, scene by scene, by long inscriptions. Formerly the ensemble was framed by a geometrical ornament similar to a Greek fret, of which a part remains, on the right.
Halberstadt Cathedral. Courtesy of the Domgemeindekirchenrat.

Charlemagne and the Philosophers. Convent of Quedlimburg, Lower Saxony, late 12th century. *This tapestry has been shortened by about one-fifth of its height. Charlemagne is shown on his throne in a diamond-shaped frame. Four ancient philosophers are represented in the corners of the tapestry. The intention was the glorification of Charlemagne, who founded the Halberstatd bishopric and was the benefactor of the cathedral. The tapestry is similar in style to that of* The Wedding of Mercury and Philosophy, *woven at Quedlimburg, about the same period, in the knotty technique.*
Halberstadt Cathedral. Courtesy of the Domgemeindekirchenrat.

established workshops in Syria whose looms produced tapestries for both the Roman empire and Iran. The archæol' ogist Pfister furnished reproductions of fabric pieces discovered at Palmyra and Dura-Europos which are presented as reps and reveal that the so-called Gobelins technique was known as early as the second century. Sir Aurel Stein discovered at Leo Lan in Eastern Turkestan numerous silk specimens of Chinese origin and very fine woolen tapestries with Hellenistic characteristics though some could well be Chinese. These relics probably date from the first century of the Christian era, but this cannot be affirmed. It appears that in Europe proper the direct influence of China was not felt until long after the Islamic conquests when the prestige of the once great Persian empire had been forgotten and when Europeans traveled to the Far East and returned with silk fabrics. Although it is true that trade existed in every period, the lack of historical documentation makes it difficult to ascertain beyond dispute the precise country of origin and the date of manufacture of much of the Eastern tapestry from before the fourteenth century.

The development of tapestry in the West before the fourteenth century

During the Crusades, the Christians marveled at the embroidered fabrics and precious silks they saw in those countries which had been converted to Islam. The booty they brought back probably included tapestries although the technique of tapestry was undoubtedly known in France before this period. The existence of tapestry is mentioned as early as the close of the eighth century, but no piece dating from the High Middle Ages has survived. Nevertheless, we possess numerous documents which describe the tapestries decorated with human figures hanging in churches and convents, especially on feast days. The terms used to describe them—*tapetia*, *aulea*, *dorsalia*, *bancalia*, *pallia*—are not precise and relate to various types of hangings which could be embroidered as well as woven. The famous QUEEN MATILDA TAPESTRY at Bayeux is actually an embroidered hanging.

In spite of the reservations of a few historians, it is believed that the most ancient example of a mural tapestry woven in Europe is a work from the Church of St. Gereon at Cologne, now divided between the Musée des Tissus at Lyons, the Germanisches Museum in Nuremberg and the Victoria and Albert Museum in London. Probably executed at Cologne at the close of the eleventh century, the tapestry's decoration consists of a series of circular motifs in which are inscribed groups representing a griffon destroying a bull; the border forms a series of stylized lion masks joined by ribbons. The manner of placing spots of color (red and green) in a crude mosaic and the clumsy treatment of the curves reveal a scarcely developed weaving technique. Yet this is an important work, for it forms a link between Byzantine art and Romanesque forms. Its very decoration with repeated motifs emphasizes the close relations which then existed between a silk fabric and a real mural tapestry.

The achievement of the three sets of tapestries of the cathedral of Halberstadt is attributed to a monastic workshop established on the banks of the Rhine. The historical sources are lacking. Judging by their stylistic character, these works date from the close of the twelfth century and the

beginning of the thirteenth. The TAPESTRY OF THE ANGELS contains depictions of the Three Angels, Abraham and the sacrifice of Isaac, and St. Michael slaying the dragon. The TAPESTRY OF THE APOSTLES represents Christ in his mandorla borne by angels, surrounded by the twelve Apostles. The third is CHARLEMAGNE SURROUNDED BY THE FOUR PHILOSOPHERS OF ANTIQUITY. The first two hangings are long and narrow (the first 1.3 yards high and 11.18 yards long, the second 1.24 yards high and 9.76 yards long) and were meant for the cathedral choir, to be hung above the stalls. The general style is that of illuminated manuscripts, that is, great stylization of modeling and systematic use of lines to indicate the form of the figures, the objects and the folds of the garments. At the close of the Romanesque period, this linear art, seen not only in tapestries but also in frescoes, was to terminate in the excesses of the *zackbrüchig* or serrated style.

The TAPESTRY OF CHARLEMAGNE is a vertical work whose composition and style are closely related to painting. It can be compared to eleventh-century illuminated manuscripts such as the *Bible of St. Calixtus* in St. Paul-Beyond-the-Walls. Here we see a definite attempt at modeling and a concern to characterize the different types represented by the philosophers in contrast to Charlemagne. This work has been related to another hanging in the cathedral of Quedlinburg, executed in a knotted technique, representing THE MARRIAGE OF MERCURY AND PHILOSOPHY from the *Satyricon* by Marcianus Capella, a late Latin writer.

The Oslo Museum of Decorative Arts contains a Romanesque tapestry which was discovered at Baldishol, in Hedmark, part of a set symbolizing THE TWELVE MONTHS. Its style recalls that of the Bayeux tapestry woven shortly after the battle of Hastings in 1066. The Oslo tapestry was doubtless woven in Norway during the first half of the thirteenth century. Its weaving peculiarities were to remain characteristic of Norwegian tapestry and, in general, that of Northern Europe, namely, a very strong geometric stylization, a certain irregularity of the outlines at the limit of a color, lively tonalities and great wealth of decoration, filling up not only the background but the garments of the figures who appear against the background of the tapestry as well.

THE MONTHS. Detail representing April. The entire tapestry measures 1.20 × 2 m. Norway, first half of the 12th century.
This tapestry, from a church in Hedmark, is, from a stylistic view, related to the tapestry of Queen Mathilda, embroidered after the Battle of Hastings in 1066 *(Bayeux Museum).*
Oslo. Kunstindustrimuseet. Museum photo.

II Europe in the fourteenth century

The Paris workshops. - The Angers "Apocalypse." - "The Nine Heroes" and "The Presentation in the Temple." - The Arras workshops. - German tapestry.

HE second half of the fourteenth century marked the beginning of the most important period for the art of European tapestry. Henceforth weaving was to be concentrated in the provinces of Central and Northern France as well as in Flanders. For centuries Paris, Arras, Tournai and Brussels were to play a leading role in this field of art and the rest of Europe acquired the habit of turning to these organized workshops. Some 150 or 200 years later, Italy, Spain, England and even Germany, which had practiced the art of tapestry since the Middle Ages, were to have recourse to Flemish and French weavers to help them establish workshops in their own countries. The fourteenth-century works which have survived are of rare perfection; the most famous one, the Angers APOCALYPSE, woven in Paris for Duke Louis of Anjou, has been called the "Sistine Chapel of Wool."

The Paris workshops

At the close of the thirteenth century Paris was an important center of textile industries. In his *Book of Trades (Livre des Métiers)*, Étienne Boileau mentioned not only counterpointers but also silk spinners, chain-purse makers, embroiderers, *tapissiers sarrasinois* (1277) and *tapissiers nostrez* or Parisian tapestry workers (1295).

In 1302 the provost Pierre Le Jumeau included in the guild of the *tapissiers sarrasinois* "another tapestry method known as high-warp workers." These were ten in number. Documents reveal that the rather restricted production was limited to tapestries for daily use such as horse saddles, sacks, cushions, bench or bed covers as well as large hangings with heraldic designed or repeated decoration, chiefly leaves and plant motifs. It was not until about 1360 that certain Parisian documents mentioned for the first time the presence of tapestries with historical subjects.

Paris was then the intellectual capital of the West and the setting was favorable to every artistic activity. Under Charles V (1364-1380) the art of tapestry prospered. The inventory made during the final years of his reign (about 1379-1380) reveals how eagerly the king sought for precious tapestries with little concern about whether they were woven in a French or Flemish workshop.

In addition to innumerable "shaggy carpets" *(tapis velus)*, there is mention of more than one hundred and thirty armorial tapestries, as well as thirty-three large hangings, each comprising several pieces, kept in the Louvre palace and known as image tapestries *(tapis à images)*. Charles VI had the same taste as that of his father. In the French court other great lords such as the dukes of Anjou, Berry and Orléans ordered hangings. Meanwhile Philip the Bold (d. 1404), the first of the Burgundian patrons, acquired a number of tapestries for his furniture repository.

Three great names are associated with the history of tapestry during the final quarter of the fourteenth century: Nicolas Bataille, Jacques Dourdin and Pierre de Baumetz.

As a citizen of Paris, Nicolas Bataille was a manufacturer, a merchant and a middleman. Between 1387 and 1400, the approximate date of his death, he delivered some two hundred and fifty *tapisseries* and *tapis* of various values. As supplier to the royal family by appointment, he took service with Duke Louis of Anjou, for whom he had already undertaken commissions before 1373, and who made him *valet de chambre*. It was from Nicolas Bataille that the duke commissioned the famous Angers APOCALYPSE.

Jacques Dourdin (d. 1407) also represented the Parisian industry and by 1386 had produced a number of tapestries for the Duke of Burgundy. Dourdin joined Bataille in the weaving of the famous JOUTES DE SAINT-DENIS to commemorate the reception of the Duke of Orléans, brother of Charles VI, and of his cousin Duke Louis of Anjou, in the Order of Chivalry in 1389.

As for Pierre de Baumetz (d. 1412), although residing in Paris, his name is not included in the royal accounts. He appears to have been exclusively attached to the service of the Duke of Burgundy to whom he delivered not only hangings with religious or heroic subjects, including a HISTOIRE DE LA PASSION DE NOTRE-SEIGNEUR (1385) and a HISTOIRE DE BONNE RENOMMÉE (1389), but also works decorated in a more simple manner, tapestries with figures of knights and ladies or cushions like green fields scattered with white sheep under a gold-colored hawthorn tree.

The Angers Apocalypse

The finest fourteenth-century hanging is certainly the Angers APOCALYPSE. This monumental set was woven at Paris which was not only one of the most important production centers but also the leading tapestry market in Europe. Made for Duke Louis of Anjou (1339-1384), brother of Charles V, this set, commissioned from Nicolas Bataille, originally consisted of seven hangings, each about sixteen and a half feet high, and of lengths up to about eighty feet. Duke Louis showed great interest in this tapestry set. The designer was Jean de Bondolf, known as Jean or Hannequin of Bruges after his native city. He was Charles V's official painter, and like many other artists from Flanders during this period, he was active in Paris from 1368 to 1381. The

The Angers Apocalypse
GREAT PERSONAGE BENEATH A CANOPY
A similar figure, almost identical, is seen at the beginning of each piece. Wearing a turban and wrapped in a great cloak, he is seated beneath a high Gothic canopy; before him is a book lying open on a stand.
Angers. Musée des Tapisseries. Photo Hachette.

rival of Jean Pucelle, Hannequin of Bruges was among the most outstanding artists of his time and played an important role in the development of painting. His *Bible historiée*, dated 1371, had been offered by Jean de Vaudetar to Charles V.

As for the cartoons for the tapestry set, we know that Charles V had lent him a thirteenth-century *Apocalypse* (this is mentioned in an inventory made in 1380), but the painter turned for inspiration to other manuscripts dealing with the apocalyptic theme, many of them now in Paris, Namur and London libraries and notably in those of Cambrai and Metz. It is clear that no single manuscript can be said to be the true and unique source of the designs prepared by Hannequin of Bruges.

Can a precise date be given to the execution of the set of hangings? The duke's accounts mention payments to Hannequin of Bruges from 1375 to 1379 "for portraits and models made by him for the aforesaid *tapis* of the History of the Apocalypse." As for Nicolas Bataille, he was paid in 1377 and again in 1379 for the execution of two, then of three tapestries. The final date is uncertain and has been placed about 1380, the year Duke Louis became King of Sicily. In fact, alongside the cross of Anjou we do not yet see that of Jerusalem, the emblem of the duke's new kingdom.

During the entire Middle Ages the Apocalypse was a source of inspiration for painted and sculptured works. The men of that period were greatly attracted by the allegories related in the story of the vision of St. John which in the words of St. Augustine "contains the whole time which has elapsed since the ascension of Our Lord Jesus Christ until the end of the world." When we read the text established by Lejard in the translation made by Lemaistre de Sacy, in regard to each reproduction of the corresponding tapestry, we are surprised by the eminently suggestive power of these evocations which are veritable programs for a vast representation. A man of the Middle Ages like Duke Louis of Anjou was the first to be impressed by this. The text is certainly one of much beauty and poetry, but the images of the tapestry match it in scale and majesty. Like every prophecy, that of the Apostle John contains some obscurity and a first glance at the ensemble leaves us somewhat confused. It is clear that the number seven mentioned in the writings of the Evangelist symbolizes perfection. The number is used here intentionally with its series including seven broken seals, seven blasts on the trumpet, seven empty cups, seven plagues, seven victories. As to the identification of the seven important figures seated beneath a Gothic canopy, there has been no agreement. Some exegetes see in them the bishops, guardians of the Seven Churches of Asia. "Blessed is he that readeth, and they that hear the works of this prophecy, and keep those things which are written therein: for the time is at hand" (Revelation).

The ensemble originally consisted of about one hundred and five scenes; sixty-seven of these have been preserved, some intact, others in part. They were arranged in two rows and Gothic letters beneath each *tableau* explained the subject. These captions, however, have completely disappeared along with the band of ground once decorated with flowers, plants and animals; the bands of sky with their angels are more or less reduced in area.

The subjects as well as the style of the tapestries are related to illuminated manuscripts. The older tapestries represent figures against a solid background, alternatively red and blue,

he Angers Apocalypse
HE PROSTITUTE

he angel carries St. John away into the wilderness, here he sees the prostitute. "So he carried me vay in the spirit into the wilderness: and I saw a oman sit upon a scarlet coloured beast, full of ames of blasphemy, having seven heads and ten rns. And the woman was arrayed in purple and arlet colour, and decked with gold and precious ones and pearls, having a golden cup in her hand ll of abominations and filthiness of her forni-ation."

ngers. Musée des Tapisseries. Photo Hachette.

T. MICHAEL AND THE DRAGON

t. Michael and his angels fighting against the agon, who was cast into the earth. "And there as war in heaven: Michael and his angels fought ainst the dragon."

ngers. Musée des Tapisseries. Photo Hachette.

HE WOMAN AND THE SERPENT

And the serpent cast out of his mouth water as a ood (persecutions) after the woman, that he might use her to be carried away of the flood. And the rth helped the woman, and the earth opened her outh, and swallowed up the flood which the dragon st out of his mouth."

ngers. Musée des Tapisseries. Photo Hachette.

while the others have backgrounds filled with rare plants and stylized trees designed with a strong contour of which the forms, consisting of flat outlined surfaces stand out strongly. This powerful mode of expression is heightened by a range limited to some fifteen colors. The differences of background value are explained by the fact that the dyeing baths were prepared according to requirements. Today the strong colors, such as blue, red and green, have lost some of their quality, but the pleasant harmony remains with the other broken tones, browns and light gray, which also have faded.

The execution of the tapestry itself reveals not only great care but also a chaste quality. Even at this early date we seem to catch a glimpse of that law of French taste, the simplicity of this great art excluding extraneous effects and remaining faithful to fine craftsmanship. Although the style and iconography of the APOCALYPSE closely relate it to the art of illuminated manuscripts, the tapestry is in itself a monumental artistic expression. As long ago as 1400 the Arles bourgeois Bertrand Boisset wrote: "No one can relate or describe the value, the beauty and the nobility of these fabrics."

The Nine Heroes and The Presentation in the Temple

There remain only a very limited number of tapestries whose style can be compared to that of the APOCALYPSE. The principal set is that of THE NINE HEROES now exhibited at the Cloisters, a branch of New York's Metropolitan Museum of Art. Originally it consisted of three large hangings which were cut up and were long utilized as curtains in the Château de Martinvast, near Cherbourg.

Like the APOCALYPSE, the set of THE NINE HEROES is an illustration of a written text, that of a chivalric theme much appreciated by the nobility in the fourteenth century. It was a *jongleur* named Jacques de Longuyon who about 1310 popularized this *Histoire des Neuf Preux* (Story of the Nine Heroes) by adding to the *Roman d'Alexandre les Vœux du Paon*, a courtly poem relating the exploits of Porus, the bravest hero of former times. Imbued with the ideas of his period, Jacques de Longuyon was familiar with the symbolic value of the number three and the combination three times three. Thus, in order to identify his heroes, he chose three pagan ones (Hector, Alexander and Cæsar), three Hebrew ones (David, Joshua and Judas Maccabeus) and three Christian ones (King Arthur, Charlemagne and Godfrey de Bouillon). This theme of the Nine Heroes was often used in the Middle Ages to decorate works of art, not only tapestries but also statues, playing cards, manuscripts and stained-glass windows. As part of his table decoration Duke Jean de Berry had a *nef* decorated with "Nine Heroes" and to wash his hands during the meal a basin on which the heroes were represented in red enamel. Although we lack precise information, it is quite possible that the tapestry set in the Cloisters was executed for him, since on the piece representing the Hebrew heroes are banners bearing the duke's arms.

THE NINE HEROES presents similarities with the APOCALYPSE, notably in the weaving and coloring. Among the number of restricted colors, we find the same gray for the stone, the same tones of red which after centuries have turned pink and, above all, the same strong

The Angers Apocalypse
THE REVELATION OF ST. JOHN
The apostle is about to write to the seven churches in Asia to inform them of his visions. "John to the seven churches which are in Asia: Grace be unto you, and peace from him which is, and which was, and which is to come."
Angers. Musée des Tapisseries. Photo Hachette.

blue, at times so dark that it appears black, against which emerges the very clear design of the figures. We are also struck by similarities in the style of the figures, the treatment of the architectural decoration, the rendering of the butterflies and *rinceaux* which form the background decoration in both sets. James J. Rorimer, the late Director of the Metropolitan Museum of Art, believed that these two sets may have been woven under the same direction, and the name of Nicolas Bataille has been suggested. The Duke de Berry, as previously mentioned, was also a client of the famous Parisian merchant. As for the name of the painter who designed the cartoons, we lack factual information, but the style reveals the influence of André Beauneveu, whose role at the Duke de Berry's court was similar to that of the Superintendant des Beaux-Arts.

The Musées royaux d'Art et d'Histoire at Brussels has a piece of a third set closely related to this group of tapestries and entitled THE PRESENTATION IN THE TEMPLE. Style, coloring and technique have made this relationship possible although it is not confirmed by any text. This piece is too high to be an antependium as was formerly supposed, but on the bottom of the preserved tapestry, which is only a section of the original work, we find the remains of an angel's wing, thus enabling us to suppose that the complete tapestry was

The Angers Apocalypse
The angel carries St. John away into the wilderness, where he sees the prostitute. Detail.
Angers. Musée des Tapisseries. Photo Hachette.

(Overleaf)
THE PRESENTATION IN THE TEMPLE. 1.53 × 2.85 m. Paris, last quarter of the 14th century. ▶
The Virgin, in the center, presents her son standing on the altar to the aged Simeon. On the left are Joseph and a young woman, holding a candle. The style, color and technique relate this work to the Angers Apocalypse.
Brussels. Musées royaux d'Art et d'Histoire. Photo A.C.L.

40

The Nine Heroes
Paris, 14th century.

According to James J. Rorimer, this set of three tapestries was probably woven in the workshop of Nicolas Bataille about 1385 *for the duke, Jean de Berry. It illustrates a chivalrous theme highly appreciated by the nobility of the 14th century, that of the Nine Heroes, popularized by the* jongleur *Jacques de Longuyon in his* Vœux de Paon (1310). *A similar tapestry devoted to nine heroines probably belonged to the King of France, Charles VI. In bad condition, these pieces were acquired and repaired by the Metropolitan Museum of Art in* 1952.

King Arthur. Detail. The entire tapestry measures 3.04 × 3.51 m.
This detail represents the head of King Arthur against a background of Gothic architecture.
Metropolitan Museum of Art. The Cloisters Collections, Munsey Fund, 1932, and gift of John D. Rockefeller, Jr., 1947. Museum photo.

The Nine Heroes
DAVID AND JOSHUA
The two Hebrew heroes, Joshua on the left and David in the center (Judas Maccabaeus is not shown), are enthroned. By their height they dominate a host of courtiers and warriors placed around them beneath arcades. The upper section is adorned with small figures treated in a similar manner, including a woman playing the harp and an archer.
Metropolitan Museum of Art. The Cloisters Collection, Munsey Fund, 1932, and gift of John D. Rockefeller, Jr., Munsey Fund and George A. Douglas. Museum photo.

designed on two superimposed rows similar to the design of the APOCALYPSE. This may be a fragment of a set of LA VIE DE NOTRE-DAME for which the Duke of Anjou had paid Nicolas Bataille in 1379. It is an outstanding achievement if only for its graceful figures. On seeing the tapestry with its subtle expression of the twin significance of the presentation in the Temple, with its joy and pain, we are reminded of the striking words uttered by Simeon: "...Behold this child is set for the fall... and for a sign which shall be spoken against."

The Arras workshops

In the fourteenth century the Arras tapestry industry enjoyed an international fame comparable to that of the Gobelins in the seventeenth. Works of Arras origin were appreciated to such an extent that in Italy the word *arrazzo* and in Spain *drap de raz* were used to designate tapestry. A text dated 1313 contains the first mention of the term high-warp applied to an Arras work. A great vogue for high-warp tapestry soon sprang up among the wealthy bourgeois of that city. To understand the history of tapestry at Arras we must consider it in relation to the history of local trade, especially what the Florentines called "the art of wool."

Cloth weaving at Arras dates from the very origin of the international cloth trade. As early as the thirteenth century merchants dealing in Arras goods were to be found at every stage of the commercial route which extended from Flanders to the banks of the Mediterranean and it was they who prepared the way for others. During the course of centuries this preeminence increased and the cloth trade developed in other northern cities. When Brabant took the lead, the sale of cloth at Arras was reduced. As shrewd businessmen, accustomed to speculations and monopolies in the various branches of economic activity—wine, beer, cloth, weapons—the aristocracy and principal citizens of the town decided, with a view to counteracting the competition, to create a trade in luxury goods. The result was a splendid efflorescence of tapestries. This time quality won out over quantity and restored the town's commercial status.

Arras was also a notable artistic center. Although the school of illuminated manuscripts was then famous at Paris, a group of talented fresco artists were active at the Château d'Hesdin, the residence of the counts of Artois. The members of the great Arras export trade soon realized that tapestry could become for them a first-class source of wealth. Until the sixteenth century the "fine Arras thread" was to remain the highest woolen mark for high-warp tapestry. Conditions were ripe for such development; fashion intervened as well as a form of snobbery to the extent that the great lords had unbelievable reserves of tapestries. When the Duke of Burgundy displayed his tapestries in his Paris *hôtel*, he had them hung one above the other to the great admiration of his visitors.

The tapestry names familiar to us are those of middlemen entrusted with transactions, such as Mouchy, Boursette and Walois, members of the aristocracy, the *poorters* who, after paying painters and weavers, kept a certain profit added to the capital from wine and cloth in which they also traded.

By his marriage Philip the Bold

ST. MAURICE. Switzerland, first half of the 14th century.

This tapestry depicts St. Maurice in armor beneath a simplified trilobate arcade. He is surrounded by symbols of the four evangelists and eight other symbolical animals (only four of which are shown here) inscribed in medallions designed in two rows.

Thun. Historisches Museum. Museum photo.

became one of the most powerful princes of Christianity. This alliance between Burgundy and Flanders created close relations which were to have considerable influence on the development of art and industry in both countries. The duke bought a great number of tapestries for his own use and generously presented them as gifts to his friends.

In this manner he negotiated the freedom of the French nobles captured at the battle of Nicropolis by sending their captor rich tapestries with figures. It would indeed be tedious to list every hanging once in the possession of Philip the Bold. The state summary of the tapestries, historiated or with figures found in his château after his death, in 1404, include some seventy-five high-warp tapestries and the majority were to reappear in the inventories of his successors. Among these the famous BATTLE OF ROOSEBEKE, which no longer exists, had been woven by Michel Bernard of Arras in 1387, five years after the event it commemorates, the victory of Charles VI and Louis de Mâle, brother-in-law of Philip the Bold, over the rebellious Flemings. This gigantic piece measured about four thousand square feet. Difficult to handle and to raise, its weight soon led to its destruction. In 1402 Duke Philip decided to have it cut into three pieces, after which each of these was divided into two, but the result still proved too heavy. In this condition it figured for the last time in the inventory of the emperor Charles V, in 1536, where it is described as "very old and worn."

German tapestry

Until the fourteenth century, the Germanic countries lacked workshops comparable to those of Paris and Arras. Of this period we have only disseminated works and it is difficult to determine where they were woven. The chief source of information lies in the arms of their owners who are often portrayed. These weaving regions were found in the South at Lake Constance, in Northern Switzerland, Alsace and Franconia, countries which were to remain the great centers of fifteenth-century German tapestry. The spirit in which these tapestries were executed differed considerably from the works we have previously studied. They were not destined to be exported for some wealthy prince, but were executed in convents for personal needs or for use in neighboring convents. There were also itinerant masters whose clients were members of the clergy, aristocratic families or less important German lords.

Often rather long and not very high, these tapestries were woven on small looms and were used as antependia or as narrow bands of tapestry *(dosserets)* to adorn the backs of choir stalls and protect their occupants from draughts. They were used for similar requirements in private dwellings. Known as *Heidnischwerk-Tücher* (pagan tapestries), they are often listed in ancient inventories or in accounts of the representations with figures of that period. We will mention a few examples whose examination reveals the different artistic tendencies of the fourteenth century and which form a prelude to the art of fifteenth-century German tapestry. The TAPESTRIES WITH BIRDS in Fribourg and THE TAPESTRY OF ST. MAURICE in the Historisches Museum at Thun have repeated decorative motifs and clearly seem to have been directly inspired by Byzantine silk fabrics. But in the Thun tapestry we find a central compo-

LES JEUX. 1.60 × 3.94 m. Alsace, last quarter of the 14th century.
This large composition represents men and women enjoying social games. The landscape (architecture of castles and convents, a background of trees and flowers) is well designed. The elegant, graceful figures are treated in the "international style." On the right of the tapestry are the coats-of-arms of the Diehl de Spire family.
Nuremberg. Germanisches National Museum. Museum photo.

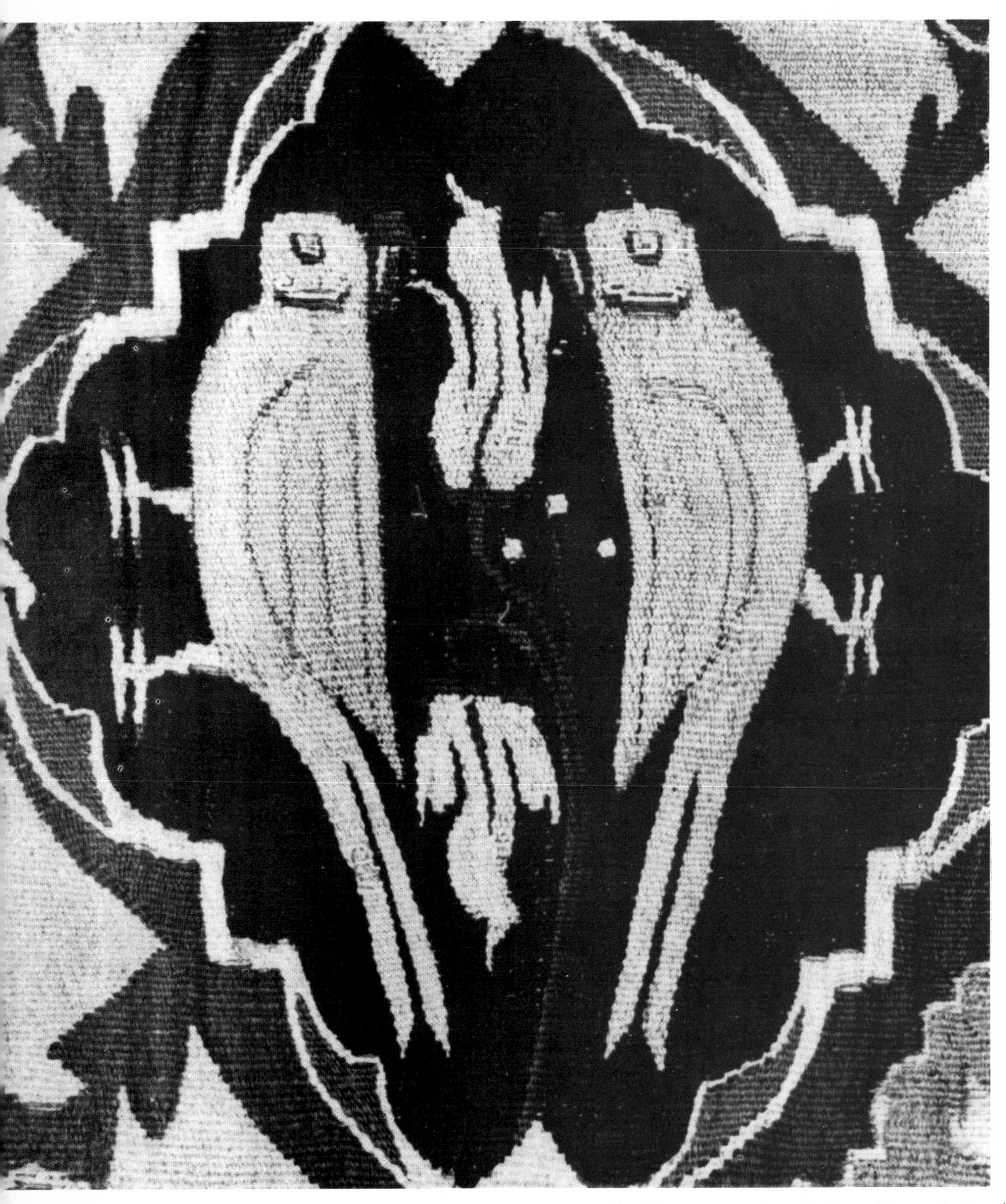

TAPESTRIES WITH BIRDS. Detail. Germany, first half of the 14th century.

This motif of birds arranged back to back seems to have been inspired by Byzantine silken fabrics.
Fribourg. Town collection. Photo H. Weber.

THE PROPHETS. 0.62 × 4.36 m. Franconia, late 14th century.

This tapestry was once in the church of St. Lawrence in Nuremberg. It represents a series of prophets in a banderole decor with inscriptions. The style of the figures bears comparison with that of the Bohemian School in the 14th century.

Nuremberg. Germanisches National Museum. Museum photo.

sition in relation to the figures of St. Maurice.

The finest and most representative work is no doubt the famous hanging of LES JEUX (GAMES) woven in Alsace at the close of the fourteenth century and now in the Germanisches National Museum in Nuremberg. This rich composition with numerous figures represents games played by a group of lords and ladies at the foot of the ramparts of a fortified town. The types of slender, slightly bent figures recall the international style which influenced both French painting and that of Northern Italy. This tapestry reveals certain peculiarities: a feeling for space with a notation of landscape ignored in earlier tapestries as well as a technique found only in Alsace—the faces are not woven but left to be subsequently embroidered.

From the same period we have THE TAPESTRY OF THE PROPHETS woven at Nuremberg for the church of St. Lorenz and now part of the collection of the Germanisches National Museum. This piece is not isolated but integrated into an entire ensemble of tapestries woven in this Franconia region in the early years of the fifteenth century. This time, however, we clearly see the influence of painting; the art of the Bohemian court had spread towards the South and West. The prophets with a very characteristic expression are shown in agitated attitudes and their large hands acquire unexpected importance. On glancing at these light figures which stand out against a dark blue background, we cannot help recalling the APOCALYPSE, the most famous tapestry of that century in the West.

III The Arras and Tournai workshops in the fifteenth century

Decline of the Paris workshops. - Predominance of the Arras workshops, then those of Tournai. - Patronage of the dukes of Burgundy and of great lords. - Sources of inspiration. - The cartoon painters. - Development of style in the Arras and Tournai productions until the death of Charles the Bold. - The close of the great Tournai period.

NTIL the middle of the fifteenth century the Arras workshops, which had superseded those of Paris, were very active and looms were set up in other woolen centers then at the height of their prosperity, cities such as Bruges, Douai, Ghent, Courtai, Lille and above all Tournai and Brussels. These last two soon eclipsed Arras in producing masterpieces which reveal the influence of the great painters of the Franco-Flemish school such as Campin, Van Eyck and Van der Weyden. With their monumental quality and decorative character, these tapestries rank among the finest and most astonishing that have ever been created.

Decline of the Paris workshops — Predominance of the Arras workshops, then those of Tournai

The prosperity of the Paris workshops lasted only a short time. The disorders created by the Hundred Years' War and above all the occupation of Paris by the English ruined the city. In 1422 Guiffrey noted that the tapestry guild included no more than two representatives. During the reign of Charles VII not a single tapestry was made at Paris for the king. In 1412 the weavers left to set up their looms at Lille and in the following year at Pau; 1419 saw them at Mantua and finally in 1455 they went to Rome.

This state of affairs was to prove advantageous to Arras, the great rival since the fourteenth century. In the first half of the fifteenth century, Arras supplied the House of Burgundy with tapestries. From 1423 to 1467 there were in fact no less than fifty-nine master tapestry artists in the Artois capital. The prosperity enjoyed by Arras lasted until the middle of the century, but political events along with customs regulations decreed by the dukes of Burgundy were seriously to affect the tapestry workshops. How-

The Story of St. Piat and St. Eleuthère
Arras, 1402.
This set originally consisted of two large tapestries, each composed of nine scenes with explanatory text; fourteen have been preserved.

PREDICATION SCENE. 1.86 × 2.82 m.
This scene depicts St. Piat in the pulpit addressing a group of converts consisting of members of the Irénée family, one of whom was Eleuthère's parent.
Tournai Cathedral. Photo A.C.L.

THE ANNUNCIATION. Arras (?), early 15th century.
This tapestry may have been woven after a cartoon by Broederlam. It was probably made for Philip the Good, who offered it to Martin V.
Detail of THE ANNUNCIATION representing the Virgin's hands.
Metropolitan Museum of Art. Gift of Harriett Barnes Pratt, 1949. Museum photo.

ever, the decline was gradual, for despite the consequences of the siege of 1477 by Louis XI's soldiers, the looms remained active until after 1528.

Simultaneous with the decline of Arras was the ascendancy of Tournai, the second great tapestry center in the Burgundian estates. After 1450 Tournai achieved considerable importance and retained this advantage until the close of the century. To distinguish between tapestries woven at Tournai and Arras is difficult, for we have little documentary evidence to prove that a tapestry was woven at one center rather than the other. Yet there is no doubt that THE STORY OF ST. PIAT AND ST. ELEUTHÈRE was woven at Arras in 1402 for the cathedral of Tournai. On the other hand, we know it was from the Tournai workshops of Robert Dary and Jean de L'Ortye that Philip the Good in 1449 commissioned the famous GIDEON set for the Order of the Golden Fleece; the cartoons were executed by the painter Bauduin de Bailleul. These

The Knight of the Swan. Tournai, mid-15th century.
THE KNIGHT ELIAS AND HIS BROTHERS
The scene represents Elias, son of King Oriens and Princess Beatrice, who was the sole person to retain his human form. He fed his brothers who were changed into swans.
Cracow. Wawel Castle. Photo Emil Rachwal.

two examples reveal the link between the two great tapestry centers and are evidence of their numerous relations during the Middle Ages. The art of weaving practiced at Tournai since the close of the thirteenth century developed to such an extent that in 1398 a regulation was published concerning its production. This is the oldest known ordinance to regulate the art of tapestry; it is also important for listing the names of the great merchant families who were in charge of their own workshops during the fourteenth century.

Patronage of the dukes of Burgundy and of great lords

During the long period when royal power was weakening in France, the House of Burgundy fostered the tradition of taste and magnificence. By the second half of the fourteenth century Philip the Bold had already proved himself a great patron. His son John the Fearless followed the tradition by commissioning from Ryfflard Flaymal THE BATTLE OF LIÈGE which was no doubt inspired by the huge BATTLE OF ROOSEBEKE woven by Michel Bernard of Arras for his father. The reign of Philip the Good proved to be a glorious one for the art of tapestry. Thanks to the inventory made at Dijon we know that as early as 1420 the duke had in his possession many splendid tapestries which then formed an unmatched ensemble. This collection was constantly enriched by personal orders. Jean Chevrot, Bishop of Tournai, president of Philip the Good's grand council and patron of the city's workshops, negotiated the duke's earliest orders such as the famous GIDEON set which no longer exists. Guillaume Fillastre, who succeeded the bishop in these duties, continued this policy. Monumental sets with figures, commissioned in Tournai, became the basis of the fame enjoyed by the city's workshops.

From 1450 to his death in 1493 Pasquier Grenier, at first a mere artisan, then middleman and finally merchant on a grand scale, was chiefly responsible for supplying the Burgundian court; but he also had clients in Bruges and Antwerp, the two most important Flemish cities. Among the surviving tapestries commissioned by the Burgundian court we are certain of two sest sold by Pasquier Grenier to Philip the Good. The first, in 1459, is THE STORY OF ALEXANDER, two hangings of which have been preserved and are now in the Palazzo Doria in Rome. The other, bought in 1462, is THE KNIGHT OF THE SWAN, destined for the Cardinal of Arras. (Originally the word *cygne* was misspelled in the ancient inventories to become *Chine* and this fact explains why the work was then known as THE KNIGHT OF CHINA.) One fragment of THE KNIGHT OF THE SWAN belongs to the Museum für angewandte Kunst in Vienna; a second and more important fragment is in the church of St. Catherine in Cracow.

Philip the Good did not house the major part of his tapestry collection, the upkeep of which necessitated no less than six guards aided by twelve servants, at Brussels, but, in 1440, he built a vaulted construction in his Hôtel d'Amboissenelle at Arras. Despite

The Passion. Arras (?), first quarter of the 15th century. Gold thread.
Second piece. CHRIST BEARING THE CROSS. THE CRUCIFIXION AND SCENES FROM THE GLORIOUS LIFE OF CHRIST. 4.15 × 8.15 m.
Cathedral of Saragossa. Tapestry Museum. Photo courtesy of the Perigrinaciones marianas Nuestra Señora del Pilar.

La Geste de Jourdain de Blaye
3.28 × 3.80. Arras (?), about 1390-1400.
This tapestry is probably the sole extant piece of a set illustrating the geste *(romance) of Jourdain de Blaye, a free adaptation of* Appolonius de Tyr, *which like other chivalrous romances enjoyed much success in the Middle Ages. The tapestry gives no indication of origin, although the Arras workshop is a likely source because of its similarity in style to the* Story of St. Piat and St. Éleuthère, *the sole set whose Arras origin is indisputable. This tapestry represents Fromont's visit to Girat; various episodes are explained in verse found in the upper part. The large figure standing apart appears to be that of the narrator.*
Padua. Museo Civico. Museum photo.

Hunting Tapestries
Bear and Beaver Hunt (detail) and Swan Hunt. 4.24 × 11.60 m.
Victoria and Albert Museum. Museum photo. Crown copyright.

the disorders which troubled his reign, Charles the Bold continued to grant the decorative arts the same patronage that had been shown by his father. In 1469 he ordered his *garde tapissier* Garnelot Pouclet to spread out all the hangings both at Arras and Lille and to make a new inventory. More than one precious hanging was added to the great collection in the châteaux in Burgundy and Flanders. In 1472 the *Vrije* of Bruges asked Pasquier Grenier for a set of The Trojan War to present as a gift to the duke. We know that some of these tapestries were part of the booty taken by the Swiss from the baggage of Charles the Bold after the disasters of Granson, Morat and Nancy. After these events and the death of Charles the Bold in 1477, Tournai ceased to produce work for the Burgundian court.

In addition to these commissions by the dukes of Burgundy we must mention those ordered by the French court. The Presentation of the Roses, now in the Metropolitan Museum of Art, was doubtless woven for Charles VII and perhaps for the Château of Loches. Among important ecclesiastical dignitaries who were great tapestry collectors were such men as Guillaume Fillastre, Abbot of Saint-Bertain at St. Omer, who presented the church of the same name with the set of hangings entitled The Old and New Testaments, certain fragments of which still exist at St. Omer. A set of Famous Women was owned by Ferry de Clugny, Bishop of Autun. Only fragments of this tapestry now remain.

Sources of inspiration — The cartoon painters

It is difficult to classify fifteenth-century Franco-Flemish tapestries, for it is almost impossible to determine the distinctive characteristic of each center. Despite the numerous studies devoted to this subject, the origin of many of the tapestries remains obscure and art historians differ in their opinions. Yet these fifteenth-century works are today among the most admired achievements in the art of tapestry. They correspond to contemporary taste by their fullness and also by a general impression of vigor. When we consider the number of such great tapestries, we cannot help but express our surprise and wonder how such huge works could have been woven. We must remember that the tapestries which still exist were originally part of a set or of *chambres*, as they were then called. Without borders, they were unrolled on the walls and, like frescoes, covered the entire surface. Their wealthy owners did not intend them for specific habitations but had them transported from place to place not only to their châteaux but also to various camps during their military campaigns. Nails in the walls enabled servants to hang or to remove the tapestries with equal ease.

Drawing upon a variety of subjects, these tapestries were originally meant to illustrate a story in several episodes. The art of tapestry, we see, was therefore a very lively one and had an instructive character. "In the fifteenth century as in the thirteenth," wrote the historian Emile Mâle, "not a single artistic work was unexplained by a book, the artists invented nothing. Medieval art was never a futile game." The performance of the so-called "mysteries" exerted a certain influence, and as we study a tapestry, many details of costume and decoration recall these religious dramas which were performed in front of a church or in the interior for the edification of the faithful. But a number of subjects were inspired by literary sources. The GESTE DE JOURDAIN DE BLAYE in the Museo Civico at Padua was based on the famous medieval *Fable d'Apollonius de Tyr*. The narrator himself is represented, standing in one corner of the tapestry. The OFFERING OF THE ROSE in the Musée de Cluny took its inspiration from the poem *Le Roman de la Rose* by Guillaume de Lorris. The *Livre des Chasses* (1370) by Gaston de Foix known as Gaston Phébus is the origin of hunting tapestries such as the splendid HUNTS OF THE DUKE OF DEVONSHIRE in the Victoria and Albert Museum. As for THE STORY OF ALEXANDER, now in the Palazzo Doria in Rome, the subjects are derived from the *Livre des Conquestes et Faits d'Alexandre le Grand* by Jean Wauquelin. THE STORY OF HERCULES is divided into three pieces, one of which is in the Musée des Gobelins, another in the Musées royaux d'Art et d'Histoire of Brussels, and the third in a private collection. The composition was inspired by the *Recueil de Troie depuis sa fondation jusqu'à nos jours* written in 1464, at the instigation of Philip the Good, by his chaplain Raoul Lefèvre. The strange subject of THE DANCE OF THE WILD MEN, now at

(Overleaf)

Hunting Tapestries
Arras or Tournai (?), mid-15th century.
The subjects of this tapestry, which consists of four pieces, are: the hunt of the bear and boar (the oldest); the hunt of the bear, otter and swan; the hunt of the falcon; the hunt of the roe-deer and heron (the most recent). All were inspired by the manuscript illuminations of Gaston de Foix's Livre de Chasse.
THE HUNT OF THE BEAR AND BOAR. 4.09 × 9.90 m.
Victoria and Albert Museum. Photo Carlton Studios. Crown copyright.

Saumur, has long intrigued tapestry specialists. Some have sought for a relationship with the notorious "Dance of the Burning Men" at the Hôtel Saint-Pôl in 1393 in which Charles VI almost perished. According to Roger-Armand Weigert, the piece must represent a scene from some courtly romance which has yet to be identified.

Unfortunately, we do not know the names of the painters who furnished the cartoons for the tapestries. Here again we encounter lapses and much imprecision. There is no doubt, however, that during this period the art of tapestry was still related to that of illuminated manuscripts. The art of the Limbourg brothers, the illuminators of the Duke de Berry's *Très Riches Heures* (Musée de Chantilly), is quite similar to that of certain tapestries such as the SCÈNES DE ROMAN in the Musée des Arts décoratifs, Paris, the OFFERING OF THE HEART in the Musée de Cluny and the HUNTS in the Victoria and Albert Museum. Here we find the same luxuriously dressed figures, the same animals represented in their familiar attitudes in the center of a flowerbed. The miniature, however, succeeds in creating a feeling of space by a true representation of the landscape, whereas the tapestry remains a decoration against which the figures with their elegant outlines are placed flat rather than integrated into the ensemble.

It is impossible not to imagine the participation of famous artists in the preparation of the cartoons. We know that in 1398 Melchior Broederlam executed for the Burgundian court the cartoons for a set of SHEPHERDS AND SHEPHERDESSES which was woven by Huart de Walois. One historian believes him to be responsible for the tapestry of THE ANNUNCIATION now in the Metropolitan Museum of Art with its many similarities to the painting

Court Scenes. Arras (?), about 1420.
This tapestry consists of five pieces illustrating romantic scenes whose subjects were inspired by seigniroal life. They are related to the scenes in the Calendrier des Très Riches Heures *of the Duc de Berry. The tapestries have marked similarities with the* Don du Cœur *now in the Musée de Cluny, Paris.*

Tapestry detail. Height 1.59 m.
Richly dressed figures in a flowered garden, at the foot of ramparts.
Paris. Musée des Arts décoratifs. Museum photo.

entitled "The Annunciation" from the altarpiece by Broederlam at Dijon. The realistic contribution noted in the treatment of landscape and accessories in THE STORY OF ST. PIAT AND ST. ELEUTHÈRE in the cathedral of Tournai recalls the art of Van Eyck. The names of Robert Campin of Tournai and Bailleul of Arras, who executed the cartoons of the GIDEON set, have been suggested in regard to a whole group of tapestries, including THE KNIGHT OF THE SWAN in Vienna and Cracow and THE BATTLE OF RONCEVAUX in Brussels. It is thought that THE STORY OF ST. PETER, offered in 1460 to the cathedral of Beauvais by its bishop, Pierre de Hellande, was woven at Tournai and that the cartoons were painted by Henri de Beaumentiel in 1443 after the designs by Robert Campin. Tournai had a number of specialized cartoon painters, including not only Campin but also his pupil Jacques Daret.

Did Roger van der Weyden really paint tapestry cartoons as certain authors believe? According to Mme. Crick-Kuntziger nothing is less certain, though she admits that he played an inspiring role. The famous tapestry of THE STORY OF TRAJAN AND HERKENBALD (or ARCHAMBAULT) in the Historisches Museum of Berne was executed after two paintings of "Justice" done at different periods by Roger van der Weyden. They were destroyed when Brussels was bombarded by Maréchal de Villeroi in 1695. Yet these paintings were reproduced in tapestry closely following the original and this appears to prove the existence of professional cartoon designers acting as middlemen for painters and weavers. We must also mention the series of drawings divided among several collections; some of them in the Louvre may be the sketches for the first drawings *(petits patrons)* for a set of THE TROJAN WAR. It is undeniable that style relationships existed between painting and tapestry in the final quarter of the fifteenth century. The figures have the same elegant proportions and fine hands and, above all, long faces with heavy eyelids whose expression reflects a deep melancholy.

Development of style in the Arras and Tournai productions until the death of Charles the Bold

The only tapestry produced by the Arras workshops of which we are certain is THE STORY OF ST. PIAT AND ST. ELEUTHÈRE, now in the cathedral of Tournai. Commissioned by Toussaint Prier, canon of the cathedral, it was executed by Pierrot Ferré, work being completed in 1402. This tapestry exalts the legends of the first persons to spread the Christian doctrine in the Tournai region. The preserved pieces reveal a quality of weaving which Guillaume Janneau has noted as special to the fifteenth century and which differentiated it from the art of the previous century. Whereas on studying the APOCALYPSE we are impressed by its intellectual quality, here in the set of ST. PIAT AND ST. ELEUTHÈRE we feel its emotional effect. The contrast of material was meant to vary the weaving which belonged only to this period: a drapery falling in heavy folds expressed by long hatchwork is seen alongside a mail tunic rendered in light touches.

The GESTE DE JOURDAIN DE BLAYE in the Museo Civico at Padua is unanimously attributed to an Arras weaver of the first quarter of the fifteenth century. This piece illustrates the fantastic legends which the chatelaine and members of the court enjoyed hearing from the troubadours. The very high horizon line leaves a narrow band of sky represented by stylized clouds; the figures appear flat against a decoration consisting of hills, stylized trees and architectural motifs. Five pieces of COURTLY SUBJECTS heightened by gold thread (Musée des Arts décoratifs, Paris) and THE OFFERING OF THE HEART (Musée de Cluny) are characteristic of the Arras style during the beginning of the century. Naturalistic realism is suggested rather than expressed; we find a serene poetical quality in these much appreciated subjects. But development is already evident; we observe an enlargement and a kind of organization of the subject in the beautiful and impressive PASSION attributed to Arras (about 1420-1430) and presented by Dalmacie de Mur to the cathedral of Saragossa. The different episodes of THE CRUCIFIXION are contained in a single tapestry. Various groups of figures are surrounded by sections of ground with "kidney-shaped flints" and bush, while architectural motifs close the background. In this representation the artist has tried to give some cohesion to the composition which becomes easier for us to understand than in the works previously mentioned.

The famous four tapestries of THE HUNTS OF THE DUKE OF DEVONSHIRE which date from about 1440 rank among the finest examples of the early Tournai style still under the influence of Arras art. Certain historians attribute them to Arras and perhaps to Jean Walois' workshop, which specialized in hunting scenes. Other historians believe that these tapestries might have been executed in 1445 on the occasion of the marriage of Marguerite of Anjou, daughter of King René, and Henry VI of England, and that it was for this reason that it has existed in England for centuries. The tapestries consist of four hangings devoted to THE HUNT OF THE DEER, OF THE OTTER, OF WILDFOWL, OF THE BEAR. Like every tapestry of this period, it is without a border, but these four scenes are limited by motifs which are part of the landscape. The horizon line is very high and the figures stand out against a background covered with vegetation; the design is deliberately free but leaves no room for improvisation.

The characteristic Tournai style asserted itself about the middle of the century and became evident in an accumulation of figures which extended from top to bottom of the tapestry leaving no room for the sky. The special "kidney-shaped flints" are now replaced by fleurettes and plant motifs less schematic than those chosen early in the century. The scenes are even closer and the figures superimposed before a more reduced landscape. This horror of empty space is perhaps more evident in the battle scenes than in the courtly ones; the clothing is treated with much richness, including luxurious armor often with a border of precious stones, sumptuous velvet and pomegranate-decorated brocade of Italian origin. Similarly, the physiognomic style is strongly individualized—for example, a man with a sharply hooked nose is shown close to a woman wearing a hennin with transparent veil.

The Story of St. Peter
Arras or Tournai (?), about 1640. Silken thread.
Originally consisting of ten pieces, this tapestry was woven at the bequest of Pierre de Hellande, Bishop of Beauvais from 1444 to 1461. Six pieces remain in the Beauvais Cathedral, the seventh is in the Musée de Cluny, Paris, the eighth is in the Museum of Fine Arts, Boston, while fragments can be seen in the National Gallery of Art, Washington, D.C. The tapestry was probably executed at the end of the Hundred Years' War, as is evident by the word Pax *woven several times on each piece.*

THE DECAPITATION OF ST. PAUL. 2.71 × 2 m.
Boston. Museum of Fine Arts. Museum photo.

Paix.
Michi viue
xp̄s est et mori lucrū
Paix.

titus

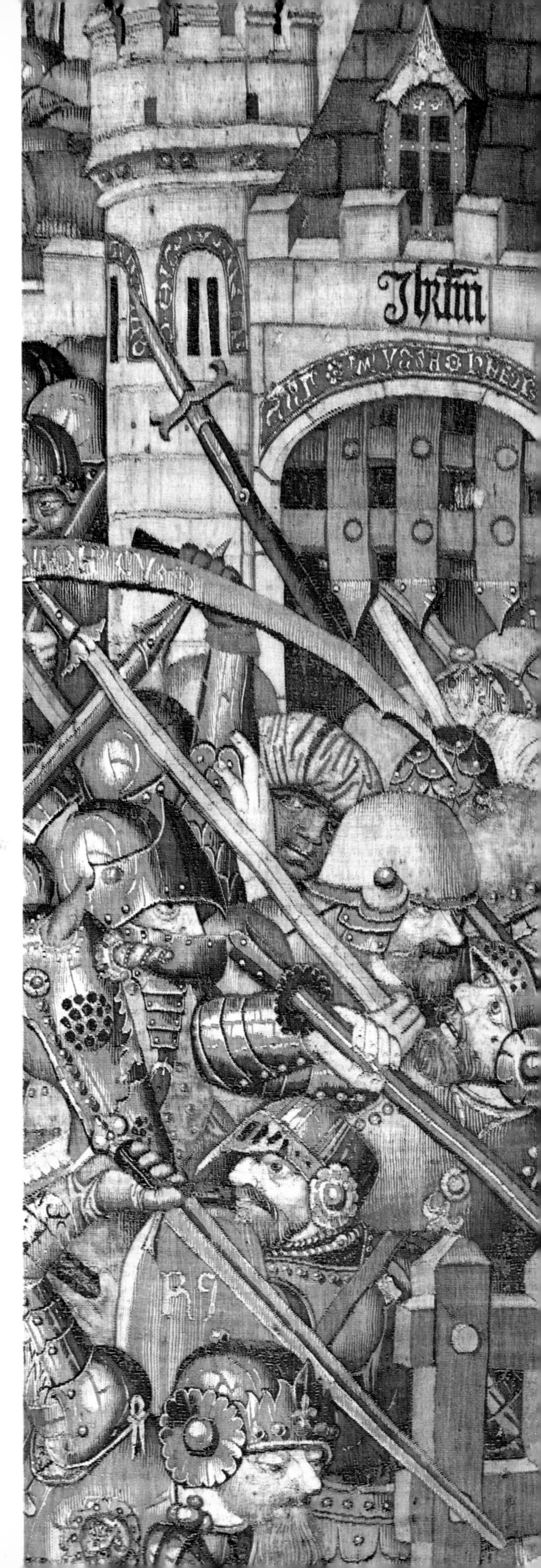

THE CAPTURE OF JERUSALEM. Arras or Tournai (?), mid-15th century.

This tapestry is part of one of the ancient cycles frequently interpreted by Arras and Tournai weavers. Remains of the same tapestry exist in the Musée des Arts décoratifs, Lyons, the Museum of Decorative Arts in Vienna, and in private collections. The inscriptions as well as the capital letters "J.R." or "R.J." remain to be satisfactorily explained. The tapestry shows an inextricable mêlée of warriors in a rather imaginative architectural décor representing Jerusalem.

Saumur. Church of Notre-Dame-de-Nantilly.
Photo Hachette.

childeriq et de la Royne baronne sa
femme apres la mort son pere fu couronne Roy en grad magnificence
par tous les pais gens de guerre et les
tendant aller asegier la cite de soissons

The Story of Strong King Clovis

Arras or Tournai (?), mid-15th century. Silken thread.

This tapestry originally consisted of six pieces. Some have recognized King Clovis as Charles VII, but this theory remains to be confirmed. In 1468 the six pieces together with other tapestries decorated one of the rooms in which Charles the Bold and Margaret of York were married. Found in the emperor's baggage after the hasty raising of the siege of Metz in 1552, the set was acquired by Duke François de Guise, then by his brother Charles, Cardinal of Lorraine, who offered it to the cathedral of Rheims in 1573. Three pieces of this tapestry were still extant in 1840; today there are only two.

Right section of the first piece: *Clovis attacking Ragnacaire, King of Cambrai, beneath the walls of Soissons. Assault of Soissons, hand-to-hand combat between Clovis and Syagrius, the Roman king.*

Rheims. Musée de l'Œuvre Notre-Dame. Photo L. Giraudon.

The Story of Strong King Clovis
Detail. Face of a Dead Soldier.
Rheims. Musée de l'Œuvre Notre-Dame.
Photo Giraudon.

THE BATTLE OF RONCEVAUX. Large tapestry fragment. The whole measures 3.78 × 5.69 m. Tournais, third quarter of the 15th century.
This detail shows Roland in the midst of the battle desperately blowing his horn. His armored shoulder pieces are distinctly marked with the fleur de lis, the heraldic emblem which recalls Roland's relationship with Charlemagne, King of France as well as emperor. It may also signify that at the time this tapestry was executed Tournais belonged to France. Another fragment is now in the Bargello Museum in Florence.
Brussels. Musées royaux d'Art et d'Histoire.
Photo A.C.L.

The Story of Caesar. Tournai (?), about 1465-1470. Silken thread.

Consisting of four pieces, this tapestry may have been commissioned by Charles the Bold to decorate his throne room. Some have read in this an allusion to the role of the "Burgundian Caesar" played by the duke himself. This set formerly belonged to the cathedral of Lausanne. In 1537 it was brought to Berne along with the rest of the treasure as war booty.

The Crossing of the Rubicon and the Battle Against Pompey. 4.30 × 7.56 m.

Caesar, on the left, leading his cavalry, approaches the Rubicon, from which a woman, symbolizing the city of Rome, suddenly appears. On the right is a view of the decisive battle at Pharsalus between Caesar and Pompey.

Berne. Historisches Museum. Museum photo.

Guillaume Janneau mentioned a technical method which is quite characteristic of this kind of tapestry: the use of pure blues strong in tone in large areas to exploit the greatest intensity of their spreading effect. A characteristic form of weaving was adopted. The long streaks formed by the hatching to pass from one color to another were replaced by heavy hatching stopped short, creating a special mirror effect known as "Tournai blues" *(bleus tournaisiens)*.

The Story of Mighty King Clovis (Rheims) and The Battle of Roncevaux (Brussels) as well as The Capture of Jerusalem (Saumur) represent an inextricable network of armored warriors locked in furious combat killing one another with spear or sword. These tapestries are perfect examples of æsthetics taken to the extreme of completely filling up the surface by the use of overlapping figures although each is designed with surprising judiciousness. One of the most spectacular sets is The Story of Cæsar in the Historisches Museum at Berne, representing Cæsar crossing the Rubicon and his battle with Pompey. Probably ordered by Charles the Bold to decorate the walls of his throne room, this tapestry was inspired by a French epic poem entitled *L'Ecriture Sainte et les Faicts des Romains* which was one of the duke's favorites. Here the epic theme of Cæsar's life finds its apogee, the tapestry glorifies the Roman general and, in an allusive manner, the duke is suggested as the Cæsar of the Burgundian period.

Other sets such as The Knight of the Swan (Vienna and Cracow) and

THE JUSTICE OF TRAJAN AND HERKENBALD OR ARCHAMBAULT. 4.61 × 10.53 m.
Tournai, about 1460. Woven in gold and silk.
This tapestry, with certain changes, was woven after the paintings of Justice *which Roger van der Weyden (1399/1400-1464) had created for the Brussels Town Hall; they were destroyed in 1695. The subjects were in praise of two model judges, Trajan and Archambault. On the left Trajan condemns to death one of his soldiers who had killed a widow's son. The other two scenes relate events much later in date. Pope Gregory the Great kneels before the altar of St. Peter's and implores the salvation of the pagan emperor. On the right of a slender column, the same pope, surrounded by ecclesiastics, contemplates Trajan's skull, the tongue which had pronounced the wise judgment having been miraculously preserved. The other scenes are devoted to the justice of Archambault. This noble lord learns on his deathbed that his nephew had seduced a maid of honor. He at once takes justice into his own hands and slashes the young man's throat. The bishop refuses Archambault the last sacraments, but a miracle takes place and the refused host adheres to Archambault's tongue. The man above the page, in the upper corner of the last compartment of* The Justice of Trajan, *may be a portrait of Van der Weyden himself.*

HERKENBALD SLASHES HIS NEPHEW'S THROAT. Detail.
Berne. Historisches Museum. Museum photo.

THE ADORATION OF THE MAGI. 3.68 × 3.85 m.
Tournai (?), about 1440-1455.

The cartoon of this tapestry is also attributed to Roger van der Weyden. Like the preceding tapestry, this piece was brought from Lausanne to Berne, in 1537, after the conquest of the Vaud country by the Bernese troops.

Berne. Historisches Museum. Museum photo.

The Seven Sacraments

Tournai, third quarter of the 15th century.

This tapestry once consisted of two superimposed rows: above, the prefigurations of the sacraments in the Old Testament; below, the Seven Sacraments. Fragments are in the Metropolitan Museum of Art, the Victoria and Albert Museum and in the collection of William Burnell in England. The tapestry may have been executed by Pasquier Grenier, who about 1475 offered it to the church of Saint-Quentin in Tournai.

MARRIAGE. Detail of the central part.

Metropolitan Museum of Art. Gift of J. Pierpont Morgan. Museum photo.

◀ **The Vengeance of the Rescuer**
THE IMPERIAL MESSENGER BEFORE PILATE
3.56 × 2.70 m. Tournai, third quarter of the 15th century. Silken thread.

This tapestry is the only one to have survived a set, now lost, entitled The Vengeance of the Rescuer, *related to the legend of Pilate. It depicts the arrival in Jerusalem of a messenger from Tiberius. Above, on the right, a great storm diverts the ship carrying the messenger, who arrives too late, after the death of Christ. He is greeted by Pilate in whose presence he kneels on one leg. Above, on the left, we see him within the city with a man who is probably Joseph. The emissary, following the texts, questions the latter on the resurrection of Christ. This tapestry is strongly related in style to* The Knight of the Swan.
Vienna. Osterreisches Museum für Angewandte Kunst. Photo Anton Fesl.

THE PRESENTATION OF THE ROSES. Detail. The whole tapestry measures 2.76 × 3.35 m. Tournai (?), about the mid-15th century.

Figures dressed in the period of Charles VII are represented against a background divided into vertical bands of white, red and blue, adorned with roses.
Metropolitan Museum of Art. Rogers Fund, 1909. Museum photo.

WOODCUTTERS. 3.20 × 5.10 m. Tournai, third quarter of the 15th century. Silken thread.

Attributed to the workshop of Pasquier Grenier, this tapestry bears the coat-of-arms of Nicolas Rolin, chancellor of Burgundy from 1422 to 1461. It represents woodcutters at work in a forest filled with wild animals.

Paris. Musée des Arts décoratifs. Museum photo.

The Story of Carrabara (or of the Egyptians)
Tournai, late 15th century.

◀ SALE OF CHILDREN. Detail.

An Egyptian woman, at the left, has just given a child to a man, who holds it in a fold of his cloak.
Gaasbeek Castle. Photo Duerinckx.

VILLAGE FAIR SCENE. The ensemble measures 3.45 × 4 m.
Gaasbeek Castle. Photo Duer inckx.

(Overleaf)

The Morality of Supper and Banquet
Tournai, early 16th century.

There now exist only five tapestries of the nine pieces which formerly constituted this set. It may have been acquired by Duke Antoine de Lorraine about 1511. The subject was inspired by La Condamnation de Banquet *by Nicolas de la Chesnaye which was published in 1507 in Paris, a morality whose aim was to show the inconveniences of hearty eating.*

THE FEAST GIVEN BY BANQUET, second piece in the set. 3.25 × 5.50 m.

Banquet, an elegant lord, is standing in the center of the composition, facing a table where Friandise, Gourmandise, Accoutumance and other guests are seated. On the sumptuously decorated table stands a ship whose mast supports a Venus. Behind and around the spectators is a group of musicians. On the left, in the background, is a buffet with its elegant and rich dishes. Below the sideboard, we see Banquet who treacherously gives the signal for the hideous troupe of sick persons, eyeing the unfortunate guests, to enter the room of festivity. Among the sick are Fever, Apoplexy, Gout, Gallstone and Colic. Above, on the right, Banquet is arrested. ▶
Nancy. Musée lorrain. Photographic Archives.

banquet et sa route
lassemblee toute
Les trois folz ont gran
De cherchez leur mal
Quant ont a bien
A la fin fault tourn
banquet
gourmandise

Sy a vous volles avoir plaisance
Bien laurez vous pour ung tandis
Mes gens qui preuent leur silence
En fin le treuuent puis mauldit
banquet
je vous plaige

The Morality of Supper and Banquet

THE FEAST GIVEN BY BANQUET

Detail. Young man with his elbow on a side-board laden with goldsmiths' work.

SHEEP SHEARING. Detail. The whole tapestry measures 1.65 × 2.24 m. Tournai, about 1460-1475. Silken thread.
This tapestry may have been a part of a set of Months. *Sheep shearing, in medieval calendars, was generally associated with the month of June.*
Brussels. Musées royaux d'Art et d'Histoire.
Photo A.C.L.

◀ PICKING ORANGES. Detail of a tapestry fragment. The whole measures 3 × 1.70 m. Tournai, late 15th century. Silken thread.
Amsterdam. Rijksmuseum.

THE SEVEN SACRAMENTS (Metropolitan Museum of Art) reveal a different tendency. Here each scene is separated by an architectural frame. A similar method was used in THE STORY OF TRAJAN as well as in THE STORY OF ESTHER AND AHASUERUS, and results in an improved composition. In THE ADORATION OF THE MAGI (Berne), the figures are grouped as though in an easel-picture painting, but the horizon line is completely closed. The scene takes place against a background which reveals a preference for decoration. This same decorative concern is evident in THE PRESENTATION OF THE ROSES in the Metropolitan Museum of Art. The tapestry is treated as a surface which relates it to a fabric. A number of figures are arranged without any coherent spatial relationship against a background consisting of vertical bands of various colors, powdered with rose sprays. This method of representing isolated figures against a solid background is far removed from the researches made by painters during that century and heralds the *mille fleurs* tapestries.

The close of the great Tournai period

The end of the fifteenth century saw a decline in the production of Tournai tapestry, although workshops in the city remained active throughout the sixteenth century and afterwards. Pasquier Grenier died in 1493 and his son became head of the workshop. But the great *entrepreneur* was to be Arnould Poissonnier and his most important client, emperor Maximilian I, though he remained in touch with the Western market and had business dealings with important Antwerp merchants, including Cornelius van Bombergen.

In 1504 the Archduke of Austria, Philip the Fair, bought from Grenier a set *"à la manière du Portugal et de l'Indye"* which celebrated the commercial enterprise of the Portuguese in the East Indies. This set has been related to the famous PORTUGUESE CONQUESTS, now in the collegiate church of Pastrana, a town in the province of Guadalajara, Spain. These three hangings, each about thirty-six feet long, are in the tradition of battle sets such as THE BATTLE OF ROOSEBEKE. Their subjects, with giraffes, leopards and ships, enjoyed great success and several tapestries were woven on the theme of "people and beasts after the manner of Calicut." Other themes such as THE STORY OF CARRABARA (also known as THE STORY OF THE EGYPTIANS) show scenes of bohemian life and reveal this taste for exoticism.

Among the subjects woven at Tournai, we must also mention the *moralités*, especially THE MORALITY OF SUPPER AND BANQUET. The most famous is the set of five tapestries in the Musée Lorrain at Nancy which foreshadows sixteenth-century art. During this period artistic creation and activity declined at Tournai. The same subjects continued to be treated, such as ESTHER, CÆSAR, WOODCUTTERS and VERDURES. The tapestries of the WOODCUTTERS with the arms of the Chancellor of Burgundy, Nicolas Rolin (Musée des Arts décoratifs, Paris) and THE SHEEP SHEARING (Musées royaux d'Art et d'Histoire, Brussels) are good examples of this production which is at once fascinating and of respectable quality.

Fifteenth-century tapestry was not a privileged technique restricted solely to Arras and Tournai. The art of weaving was already practiced in every city of northern France and in the southern Netherlands. In addition to Lille, Valenciennes, Douai, Ypres, Middleburg and Alost, whose activity during that century cannot be denied, Bruges produced an important number of tapestries. The dukes of Burgundy ordered numerous sets and foreigners, notably the Medici, commissioned them as well. There is no doubt that the superiority of the Bruges school of painting contributed to the fame of its tapestry.

THE DANCE OF THE WILD MEN AND WOMEN. Detail.
The author and origin of this tapestry are unknown, and it has been impossible to identify this group of men and women, some of whom are wearing animal skins. For a time it was said to have been a reminder of the notorious Dance of the Burning Men at the Hôtel Saint-Pol in 1393. *According to Roger-Armand Weigert it represents a scene of some courtly romance.*
Saumur. Château. Musée des Arts décoratifs. Photo Hachette.

THE DANCE OF THE WILD MEN AND WOMEN. 3 × 5 m. Tournai (?), second half of the 15th century. Saumur. Château. Musée des Arts décoratifs. Photo Hachette.

IV Tapestry at the dawn of the Renaissance

Rise of the Brussels workshops in the second half of the fifteenth century. - Paintings reproduced as tapestries. - The altarpiece tapestries. - Great tapestries with gold background. - From Gothic art to the Italianate influence of Bernard van Orley. - Tapestry workshops in France. - "Mille fleurs" tapestries. - Tapestries with armorial decoration and religious subjects. - Archaic design and the new style. - German tapestry at the close of the Middle Ages.

HE early sixteenth century was a very rich period in the history of Western tapestry. By the close of the fifteenth century a decisive change in tapestry style had taken place. Although the Arras and Tournai workshops continued in the traditions to which they owed their fame, those of Brussels turned in a new direction and developed a style which was undeniably related to painting. During the years from 1480 to 1520 a new approach to art was introduced, and without denying the Gothic heritage, it gradually began to free itself and change in form as it felt the impact of the Renaissance. This period which formed a link between the old and new witnessed the first splendid creations of Brussels tapestry.

During the sixteenth century Brussels was to retain her supremacy and fame. Despite the fine quality of her productions, France was not the leading country in the art of tapestry. Her work was characterized by the efflorescence on the banks of the Loire of the *mille fleurs* tapestries which were still in the medieval tradition and produced by workshops, probably itinerant ones, whose numerous sets timidly revealed an Italianate influence. As for the Germanic countries, they were deliberately attuned to the past and retained an archaic quality in their tapestry productions.

Rise of the Brussels workshops in the second half of the fifteenth century

Tapestry workshops existed in Brussels as early as the fourteenth century. A document dated 1379 mentions the delivery of a chamber of tapestries *(chambre de tapisseries)* by a certain Gheert Godart entitled *tapytwerer*. As at Arras, there was a relationship between the decline of cloth and the development

TAPESTRY WITH THE COAT-OF-ARMS OF CHARLES THE BOLD. Detail of the central part. The whole tapestry measures 3.06 × 6.87 m. Brussels (?), third quarter of the 15th century. Woven in silk, gold and silver.

Against a mille fleurs background this tapestry shows the complete coat-of-arms of Charles the Bold surrounded by the gold chain of the Grand Master of the Order of the Golden Fleece. On the top of the coat-of-arms is a gold helmet crowned by a crest consisting of the golden lily of France, the whole surmounted by two small Gothic "C's," facing each other and knotted by a cord of love. The tapestry was attributed to the workshop of Jean de Haze, a weaver in Brussels who, in 1466, delivered a similar set for Philip the Good, father of Charles the Bold. This tapestry was part of a set which accompanied Duke Charles during his campaigns, and was among the booty captured by the Swiss forces when Charles was defeated at Granson on March 3, 1476. Berne. Historisches Museum. Museum photo.

of tapestry. In 1447 the Brussels weavers left their wool craft or *grand métier* as it was called to form an independent guild or *legnerckersambocht*. There is no doubt whatever that the Brussels workshops rivaled those of Arras and Tournai; we have the list of inscriptions of the master tapestry weavers and apprentices in Brussels from 1417 to 1446 and they are numerous. The name of Jean de Haze is especially famous. In 1466 he was paid by Philip the Good for "eight pieces of *verdure* each having the arms of the duke, wrought in gold, in the middle, six to be used to cover the walls, one for the sideboard and one for the banquet table, 109 3/4 ells in all." One authority has identified this reference as describing a splendid piece woven with gold threads and emblazoned with the arms of Charles the Bold. But Jean de Haze probably turned to the cartoons which he had used in 1466 for Philip the Good, changing the arms and replacing them with those of his son. This sumptuous heraldic tapestry, whose background was once black, has now acquired a dark blue tone. The ground is scattered over with a seeming multitude of small flowers, symbolizing the prosperity enjoyed by the dukes of Burgundy, who during their military campaigns were often accompanied by a convoy of tapestries and precious fabrics which followed in the wake of the army. Once part of the booty taken by the Swiss from Charles the Bold during the Battle of Granson on March 3, 1476, this heraldic tapestry is now in the Historisches Museum at Berne.

In the final decade of the fifteenth century, the Brussels weavers rose to preeminence in Europe. They not only produced *menues verdures* tapestries (known today as *mille fleurs*), but also created many others with figures designed in an extremely characteristic style and of exceptional technical competence.

Paintings reproduced as tapestries—The altarpiece tapestries—Great tapestries with gold background

Brussels tapestry was now strongly influenced by painting, and the highly skilled weavers were led to follow the cartoons more closely, and in a new direction. Until then these cartoons were merely canvases painted with large figures in distemper or tempera. After the death of Roger van der Weyden, the weavers of Brussels turned for inspiration to his style and produced tapestries of average size which are true reproductions of paintings. Here we must mention such tapestries as THE BAPTISM OF CHRIST, one version of which is now in Vienna, THE VIRGIN, ST. ANNE AND THE INFANT CHRIST (Musées royaux d'Art et d'Histoire, Brussels) and especially ST. LUKE PAINTING THE VIRGIN (Louvre), the original painting of which once hung in the Painters' Guild in Brussels.

This type of tapestry was related to an entire set of smaller pieces which can be grouped under the general term of "altarpiece tapestries." We do not know the names of the workshops which executed two precious tapestries woven with gold thread and now in the treasury

The Three Coronations. 1 × 2.92 m. Northern France. Undetermined workshop. Third quarter of the 15th century. Woven in silk, gold and silver.

A reproduction of an altarpiece, this tapestry represents three scenes separated by slender columns whose capitals are surmounted by gilt statuettes. In the center is the Coronation of the Virgin; on the right, the Coronation of Esther by Ahasuerus; on the left, the Coronation of Bathsheba by Solomon. According to the ancient text of the Speculum humanae Salvationis *(The Mirror of Human Knowledge), these two episodes prefigure the Coronation of the Virgin. This tapestry was presented to the cathedral of Sens by Cardinal Louis de Bourbon-Vendôme, archbishop of Sens between 1536 and 1557. He may have inherited it from his uncle, Cardinal Charles de Bourbon, Archbishop of Lyons from 1446 to 1486. The central scene, cut off on its four sides under Louis XV (on the occasion when the tapestry replaced the* Table d'Or *sent to the Mint), was*

restored, in 1924, *by the Historical Monuments Administration to its earlier dimensions, the removed fragments having been preserved.*
Cathedral of Sens. Photo Giraudon.

(Overleaf)
The Adoration of the Magi
Detail showing the infant Christ on the Virgin's knee.
Cathedral of Sens. Photo Giraudon.

THE ADORATION OF THE MAGI. 1.38 × 3.31 m. Brussels (?), 1466-1488. Woven in silk, gold and silver.

Like The Three Coronations, *this tapestry was presented to the cathedral of Sens by Cardinal Louis de Bourbon-Vendôme. The border bears the coat-of-arms of Cardinal Charles de Bourbon, his uncle, who was Archbishop of Sens. No doubt the tapestry was meant to be used as an antependium. The cartoon is attributed to the Master of the View of Sainte-Gudule.*

Cathedral of Sens. Photo Giraudon.

The Life of Christ and the Virgin ▶

Brussels (?), early 16th century.

This tapestry consists of twenty-seven scenes divided into a long frieze of fourteen pieces which originally decorated the choir of the abbey of Canterbury. It belongs to an important group of Flemish tapestries, probably woven in Brussels, about which, unfortunately, we know very little. Recent studies have confirmed the attribution of this tapestry cartoon to Quentin Metsys.

MARY IN THE TEMPLE. Height 1.90 m.

Aix-en-Provence. Saint-Sauveur Cathedral. Photographic Archives of Architectural Management.

of the cathedral of Sens. These were offered to the cathedral by Cardinal Louis de Bourbon, Archbishop of Sens, between 1536 and 1557, but they were woven before 1448, for the cardinal had probably inherited them from his uncle Charles de Bourbon, who was already dead by that date. One of these tapestries, THE THREE CORONATIONS, includes a central scene which represents THE CORONATION OF THE VIRGIN with THE CORONATION OF BATHSHEBA on the left, and THE CORONATION OF ESTHER BY AHASUERUS on the right. These two episodes, which follow the ancient text of the *Speculum Humanae Salvationis*, foreshadow THE CORONATION OF THE VIRGIN. The second is an ADORATION OF THE MAGI. Both were used as antependia and are faithful reproductions of a painted and carved altarpiece. The names of the painters who supplied the cartoons are also unknown, but they appear to be among the followers of Roger van der Weyden or Dirk Bouts. The ANNUNCIATION and THE ADORATION OF THE MAGI (Musée des Gobelins) have been attributed to the Master of the Redemption, identified with Vrancke van der Stockt, who succeeded Roger van der Weyden as city painter of Brussels. As for the famous ALLEGORY OF THE VIRGIN MARY SOURCE OF SPIRITUAL STRENGTH, dated 1485 (Louvre), this too is a reproduction of one of these painted and carved altarpieces executed not only at Brussels but also at Antwerp, Malines and Bruges. The architectonic structure consisting of slender columns and complicated pinnacles creates the impression of sculpture. We see that as early as this period the skillful weavers managed to reproduce the effect of *trompe-l'œil.*

Among the most famous tapestries woven at Brussels during the final decade of the fifteenth century, we must mention the "Golden Tapestries," so called because of the profusion of gold thread which enrich their effect. One of the most characteristic is THE STORY OF THE VIRGIN (Spanish National Patrimony). The set consists of four pieces and the gold gives a warm tone which dominates the composition and heightens the other colors. These *vieilles tapisseries du Brabant* (old Brabant tapestries) had been brought to Spain by Philip the Fair and were later sent to Tordesillas by order of Joanna the Mad. Charles V subsequently had them in his retreat at Yuste, but Philip II ordered them to be removed to the Escorial. Several tapestry sets are related to this group. The MASS OF ST. GREGORY (Spanish National Patrimony) was probably bought by Joanna the Mad from Pierre d'Alost, the most important Brussels weaver of the period, who in all likelihood furnished THE STORY OF THE VIRGIN.

There are similarities in style between these sets and a rich tapestry entitled THE GLORIFICATION OF CHRIST now in Washington but also originally from Spain. It was acquired as early as the seventeenth century by Mazarin, then by Maréchal de Villars. Like other tapestries representing the same subject, another GLORIFICATION OF CHRIST which is without gold (Musées royaux d'Art et d'Histoire, Brussels) is composed like an altarpiece, whose various scenes are separated by slender columns to form a delicate architectonic framework. In the majority of such tapestries, the figures of angels scarcely differ from those in other sets. Their presence is linked with ancient scenic traditions and the *Biblia Pauperum.*

The Brussels workshops probably had a supply of cartoons representing the same figures.

In all of these related tapestries the composition is rather tight and fills the available space with a swelling of superimposed heads. The foreground is decorated with slightly stylized plants and there is a framelike border containing foliage, flowers and fruit which are also characteristic of the Brussels workshops. Other tapestries such as KING SOLOMON AND THE QUEEN OF SHEBA (Poldi Pezzoli Museum, Milan) are composed in a similar manner. All these tapestries are outstanding for the wealth of their execution in silk and gold. The characteristic use of fabrics, especially velvet and brocade decorated with pomegranates, creates a notable surface unity by closely linking the groups and figures.

From Gothic art to the Italianate influence of Bernard van Orley

In contrast to these precious tapestries, treated with rather mannered elegance, there existed another group which is outstanding for the rhythm of the figures. They reveal the influence of the painter Quentin Massys, also known as Matsys. Tapestries such as THE LIFE OF THE VIRGIN (two pieces are now part of the Spanish National Patrimony), THE MARRIAGE OF ST. CATHERINE (the Vatican), THE BEWAILING OF CHRIST (Kunsthistorisches Museum, Vienna) and the important set, THE LIFE OF CHRIST AND OF THE VIRGIN, in the cathedral of Aix-en-Provence, are peaceful and solemn compositions with their clear symmetry in which the figures are juxtaposed on a narrow scene. The relationship of the Antwerp school of painting and the Brussels tapestry workshops is evident; this marked the beginning of a tradition which was to last until the seventeenth century.

The Musées Royaux d'Art et d'Histoire in Brussels houses THE JUSTICE OF ARCHAMBAULT which is of exceptional interest in the history of tapestry, for in addition to its artistic value, its origin is perfectly known. Woven for the Brotherhood of the Holy Sacrament, it was paid for in 1513 and the accounts list three names: Jan van Roome of Brussels, the painter responsible for the project; Master Philippe, who designed the cartoons; and Leon de Smet, the weaver. Characterized by a great number of figures all closely arranged in a composition in which depth has been deliberately dismissed, this work, definitely of Brussels origin, has enabled us by comparison to attribute to Brussels a number of pieces executed prior to May 18, 1528, the date of the edict requiring the weavers to include the city's mark. There are a number of tapestries in European and American collections with important ties to the style of THE JUSTICE OF ARCHAMBAULT, namely, the presence of majestic figures with plastically draped garments which, although dating from early in the sixteenth century, reveal a certain archaic quality and the absence of perspective. Nevertheless, we find in these tapestries a timid attempt to use Renaissance forms, especially in the decoration of the architectural motifs.

Many tapestry subjects were inspired by fifteenth-century literary works such as *The Triumphs* in which Petrarch (1304-1374) in an allegorical form described the philosophical and moral values to which he was attached. Others included the poems by Guillaume de Digulleville written from 1300 to 1358, *Le Pèlerinage de la vie humaine*

THE GLORIFICATION OF CHRIST, KNOWN AS THE "MAZARIN TAPESTRY." 3.30 × 3.90 m.
Brussels, about 1500. Woven in silk, gold and silver.

The composition forms a triptych whose parts are separated by slender columns. In the center of the upper part, Christ is represented enthroned, surrounded by angels. The left lower part shows Octavius Augustus consulting a sibyl who points out to the kneeling emperor (in the rear scene) the Virgin and Child appearing in the sky. Above this compartment we see the foundation of the altar on the Capitoline Hill (Santa Maria de Capitolo in Rome). The right part of the tapestry depicts, below, the marriage of Esther and Ahasuerus and, above, Esther ordering the banquet. This tapestry once belonged to Cardinal Mazarin.
Washington, D.C. National Gallery of Art, Widener Collection. Museum photo.

(Overleaf) ▶
THE MASS OF ST. GREGORY. 3.36 × 4.04 m. Brussels, about 1500. Woven in silk, gold and silver.
The iconographic theme illustrated by this tapestry enjoyed much success during the 15th and 16th centuries. One day, when Gregory was celebrating mass in the Basilica of the Holy Cross in Jerusalem, where the relics of the Passion were kept, one of the assistants began to doubt the true presence of Christ in the host. At that moment Christ, answering the Pope's prayer, descended to the altar, surrounded by the instruments of his torture. This is among the richest tapestries with gold background woven in Brussels in the early 16th century, and was probably purchased by Joan the Mad from Pierre d'Alost to offer to her mother, Isabella of Castile.
Madrid. With the courtesy and authorization of the Spanish National Patrimony.

ROLAUT

The Triumphs of Petrarch

Petrarch's allegorical poem, The Triumphs, *published in 1470, inspired the cartoons for this tapestry which consists of the Triumph of Love, the Triumph of Chastity over Love, the Triumph of Death over Chastity, the Triumph of Fame over Death, the Triumph of Time over Fame, the Triumph of Eternity. The most celebrated sets are now in England at Hampton Court and at the Victoria and Albert Museum.*

THE TRIUMPH OF FAME OVER DEATH. Detail. The entire piece measures 4.45 × 8 m. Brussels, about 1510-1520. Woven in silk.

Fame, crowned, sounds the trumpet to raise the famous dead who emerge from their tombs. These include Roland, Pyrrhus and Galahad.
Amsterdam. Rijksmuseum. Museum photo.

The Victory of the Virtues
The theme of this tapestry, consisting of four pieces, was borrowed from The Combat of Vices and Virtues.
DANCE. Detail. Brussels, about 1520. Woven in silk.

On the left, a group of young women and men singing to musical accompaniment; in the center, a young woman dancing before her admirers. The figure standing behind her, his hands raised in admiration, recalls Martin Luther. These tapestries were once in the cathedral of Palencia.
Brussels. Musées royaux d'Art et d'Histoire. Photo A.C.L.

The Story of the Redemption
The eight pieces of this tapestry depict the story of Christianity according to themes borrowed from the medieval theater.
The Creation of the World. The entire piece measures 4.20 × 7.85 m. Brussels, about 1500-1515. Woven in silk.
The divinity, represented as three identical figures, develops in a flower bed. The Trinity appears six times for the six days of the Creation.
San Francisco. The Young Memorial Museum. William Randolph Hearst Foundation. Museum photo.

and *Le Pèlerinage de l'âme*, which concern the conflict of the vices and virtues and which from the fourteenth century to the beginning of the sixteenth was a return to the ancient theme of psychomachy or conflict of the soul. Several of these tapestries are now in Burgos. Since the sixteenth century other examples have found their way to England, including those which Cardinal Wolsey bought in 1521 for Hampton Court. An important set was recently added to the collections of the Musées d'Art et d'Histoire of Brussels. These tapestries reveal a conception which is still utterly medieval and their fundamental themes are borrowed from the mystery and morality plays of the theater of the period. The chief mystery is that of *La Vie et la Passion de Jésus-Christ*, a version reworked at the close of the fifteenth century and the beginning of the sixteenth, based on Arnoul Gréban's *Le Mystère de la Passion.* To this must be added the complete story of *La Rédemption de l'Homme* taken from *L'Homme pécheur*, a morality then very popular in France. Homo the hero is Adam represented in the person of a young man of the period, a sort of prodigal son, who is also a popular hero of the dramatic Redemption. As a prologue *The Mystery of the Creation* was given. This is among the most fascinating themes and is used in several tapestries (cathedral of Narbonne, Young Museum of San Francisco, and Château de Haar). It represents the divinity as three identical figures developing in a flowerbed. The Trinity appears six times for the six days of the Creation; above presides the celestial tribunal framed by Mercy and Justice, while in the background sings the choir of angels. Thus was perpetuated a complete medieval tapestry tradition.

During the same period other tapestries heralded the Renaissance spirit. The early works of Bernard van Orley can in fact be dated from the

(Overleaf)

The Legend of Our Lady of Le Sablon

The subject of this set consisting of four pieces was treated only once and was inspired by Brussels religious folklore. Chroniclers relate that, in 1348, the Virgin appeared to a pious Antwerp weaver, Beatrice Soetkens, telling her to remove a statuette of the Virgin in a church in Antwerp and transport it to one in Brussels. Beatrice fled aboard a ship with the precious statuette, which was transferred with much pomp to the church of Le Sablon where it continued to perform miracles until 1580, the year of its destruction by iconoclasts. The cartoons for this tapestry are attributed to Bernard van Orley and were commissioned by François de Tassis to decorate the sanctuary where the statuette of Our Lady of Le Sablon was venerated.

THE ARRIVAL IN BRUSSELS OF THE MIRACULOUS STATUETTE. 3.55 × 5.45 m. Brussels, about 1516-1518. Woven in silk.

The composition of this tapestry is treated as a triptych: the left part shows Beatrice handing the statuette to a crowned prince wearing the Order of the Golden Fleece, none other than Philip the Good. The central part represents the procession of the statuette through the city, carried by a bard, *held in front by Ferdinand and in the rear by the future Charles V. On the right, we see the solemn installation of the statuette in the church of Le Sablon. Kneeling are Margaret of Austria, her nephew Ferdinand and her four nieces. In the foreground, represented three times, is a kneeling figure, who is none other than the tapestry donor, François de Tassis. In the center of the upper border emerges the coat-of-arms of Margaret of Austria, in the center of the left border that of Tassis, while the right border bears the coat-of-arms of Tonila Magnasco, mother of François de Tassis.*

Brussels. Musées royaux d'Art et d'Histoire. Photo Louis Loose.

The Story of the Redemption

Detail. CREATION OF ANIMALS

San Francisco. The Young Memorial Museum. William Randolph Hearst Foundation. Museum photo.

Qua magnanimus veneratus munera princeps
Excipit inflexo poplite sacra manu
AVE

V Hanc age devoto cultu venerare
Illa feret meritis premia dign

The Lady with the Unicorn

Since 1660 *the six pieces of this tapestry had been exhibited in the Château de Boussac in the Creuse region of France. These were acquired by the Musée de Cluny in* 1882. *The weaving origin of the tapestry is unknown, but it belongs to the* mille fleurs *type often attributed to the workshop along the Loire River. Mystery surrounds the meaning of the subjects represented, the general opinion being that it is a representation of the five senses.*
SIGHT. 3 × 3.10 m. Loire workshop (?), late 15th century. Paris. Musée de Cluny. Photo Giraudon.

second decade of the sixteenth century. His realistic Italianate vigor was to transform the art of tapestry. THE STORY OF DAVID (Musée de Cluny), which several authors attribute to him, reveals the progress achieved in this new direction. The importance of the central airy subject frees the adjoining scenes; the architecture richly decorated with Renaissance motifs no longer serves only as a frame but contributes to the illusion of space. The same is true of various sets which constitute THE LEGEND OF OUR LADY OF LE SABLON (Musées d'Art et d'Histoire, Brussels, and the Hermitage, Leningrad). Ordered by François de Tassis, *maître des postes impériales*, this famous Brussels tapestry dated 1518 relates one of the most stirring legends of the Belgian capital. A study of these sets reveals the personality of this painter who "upset" the traditional style of Brussels tapestry.

Tapestry workshops in France — *Mille fleurs* tapestries

The turbulent political and economic conditions which marked the early fifteenth century, among them the great plague in Paris (1418) and the English occupation, were scarcely conducive to the development of the arts, but in France tapestry enjoyed great favor during the last quarter of the fifteenth century and the beginning of the sixteenth. Members of the court, the nobility and the Church commissioned numerous tapestries and a relatively important number of these have survived. The provinces proved richer in workshops than Paris. Weavers were active in Burgundy, which had been annexed in 1477, and a hypothesis has been advanced that THE CHASTE SUSANNA (Musée Marmottan) bearing the arms of a Burgundian family may have been woven at that period. Weavers also settled in the ancient French province known as La Marche, where the weaving tradition has been maintained down to the present day. But it was chiefly in the center of France, on the banks of the Loire, that the majority of these workshops were found. Since tapestry was an art for the very rich, it is not surprising that the residences of the French kings and their court lay in this pleasant region, including Tours, Angers, Blois and Bourges. Here were grouped weavers who had come not only from Arras and Tournai but also from Paris and had established short-lived workshops, generally designated as "the workshops of the Loire" about which we really know very little.

It has been theorized that these itinerant weavers practiced their craft from city to city and from château to château, but the working conditions remain difficult to define. We merely have to imagine the cumbersome looms and stores of material needed to weave a set of tapestries often of huge dimensions.

The tapestries known as *mille fleurs*, which brought fame to these workshops of the Loire, are among the most admired productions of the period, yet their attribution to these workshops has not been unanimously accepted. Mme. Crick-Kuntziger believes that the *mille fleurs* workshop may have had its seat in Bruges at the close of the fifteenth century. Mme. Schneebalg Perelman suggests Brussels, whereas M. Salet is of the opinion that two groups must be considered, that of the *mille fleurs à fond bleu foncé* and that of the *mille fleurs à fond rose.* However the case, these tapestries with their pleasant figures designed against a background strewn with flowers are among the most fascinating dating from the close of the Middle Ages. The most characteristic is THE LADY WITH THE UNICORN which comprises six tapestries and originally hung in the Château de Boussac. It can now be seen in a specially arranged room in the Musée de Cluny. It bears the arms of the Le Viste family who were originally from Lyons and the date when it was woven has been placed at about 1500.

The significance of the six tapestries has not been elucidated and much has been written on the interpretation of the subjects. The most satisfactory is the one which sees here the representation of the five senses; the sixth tapestry with the inscription "to my sole desire" *(à mon seul désir)* may be a dedication to the woman for whom these tapestries were made. In a recent study Mme. Lanckoronska suggests that the lady with the unicorn is Margaret of York, wife of Charles the Bold, Duke

CAPVD MEDVSE
PEGASVS
PERSEVS

THE STORY OF PERSEUS. Loire or Flemish workshop, late 15th century.
Stylistically, this tapestry is related to The Lady with the Unicorn *as well as to* Famous Women *(Boston Museum of Fine Arts). The subject has not been satisfactorily identified. The coat-of-arms are those of Charles Guillard* (1456-1537), *who was associated with the Le Viste family, once the owners of* The Lady with the Unicorn.
Private collection. Photo Connaissance des Arts. R. Guillemot.

The Hunt of the Unicorn

This tapestry consists of seven hangings which once decorated the Château de Verteuil in Charente, France. Five of these were probably executed for Anne of Brittany on the occasion of her marriage to Louis XII in 1499. The first piece and another one were added when Francis I married Anne's daughter in 1514, at which time he received them. Later they were presented to his godfather François de Rochefoucauld.

THE UNICORN A PRISONER. Detail of the central part. France or Flanders, late 15th century. Metropolitan Museum of Art. The Cloisters Collection. Gift of John D. Rockefeller. Museum photo.

of Burgundy, but the reasons she proposes are not convincing. These tapestries owe their great power of fascination to the red background decorated with flowers in contrast to the dark tone of the blue-green islet strewn with flowers which serves as a sort of platform for the scene represented. In each tapestry the lady is placed in the center of the composition. Seated well in view or, more often, standing, thanks to her tall stature she dominates the lion and the unicorn which frame her as well as the girl who appears to be a member of her suite. In each tapestry the figure, richly decorated in brocade and velvet and adorned with jewels, is represented doing something different. The presence of the unicorn, which is carefully designed in its various attitudes and expressions, contributes a poetical quality to the entire composition. This fabulous four-footed beast was considered a symbol of purity in the Middle Ages. Every animal is delineated with precision and this same research and realism is revealed in the flowers strewn on the red background or on the islet. The fine, elegant design and the magnificent, luminous colors, down to the slightest detail, are evidence of a great achievement in art.

The origin of THE LADY WITH THE UNICORN remains a mystery. Similarities in style relate it to other tapestries such as the set of the FAMOUS WOMEN (Museum of Fine Arts, Boston) and above all THE STORY OF PERSEUS (private collection) which bears the arms of Charles Guillard (1456-1537). The Guillard family were closely connected with the Le Viste family who formerly owned THE LADY WITH THE UNICORN and the two tapestries may have been woven at the same period. The perfection of the decoration in the Perseus tapestry and the evident skill of its execution make it one of the noteworthy hangings of the time. As the inscriptions show, the subject is the legend of Perseus transformed by the poetic taste of the medieval age into a fairy tale.

The *mille fleurs* represent exclusively secular scenes which show nobles hunting, listening to musicians or engaged in minor occupations. The five hangings of SEIGNIORIAL LIFE (Musée de Cluny) and the three pieces of THE NOBLE PASTORAL (Louvre), as well as the various CONCERTS D'ORGUE (one in the Louvre, the second in the Musée des Gobelins and the third at Antwerp), are typical works of this pleasing form of tapestry. Against a dark background strewn with bushes and bunches of flowers we find a group of figures placed rather flat, but decoratively, against the background with no attempt at composition. For the figures, the weavers undoubtedly turned to engravings. For example, a halberdier firing, originally portrayed in an engraving by Dürer, can be recognized not only in a tapestry with a blue background in the Musée de Cluny but also in one with a pink background in the Art Institute of Chicago.

The unicorn was also the chief subject in THE HUNT OF THE UNICORN now in the Cloisters, a branch of New York's Metropolitan Museum of Art. The six hangings of this delightful set, formerly in the Château de Verteuil in Charente, all bear the initials which are said to be those of François de la Rochefoucauld, godfather of Francis I.

This splendid work, which relates the capture of the unicorn, is not really a *mille fleurs* tapestry, for the hunting scene takes place against a landscape background with the outline of a château in the distance. The late James Rorimer believed that at least four of these tapestries were woven for Anne de Bretagne on the occasion of her marriage to Louis XII in 1499. The

The Angels Carrying the Instruments of the Passion

On the three extant pieces of this important set, we see angels kneeling against a mille fleurs *background. They are carrying the instruments associated with Christ's suffering. Near each angel is a scroll with its commentary on the suffering inflicted on the Son of God. The author of these verses is said to have been King René. These tapestries have the coats-of-arms of Pierre de Rohan, bearing the Order of St. Michael, and Jeanne de San Severino, his second wife, framed by the widows' cord.*

THE ANGEL OF THE WHIPS AND THE COLUMN OF THE FLAGELLATION. Detail. The whole piece measures 1.80 × 6.90 m. French workshop, after 1513. Woven in silk.
Angers. Musée des tapisseries. Photo Hachette.

first and the last, THE UNICORN AT BAY and THE UNICORN HELD CAPTIVE, may have been subsequently added.

THE UNICORN HELD CAPTIVE is related to the *mille fleurs* tapestries. This time the fabulous and charming animal is alone, symbol of the resurrected Christ (the wounds are evident). As the symbol of the Holy Virgin and the Incarnation, the unicorn rests in the center of a small enclosure *(hortus conclusus)* and is attached by a gold chain to a tree bearing pomegranates which symbolize marriage and fertility.

Although generally used for secular subjects, *mille fleurs* tapestries were often the subject of religious themes as in THE ANGELS CARRYING THE INSTRUMENTS OF THE PASSION whose figures are represented against a *mille fleurs* background. The name of the cartoon painter has not survived, but beside each angel is a scroll bearing an eight-line inscription describing the torments which Christ willingly suffered and the moral lessons which they offer to humanity. According to a chronicler, the verses were composed by King René, the last Duke of Anjou. The tapestry, which bears the arms of Jeanne de Sanseverino, surrounded with the knotted cord indicative of a widow, enables us to assume that this piece was woven after 1528, date of the death of her husband Pierre de Rohan. The tradition of these delightful *mille fleurs* tapestries was thus perpetuated during the final quarter of the sixteenth century simultaneous with the new and "revolutionary" tapestries inspired by the cartoons made by Renaissance painters.

THE WINGED STAGS. 3.48 × 3.80 m. France, about 1430-1450.
This tapestry with its heraldic décor represents, in a fenced garden, winged stags wearing the royal French crown as a collar. They are supporting a coat-of-arms treated in a fleurs de lis manner — the personal coat-of-arms of King Charles VII.
Rouen. Musée des Antiquités départementales.
Photo Hachette

Tapestries with armorial decoration and religious subjects

Early fifteenth-century French illuminators often represented a room entirely decorated with a tapestry with repeated heraldic motifs. These armorial tapestries were easy to hang and were frequently listed in inventories. A tapestry bearing the arms of Guillaume Roger de Beaumont (Rijksmuseum, Amsterdam, and the Metropolitan Museum of Art, New York) and one bearing the arms of the Dinteville family now in the Château de Commarin offer an idea of their often unusual decoration. To this type belong the famous tapestries in the Hospice de Beaune whose weaving is attributed to an itinerant workshop temporarily established in Burgundy. They were executed about 1450 to be used at the Hôtel-Dieu of Beaune which had been founded by the Burgundian chancellor, Nicolas Rolin. Works of outstanding simplicity, bearing the arms of the founder, the two pieces woven for the chapel include a large central figure representing St. Anthony dressed as a hermit.

The extremely elegant style and skillful composition of THE WINGED STAGS (Musée des Antiquités, Rouen) grant it an important place in the field of heraldic tapestry. It represents stags in an enclosure of rose bushes, wearing the royal crown of France as a collar with the royal shield of France attached as a pendant. M. P. Martin has recognized in these emblems the motto of Charles VII. The execution of this piece can therefore be placed between the years 1430 and 1450.

The treasuries of the churches of France contain numerous sets of tapestries and their origins present a difficult

TAPESTRY WITH HERALDIC DÉCOR. Detail. France, itinerant workshop, about 1450.

Of the original thirty-one tapestries, thirty have been preserved. They were meant to cover the beds of the sick in the Hôtel-Dieu in Beaune, founded by Nicolas Rolin, chancellor of Burgundy from 1421 to 1461 and by his wife, Guigone de Salins. The coat-of-arms of the founders stands out against a red background, alternating with turtle doves and the motto Seulle.

Beaune. Hôtel-Dieu. Photo Hachette.

◀ The Life of Christ

Containing fourteen pieces, this tapestry was offered in 1518 to the abbey of La Chaise-Dieu by Abbot Jacques de Saint-Nectaire. According to the French art historian, Émile Mâle, the author of the cartoons took his inspiration from the engravings illustrating the Biblia Pauperum *and the* Speculum humanae Salvationis.

THE RESURRECTED CHRIST APPEARING TO MARY MAGDALENE. Height 2 m. France or Flanders, 1516-1518.

La Chaise-Dieu. Abbaye Saint-Robert. Archives photographiques.

problem to solve, for in the majority of cases documentation is lacking. Most of these sets with religious subjects are long and narrow; they were woven as tapestry bands *(dosserets)* to adorn the back of choir stalls and protect their occupants from draughts. Joyous tales related in a series of scenes in a setting of landscape and architectural motifs reveal all the characteristics of popular imagery. One of the most outstanding is THE LIFE OF THE VIRGIN which was intended as a gift from Cardinal Jean Rolin, son of Nicolas Rolin, to the church of Notre-Dame at Beaune. Others relate the lives of various saints by explaining their miracles after the apocryphal stories of the *Golden Legend.* These include THE LIFE OF ST. MAURILLE (Château of Angers), THE LIFE OF ST. QUENTIN (Musée de Cluny), THE LIFE OF ST. STEPHEN (Musée de Cluny) and THE LIFE OF ST. GERVAIS AND ST. PROTAIS (Cathedral of Le Mans). Here we find a timid appearance of Renaissance forms, especially in the architectural decoration. Among such tapestries we must also mention those of La Chaise-Dieu with the arms of Jacques de Senneterre, who was abbot from 1491 to 1518. Executed by weavers from La Manche or perhaps from Flanders, this set relates the life of Christ. Emile Mâle believes it to be a copy made from woodcuts illustrating two small works which were once very popular, the *Biblia Pauperum* and the *Speculum Humanae Salvationis.* As for the tapestries which were formerly in the Abbey of Le Ronceray at Angers and now divided between several collections (Musée des Gobelins, Château de Langeais, and Museum of Fine Arts, Boston), they represent THE STORY OF THE HOLY SACRAMENT and were woven in the time of the abbess Isabelle de La Jaille (1505-1518).

The Triumphs of Petrarch
(see pages 108-109)
The six pieces of the tapestry were inspired by Petrarch's poems and once were a part of the treasury of the ancient Crown of Austria. The explanatory quatrain above is in French. Two similar Triumphs are now in the Metropolitan Museum of Art.
THE TRIUMPH OF LOVE. France or Flanders, early 16th century. Woven in silk.
Detail: Mermaids Dragging the Chariot of Love.
Vienna. Kunsthistorisches Museum. Photo E. Meyer.

The Lives of St. Gervais and St. Protais
The seventeen scenes of this tapestry are divided into five pieces. They were presented by Martin Guérande, in 1509, to the cathedral of Le Mans to decorate the choir.
THE BAPTISM OF ST. GERVAIS AND ST. PROTAIS by the Bishop of Milan in the presence of St. Celsus and St. Nazarius. Height 1.50 m.
France (?), early 16th century. Woven in silk.
Cathedral of Le Mans. Archives photographiques.

Archaic design and the new style

The laws and principles which had regulated French tapestry since the early fifteenth century were maintained until about the year 1530, as is evident in two beautiful tapestries, THE LIFE OF THE VIRGIN and THE STORY OF ST. REMI, which were presented by Archbishop Robert de Lenoncourt between 1509 and 1532 to the cathedral of Rheims and to the church of St. Remi. The filling up of the surface, the wealth of detail, the lack of clarity in the arrangement of various scenes, all reveal a certain archaic design and still create the impression of a kind of "box space" as a frame for the composition.

Two other sets, however, woven at the same period, reveal new tendencies. THE KINGS OF GAUL in the cathedral of Beauvais is an interesting tapestry from many points of view. This set comprising five hangings is said to have been woven at Beauvais by a workshop probably of Flemish origin and presented to the cathedral by the canon Nicolas d'Argillières in 1530. They were inspired by a fanciful translation of Annius of Viterbo (1498), supplemented by the *Illustrations de Gaule et singularités de Troyes* printed at Lyons between 1509 and 1512. Against a background designed like some strange map with the outline of buildings in the distance, we see the figures of the kings of Gaul who were said to have reigned since the Deluge until the period which followed the siege of Troy. Despite the definite feeling for space, here again the figures are not integrated into the landscape.

The Triumphs inspired by the sonnets of Petrarch, six of which are in the Kunsthistorisches Museum, Vienna, and two similar pieces in the Metropolitan Museum of Art, appear to characterize in France the early decades of the sixteenth century. The explanatory quatrains are in French and a Touraine origin has been substituted for an Arras or Tournai one. The long fine figures, the slender female forms, the delightful harpies with fish tails dragging the chariot of love recall the aristocratic female figures in The Lady with the Unicorn and the naiads in The Story of Perseus, although mingled with these medieval forms are decorative elements borrowed from the new Renaissance style.

The Story of St. Saturnin (Musée de Tapisseries at Angers and the Château de Langeais), which was presented by Jacques de Semblançay, in 1527, to the church of Saint-Saturnin at Tours, is quite different in character. An attempt at perspective and the representation of classical architecture reveal an Italianate approach on the part of the cartoon painter, who was probably André Polaston, a Florentine painter and a former pupil of Andrea del Sarto, who was established in Tours. The Italianate features must be considered direct imports from Italy rather than the results of French assimilation of Italian formulas. The tapestry is a considerable testimony to the influence of foreign artists in Touraine and also reveals the existence of leading tapestry workshops at Tours, the importance of which increased in later years.

The Life of the Virgin
This tapestry of five pieces depicts seventeen scenes in the life of the Virgin. Commissioned by Cardinal Rolin, the cartoons were executed by Pierre Spicre in 1475.
The Visitation and the Nativity. Height 1.90 m. France (?), 1475-1500. Woven in silk.
Beaune. Collégiale Notre-Dame. Photo Giraudon.

The Kings of Gaul
This set of five tapestries was presented about 1530 to the cathedral of Beauvais by the canon Nicolas d'Argillières, whose coat-of-arms can be seen. The subject was inspired by the Illustrations de Gaule et Singularités de Troyes.

BELGIUS JASIUS AND PARIS. Detail (right section). The whole tapestry measures 2.11 × 7.59 m. France, itinerant workshop (?), about 1530. *Paris stands before a general view of the city of Paris which he has founded.* Cathedral of Beauvais. Photo Hachette.

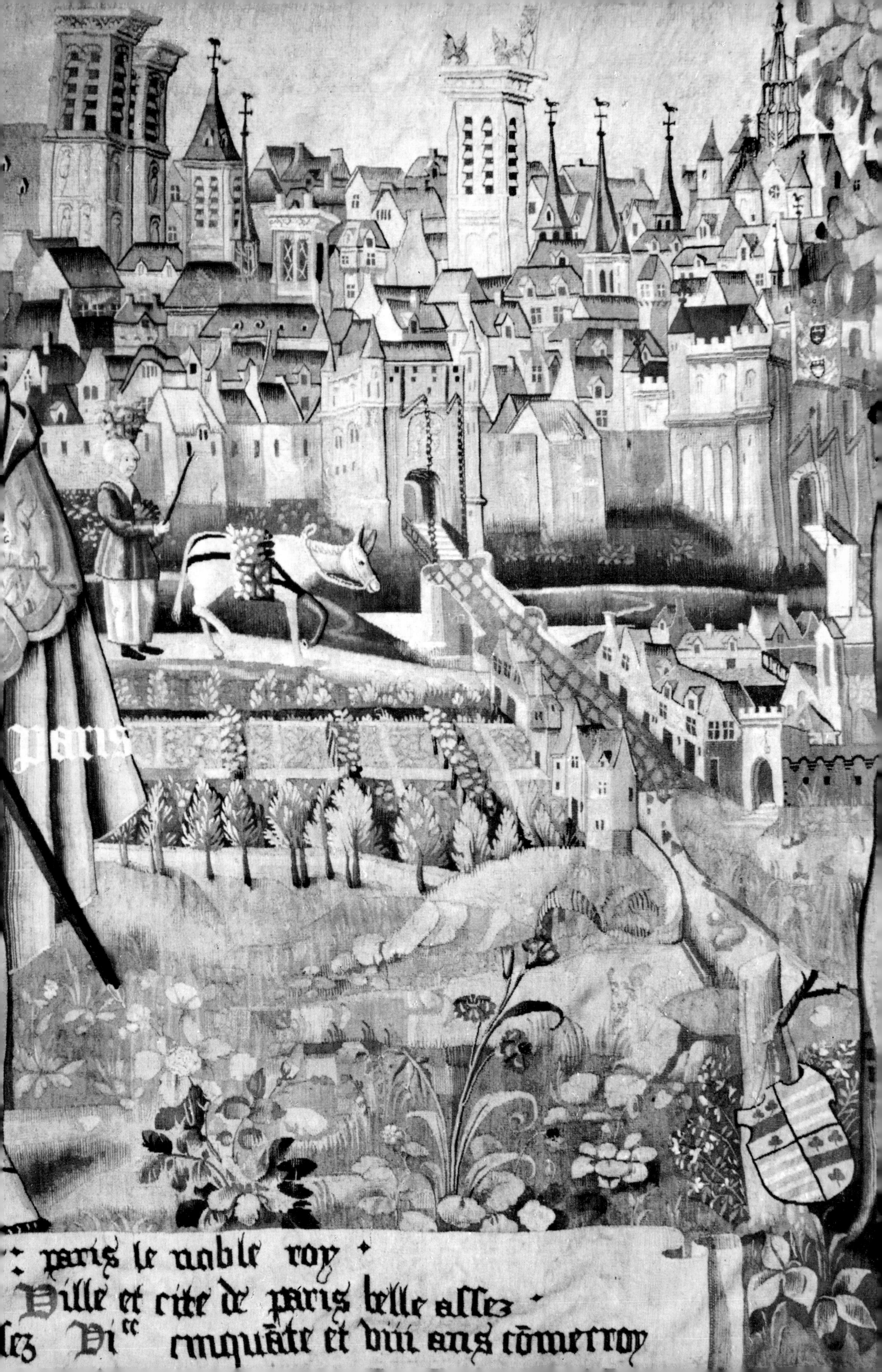

paris

paris le noble roy

Ville et cite de paris belle assez

sez VIᶜᶜ cinquãte et viii ans cõme roy

EAGLE AND OSTRICH. Swiss, 15th century. Zurich. National Swiss Museum. Museum photo.

German tapestry at the close of the Middle Ages

It was in the fifteenth century that tapestry in the Germanic countries reached its greatest development. Whereas in France and Burgundy tapestry was a luxury meant for wealthy members of the nobility and of the Church, in the Germanic countries it retained a strictly bourgeois character. Those who bought German tapestries belonged to the lesser nobility or to the bourgeoisie as in the fourteenth century, whereas the leading nobles ordered directly from the important workshops in other countries.

Production was concentrated in several centers. Although retaining a very artisanal character, the working conditions remained faithful to certain norms, namely the small loom and the use of wool with a bit of linen for the white but very few gold and silver threads, rarely silk ones. As a whole, the German weavers made little attempt to render effects which were related closely to painting but sought to achieve a decorative effect, created solely by balance of form and color with no concern for the illusions of space.

To study these styles we must turn to the graphic arts. In fact, at the close of the fifteenth century the great artists who developed engraving furnished an important variety of subjects which were used by these weavers. Moreover, nowhere else do we find such close relationship with the literature of the period. This delight in "telling a tale" is expressed in numerous secular stories in a naïve and popular style characteristic of the close of the Middle Ages. A pessimistic current mingled with a certain resignation can often be seen in certain representations in which the principal theme is taken from chivalry.

Three great weaving centers dominated German tapestry and two were closely related. The first was Basle, an episcopal city whose influence extended over the regions of the Upper Rhine, then Strasbourg in Alsace, with its widely spread culture, and finally Nuremberg in Franconia. Inspired by easel-picture painting, itself strongly influenced by the School of Bohemia, the Nuremberg productions differed greatly from those of the two Rhenish cities. Other centers on the Middle Rhine and in Swabia, such as Mayence, Trêves and Heidelberg, and various monasteries are also worth mentioning.

Altogether there are two inspirational groups. Certain tapestries decorated with religious or symbolical scenes were destined to embellish churches. These included antependia, decorative hangings or stall covers, and were woven by nuns. The others which represented secular subjects were destined to decorate bourgeois homes and had characteristic subjects such as fabulous and wild monsters or amorous scenes. They represent richly dressed young men and women holding strange animals on leashes or wild men galloping monsters. These figures are designed against a background decorated with flowers and small animals. The illusion of space has been omitted to the advantage of the surface decoration. Other tapestries also include banderoles often of great decorative value with a text to explain the scene represented. A kind of symbolism of the forces of good and evil intervenes in these representations of fabulous and wild animals. Other tapestries with secular themes known as *Minne Teppiche* were inspired by amorous themes and are related to the carved chests similarly decorated and known as *Minne Kastchen* or marriage gifts given to the fiancée. In the GARDEN OF LOVE we find amorous couples, including a woman weaving a crown for her friend, playing chess or cards. The outline of the figures is lost against a background filled with a vine-trellis decoration.

In addition to such popular themes we must not overlook the quality of the tapestries woven at Nuremberg, such as THE LAST JUDGMENT (Nuremberg Museum) and THE CRUCIFIXION at Würzburg. The weaving of the latter consists of a rich quantity of metal threads. The concern for exact reproduction of the painting, which became the chief characteristic of Franconian tapestry, was the prelude to a sudden decline. Not one work woven in the sixteenth century offers the slightest idea of the originality of tapestries produced at Nuremberg in the Middle Ages.

◀ The Garden of Love. 1.02 × 3.55 m. Basle, about 1460-1470. Woven in silk and silver. Basle. Historisches Museum. Museum photo.

(Below)
The Legend of the Count of Savoy. Fragment. 1.25 × 2.28 m. Basle, about 1477.

The scenes represented on this tapestry fragment were taken from the legend of the Count of Savoy, known by a medieval verse, Von dem Grafen von Savoi. *In the depths of poverty, the count has to sell his wife to sailors leaving for France. The countess is asked in marriage by the king, but she begs him to wait a year. A great tournament takes place in which the count is victorious. He finds his wife, they are reunited by the king and their possessions are restored to them. These episodes are explained by the text in banderoles which is read from right to left. Most of the figures are depicted as "savages."*

Besançon. Musée des Beaux-Arts. Photo Hachette.

The Combat of Vices and Virtues. Detail. Nuremberg, about 1400. Regensburg. Staadts Museum. Museum photo.

▼

THE STORY OF GUILLAUME D'ORLÉANS. Detail. Germany, middle Rhineland, first quarter of the 15th century.

Like the preceding tapestry, this one illustrates a medieval tale whose various episodes are explained in banderoles. This section depicts a tournament scene.

Frankfurt. Museum für Kunsthandwerk. Museum photo.

V The sixteenth century — tapestry during the Renaissance

The Brussels workshops and their organization. - Raphael and Giulio Romano as cartoon painters. - Bernard van Orley and his followers. - The Brussels workshops in the second half of the sixteenth century and other Flemish workshops. - Italy: the workshops at Ferrara, Mantua and Florence. - The Fontainebleau and other French workshops. - Tapestry workshops in Germany. - Tapestry in northern Europe: Sweden, Denmark and Norway.

THE sixteenth century witnessed a complete change in tapestry æsthetics in every country. THE ACTS OF THE APOSTLES, which had been woven at Brussels for Pope Leo X after designs by Raphael, marked a turning point in the art of tapestry and the development of a new style based on Renaissance painting. During the entire century the Brussels looms continued to produce tapestries based on designs furnished by important Italian and Flemish painters who were followers of Raphael. The Reformation resulted in the emigration of an increasing number of Flemish weavers who fled religious persecution and were received at foreign courts where the ruling princes encouraged them to set up looms although this activity proved short-lived. This explains the establishment of workshops in Italy in such cities as Ferrara, Mantua and Florence. The royal workshop created by Francis I at Fontainebleau also engaged Flemish weavers, while still others settled in northern Germany, Sweden and Denmark.

The Brussels workshops and their organization

For almost a century Brussels held the lead in tapestry. We admire the fine quality of its production, yet we must also remember that tapestry was not only an art but an important branch of trade. The most brilliant years lasted from about 1510 until the Religious War of 1568 when the country was governed by two regents, Margaret of Austria and Mary of Hungary. Unaided, the workshops assured the financing, the execution and the sale of tapestries, and also extended the trade in luxury goods which had developed in the West since

The Acts of the Apostles

In order to decorate the Sistine Chapel, Pope Leo X commissioned Raphael to create ten tapestry cartoons, whose subjects were inspired by the Acts of the Apostles. These cartoons were delivered at the end of 1516 and the first seven tapestries, woven in Brussels, were finished by 1519 and exhibited in the Sistine Chapel during the Christmas festivities. It is worth indicating that their fine borders decorated with grotesques were also executed from designs by Raphael. The cartoons themselves are now on exhibition in the Victoria and Albert Museum.

The Miraculous Draught of Fishes. 4.40 × 4.96 m. Brussels, workshop of Pierre d'Alost, 1516-1519. Woven in silk and gold.
Rome. Vatican Museum. Photo Alinari.

The Handing of the Keys to St. Peter. Brussels, worskhop of Pierre d'Alost, 1516-1519. Woven in silk and gold.
On the original cartoon, the robe of Christ was of a single color, which the weavers heightened with gold stars.
Rome. Vatican Museum. Museum photo.

the fourteenth century. Owing to the cost of material and the slow rate of production, the creation of tapestries was concentrated in the hands of wealthy merchants who monopolized important enterprises but frequently turned to smaller workshops for the execution of large sets.

After the enormous success of THE ACTS OF THE APOSTLES, the Brussels weavers were unable to fill the orders which they had received from every country. The tapestry industry found itself in need of protection against frauds and imitation during this great period of prosperity and the first half of the century was marked by a series of regulations. The first edict of 1525 promulgated by the Brussels magistrates prohibited the manufacturers from blending the heads of figures in valuable pieces and, in addition, assured the weavers exclusive property of their models by forbidding copies to be made by their competitors. In 1528 a new regulation required that each piece bear the city's weaving mark consisting of a shield of plain gules (the original arms of Brussels) between two letter B's which signified "Brussels Brabant." This same edict obliged the manufacturers and merchants to use a special signature consisting of the monogram of a master weaver. It consecrated and completed the earlier regulations and in a way became the fundamental statute of the Flemish industry of this period. In 1544 the imperial charter granted to the tapestry artisans in the Netherlands confirmed these regulations.

The economic and working conditions were such that the management of workshops was possible only for a small number of masters. The names which dominate this century are those of Pierre d'Alost, the Pannemaker family, and François and Jacob Geubels. The industrial heads were quite familiar with the art of weaving but often added other trades. A man like Pierre d'Alost had dealings not only with bankers such as

The Triumph of the Gods
Only three hangings exist of a tapestry of seven pieces which was purchased by Louis XIV before 1673 and listed in the Royal Inventory as The Triumph of the Gods. *The style of the borders is characteristic of Flemish workshops, whereas the principal subjects are distinctly Italian (the workshop of Raphael). In fact, this may be a tapestry woven in Brussels about 1570-1575 for Pope Gregory XIII from the one now in Windsor Castle, itself inspired by the celebrated* Grotesques *of Pope Leo X, now lost, which was woven in Brussels about 1520 from the cartoon by Raphael's pupil Giovanni da Udine.*

THE TRIUMPH OF VENUS. 5.05 × 7.32 m. Brussels, workshop of François Geubels, about 1570. Woven in silk and gold.
Paris. Mobilier national. Photo Visages de France.

Fugger of Würzburg but also with those of Munich, for he often found himself in financial difficulty in respect to finishing an important and costly set of tapestries. The organizational work was well understood. Moreover, there were several categories of weavers paid according to various rates. The weaving of flesh and faces was considered the most delicate work and therefore paid at a higher rate than that of landscape and costumes. Painters and cartoon designers remained in close contact with the weavers, yet their profession was judged differently. This same division into specialties existed in the painter's studio; the man responsible for the figures was not the same one who painted landscapes or borders. Such organization led to rapid execution and enabled these artists to create the huge sets which today arouse our admiration.

Raphael and Giulio Romano as cartoon painters

In the early years of the century Brussels ranked as the leading weaving center and it was not surprising that Pope Leo X should turn to her workshops to execute THE ACTS OF THE APOSTLES. This commission was in a way a supreme consecration of the skill of these Brussels weavers. This set, which greatly influenced the history of tapestry, was destined to complete the decoration of the lateral walls of the Sistine Chapel which was consecrated in 1483. The design of the cartoons was entrusted to Raphael, who had painted the famous frescoes in the Stanza della Signatura and the Stanza dell'Incendio in the Vatican. Completed in the final months of the year 1516, the designs were at once sent to Brussels to be woven and on Christmas Day 1519 seven of the ten pieces were presented at Rome. These designs now in the Victoria and Albert Museum appear not to have been executed entirely by Raphael, who probably had turned to his chief pupil Giulio Romano, aided by Tommaso Vincidor and Gian Francesco Penni. The weaving was entrusted to Pierre d'Alost, whose important role has already been mentioned.

We have only a partial idea of these works now in the Vatican, for they have suffered a great deal. Yet contemporary accounts mention the tremendous enthusiasm they aroused when they were exhibited at Rome. THE ACTS OF THE APOSTLES created considerable interest and the set was copied down to the eighteenth century not only in the Brussels workshops but also in those of Mortlake in England as well as in the Gobelins and Beauvais factories in France. Traditional tapestry æsthetics had been drastically changed. The medieval method of grouping figures in several scenes on the same piece, covering the entire surface often in a confused manner, now gave way to a powerful and well-arranged composition, whose figures appear to move in real space, creating the illusion of depth. Raphael had conceived these designs as a monumental composition treated in a general manner without detail. According to the expression of M. R. A. Hulst, "it tends towards the eternal," and represents figures nude or wearing artistically draped dark tunics arranged in a decoration of classical artistic inspiration or else in a vast landscape dominated by a dark sky. Confronted by such unusual compositions treated in a spirit

The Hunts of the Emperor Maximilian
Mystery surrounds the origin of The Hunts of the Emperor Maximilian *which consists of twelve pieces, but its importance suggests a royal commission. The cartoons were made by Bernard van Orley. The tapestry probably belonged to the Guise family as early as the 16th century. These twelve hangings, which follow the calendar months and the signs of the zodiac, are partly inspired by a late 14th century book on hunting printed in the 15th century,* Le Livre du Roi Modus et de la Reine Ratio. *This tapestry enjoyed such success that several copies were woven in the Gobelins workshops.*
THE BOAR'S LAST ATTACK. Detail. The dogs seize the boar by the ears. Brussels, workshop of Jean Gheteels (?), 1521-1533.
Paris. Louvre. Photo Giraudon.

(Overleaf) ▶

The Story of Jacob
The cartoons of this tapestry comprising ten hangings are by Bernard van Orley. The first series was probably woven for Charles V. The set in Brussels probably dates from 1534, having been executed in Kempeneere's workshop for the tapestry and goldsmith merchant, Georges Wezeleer.
JACOB RECEIVING THE BLESSING WHICH ISAAC MEANT FOR ESAU. 4.24 × 8.40 m. Brussels, workshop of Willem de Kempeneere, second quarter of the 16th century. Woven in silk and gold.
Foreground, in the center, Isaac blessing Jacob whom he takes for Esau. On the left, Rebecca gives instructions to her favorite son Jacob. On the right, Rebecca receives the two young goats. Background, from left to right: Jacob has just been born and seizes his twin brother by the foot. Esau sells Jacob his birthright for a dish of lentils. While Esau has gone off to hunt for the game demanded by his father, Rebecca prepares a dish of the two young goats which Jacob presents to Isaac.
Brussels. Musées royaux d'Art et d'Histoire. Photo A.C.L.

VT·PATRIARCHA
INSIDIAS·FRAT
CAVTA·FVGAM
NE·NATO·N

BENEDIXIT · ESAU ·
APTA · PARAT ·
· REBECCA · FIDELIS ·
· TELA · TIMET ·

unlike that to which they had been accustomed, the weavers found themselves faced by many problems, and yet their skill soon proved great enough to follow tapestry in its progress towards Italianism. The splendid borders of THE ACTS OF THE APOSTLES represent arabesques *(grotesques)*. This decorative motif of classical origin, rediscovered in the ruins of Nero's Golden House in 1493, was soon adopted by Raphael. The *grotesques* became very popular and inspired several tapestry sets. The magnificent DIVERTISSEMENTS DES DIEUX GROTESQUES mentioned in the inventory of Louis XIV's furniture repository and bearing the signature of Geubels' workshop which was active from 1540 to 1585, probably took up the theme from the designs for the TAPISSERIES A GROTESQUES (which have disappeared), ordered by Leo X from Brussels about 1520 from the cartoons by Giovanni da Udine.

Raphael's vigorous classicism, however, was not respected by his followers. After the master's death, the chief representatives of his school created overloaded compositions in their constant search for movement, overcrowded with accessory figures and designed with complicated foreshortening and much luxury of detail. This virtuosity often destroyed the clarity of the design. The most important set created by this circle of Raphael's immediate followers was that of the STORY OF SCIPIO, consisting of twelve scenes. Penni's sketches illustrate the deeds of war and those by Giulio Romano represent THE CHARIOT OF THE TRIUMPH OF SCIPIO and THE CAPTAINS' BANQUET, large and lively compositions full of figures. The second great set, FRUCTUS BELLI, is chiefly related to the monumental frescoes conceived by the artist for the Palazzo del Tè at Mantua. As for the JEUX D'ENFANTS, these have a purely decorative character and the pleasant theme of Cupids playing among foliage was used not only by the Brussels workshops but also by the Italian.

Bernard van Orley and his followers

Despite these large sets of cartoons, Giulio Romano's style failed to play an important role in the history of Flemish tapestry. Indeed, it was the art of Bernard van Orley, the Flemish cartoon painter, which dominated the entire century. Born at Brussels about 1488 into a painting dynasty, he probably first learned the art in his father's workshop, then made numerous paintings with religious subjects as well as portraits of the princely family for the regent Margaret of Austria, who was succeeded by Mary of Hungary. His work was much admired abroad and Dürer did not fail to pay him a visit during his journey to the Netherlands in 1520. It is very possible that during his youth Bernard van Orley may have had the occasion to visit the famous Brussels workshops which produced splendid gold and silver tapestries and thus familiarize himself with all the requirements of the art of tapestry. His activity in this field was considerable. The first great sets attributed to him, THE LEGEND OF OUR LADY OF LE SABLONS (Musées royaux d'Art et d'Histoire, Brussels), MORALIDADES, HONORES, APOCALYPSE or THE REVELATION OF ST. JOHN, cartoons designed between 1520 and 1530 (Spanish Nation-

The Seven Deadly Sins
The cartoons for this set, designed by Pierre d'Alost, illustrate the theme of the Seven Deadly Sins. The design of the triumphs which occur in the foreground are modeled after The Triumphs of Petrarch.
SLOTH. Detail. 4.50 × 7 m. Brussels, workshop of Guillaume Pannemaker, second half of the 16th century.
Sloth is represented by a winged and horned woman lying on a chariot covered with thistles and drawn by an ass.
Vienna. Kunsthistorisches Museum. Museum photo.

The Life and Exploits of Joao de Castro

Comprising ten hangings, this tapestry was copied from an older one, now lost, the cartoons being attributed to Pierre d'Alost as well as to Michel Coxcie. The subject is devoted to combats fought by the Portuguese army at the gates of the maritime town of Diu and its triumphal entry into Goa on April 15, 1547.

THE VICTORY WON AT GOA BY THE KING OF CAMBAJA. Detail. The entire tapestry measures 3.45 × 5.30 m. Brussels, workshop of Henri de Nève, late 16th century. Woven in silk and gold.

The richly dressed knight is no doubt the Indian King of Cambaja.

Vienna. Kunsthistorisches Museum. Museum photo.

al Patrimony), all reveal in the artist's manner of designing a host of figures and distributing the masses a clearer composition than that of the preceding period. The tendency to fill the entire composition, the fondness for detail and the emphasis on decorative unity —all in a well-established tradition—clearly indicate the direction towards which the artist had created these cartoons.

Later Raphael's art was to influence the work of Bernard van Orley, who changed the Italian master's style by adapting it to the Flemish spirit. The set of eight tapestries of THE STORY OF TOBIAS (Vienna) has not only a peaceful harmony but also the undeniable mark of his Italian model, THE ACTS OF THE APOSTLES. The set of THE STORY OF ABRAHAM (Madrid and Vienna) reveals a more dramatic and lively style. Here we see the teachings of Raphael fully developed; the spacing of the figures in the distance creates considerable feeling of depth and endlessly increases the field of representation. This concern for great space, increased even in relation to Raphael's compositions, is evident in THE BATTLE OF PAVIA (some drawings in the Louvre, the tapestry itself in the Museo Capodimonte, Naples) in which the battle scenes are represented as though from a bird's eye view. No longer do we have the confused mêlées of the medieval tapestries but rather a marked concern to represent historical accuracy in the modern journalistic sense of the word with respect for perspective and topography. The general style is very similar to that of the HUNTS OF EMPEROR MAXIMILIAN I (Louvre) which comprise twelve pieces woven no doubt in Gheetels's workshop before the year 1528. The subject was inspired by the *Livre du roi Modus et de la reine Ratio*, a fourteenth-century treatise on hunting printed in the fifteenth century. The entire hunting cycle takes place under each sign of the month. The clear and balanced compositions follow the laws of the new æsthetics yet reveal much concern for detail and retain all the flavor of the Flemish soil.

In THE BOAR'S FINAL ATTACK we find carefully represented not only the Soignies Forest but also the red hunting costume worn by the horseman, who is said to be Ferdinand of Austria, and even the *jaque*, the blue protective jerkin of the dog seizing the boar by the ears. Faithfully observed landscapes envelop the scenes in a startlingly luminous atmosphere, which is only to be expected when one recalls the drawings in the Louvre and the Leyden Museum which Van Orley made directly from nature. Even more clearly than the foregoing works, the set of THE STORY OF JACOB (Brussels) marks the two tendencies of this great Flemish painter: on the one hand, the purely decorative current inherent in the Netherlands and, on the other, the new attempt to make tapestry a rival of painting.

During the entire century the cartoon painters remained deeply influenced by Bernard van Orley's style and continued in his direction. It is to Pieter Coecke van Aelst (Pierre d'Alost), who was born at Alost about 1500 and died at Brussels in 1550, that we are indebted for the cartoons of THE SEVEN DEADLY SINS (Vienna) represented in the manner of the TRIUMPHS inspired by Petrarch. The arrangement of the procession and the rhythm of a handful of important figures reveal how strongly the painter followed the style created by Bernard van Orley. It is characterized by much lightness and nobly elegant forms. The set of THE STORY OF ST. PAUL, inspired by THE ACTS OF THE APOSTLES, may likewise be considered a continuation of Raphael's famous

Charles V's Campaign Against the City of Tunis

The twelve pieces comprising this set were commissioned by Charles V to commemorate his expedition in Tunis, among the most important military feats during his reign. The painter Jean Cornelisz Vermeyen accompanied the emperor on this campaign and we are indebted to him for the cartoons of this set, which enjoyed much success. The tapestry was displayed at Madrid for every important festivity organized by the Spanish court. Several copies were made, one about 1566 for Cardinal de Granvelle, another was ordered by Charles VI in 1712 from

Judocus de Vos. Finally, in 1740, still another version was woven by the Real Fabrica de Tapices of Madrid by order of the Spanish monarch, Philip V.

THE EMPEROR ENTERS THE HARBOR OF TUNIS WITH HIS GALLEYS. Brussels, workshop of Guillaume Pannemaker, 1548-1554. Woven in silk, gold and silver.
Spain. National Patrimony. Photo Ruiz Vernacci.

Vertumnus and Pomona
The Vertumnus and Pomona cycle from Ovid's Metamorphoses *was often represented by Brussels weavers in the 16th century. Of the original nine hangings only eight exist at present. This tapestry shows Vertumnus, god of the Seasons, who in various guises attempts to seduce Pomona, goddess of fruit and gardens. The cartoons are attributed to Jean Cornelisz Vermeyen.*

VERTUMNUS, DISGUISED AS A HAY GATHERER, APPROACHES POMONA. The entire tapestry measures 4.20 × 6 m. Brussels, workshop of Georges Wezeleer (?), second quarter of the 16th century. Woven in silk, gold and silver.
Detail. Bacchus Carried by His Fauns.
Vienna. Kunsthistorisches Museum. Museum photo.

The Seven Virtues
The cartoons of this set are by Michel Coxcie (1500-1592).

WISDOM. Detail. The entire tapestry measures 3.42 × 5.30 m. Brussels, workshop of François Geubels, second quarter of the 16th century. Woven in silk, gold and silver.
In this detail the figure representing Wisdom is not shown. In the foreground we see Ruth gleaning and, in the background, Gideon fighting the Midianites.
Vienna. Kunsthistorisches Museum. Museum photo.

tapestry set. THE LIFE AND EXPLOITS OF JOÃO DA CASTRO (Vienna) has been attributed to both Pierre d'Alost and Michel Coxcie. In any event, the painter responsible for the cartoons was certainly one of Van Orley's pupils. This set, which represents the Portuguese army engaged in combat before the gates to the town of Diu and João da Castro's triumphal entry into Goa in 1547, together with THE BATTLE OF PAVIA (Naples) and THE CAMPAIGNS OF CHARLES V AGAINST TUNIS by Vermeyen (Spanish National Patrimony) are among the most important historical sets woven in the sixteenth century.

In his CAMPAIGN AGAINST TUNIS, Vermeyen, another follower of Van Orley, developed the representation of fully open landscape conceived almost as a map, doubtless inspired by THE BATTLE OF PAVIA. Mme. Crick-Kuntziger also attributes to Vermeyen the famous VERTUMNUS AND POMONA (Vienna) taken from Ovid's *Metamorphoses.* The nine tapestries relate the story of Vertumnus, the ancient Roman god of the seasons, who in various forms approaches Pomona, the goddess of gardens and orchards, in order to seduce her. The divinities meet in a setting that recalls a richly decorated pergola, while in the background are vast perspectives of a garden open to distant landscape. Also attributed to Vermeyen are the cartoons of the set of

The Planets
The subject of this tapestry comprising seven pieces was doubtless inspired by engravings made in Florence about 1460 devoted to the planets and their influence on human beings.
MERCURY. 4.20 × 5.45 m. Brussels, last third of the 16th century. Woven in silk, gold and thread.
In the center, in the upper part, is Mercury enthroned on his chariot drawn by two roosters. Below, some of his protégés are enjoying their favorite occupations: on the left, a woman personifying Music plays the organ; in the upper right-hand corner, grouped beneath a covered gallery, astronomers study a celestial globe and a surgeon examines a urinal. The border is quite rich. Ornaments in Raphael-like "grotesques" are combined with flowers and fruit, following the traditional Flemish conception.
Munich. Bayerisches National Museum. Photo J. Blauel.

The Valois

This tapestry praises the short-lived reign as Duc de Brabant from 1582 to 1583 of the Duc d'Anjou, François, brother of the French king, Henri III. It represents various festivities organized at the court of Catherine de' Medici. The cartoons for the landscapes were executed by Antoine Caron, painter at the Court of France, while those for the figures in the foreground are by Lucas de Heere, painter in the service of William of Orange.

WATER FESTIVITY AT FONTAINEBLEAU. Brussels, workshop of Joost van Herselle, about 1590. Woven in silk.

Florence. Uffizi. Photo Alinari.

THE CREATION OF THE WORLD or MAN AND ORIGINAL SIN (Uffizi, Florence). These scenes of Adam and Eve in a marvelous earthly paradise are treated in a most harmonious manner.

Michel Coxcie, known as the "Flemish Raphael," is the final representative of Van Orley's school. Born about 1500, he died in 1592. His period of activity was therefore far greater than that of the first two painters. Several sets by him have survived, including that of THE STORY OF THE FIRST COUPLE (Wawel) and above all the set of VIRTUES woven in François Geubels's workshop and now in Vienna. In these static compositions with their calm and serene figures, Michel Coxcie sought for the beauty of form with a tendency to idealization.

The Brussels workshops in the second half of the sixteenth century and other Flemish workshops

Flemish production in the second half of the sixteenth century is marked by a slight artistic weakening, the new sets with figures no longer bearing the strong imprint of the preceding artists. THE EXPLOITS OF THE DUKE OF ALBA remain battle plans rather than monumental decoration and the same comment might be applied to THE CAMPAIGNS OF ARCHDUKE ALBERT which was woven about 1600 after the cartoon by Otto Vaenius, although the attention given to detail destroys the unity of the ensemble. Flemish tapestries generally reveal a dwindling of figures to the benefit of the decoration which is enriched either by much detailed *verdures* or by the contribution of architectural motifs and decorated buildings. Gradually landscape invades tapestry, as is evident in sets such as THE STORY OF ROMULUS AND REMUS, THE PLANETS and TRISTAN AND ISOLDE. The finest and most decorative set woven during the final quarter of the century is doubtless that of THE VALOIS (Uffizi, Florence). The backgrounds are closely related to the drawings by Antoine Caron, but the painter who designed the cartoons was certainly Lucas de Heere, then working at Antwerp. With their undeniable poetical quality, these eight pieces recall the magnificence shown by Catherine de' Medici at her court and represent in the foreground faithful portraits of the Valois family. At the close of the century Brussels compositions became complex and complicated as the result of deliberate confusion, the painters returning to the principle in vogue during the previous century of totally filling up the space to the point of unreadability.

In addition to such grand historiated sets there existed another kind of tapestry of purely decorative character, namely, the *grotesques*. The GROTESQUE MONTHS now in the Kunsthistorisches Museum, Vienna, was sold in 1574-1575 to the Duke of Lorraine by a certain Joost van Herseele. Different from the set commissioned by Leo X, it comprises twelve pieces each dedicated to one of the months; represented against a fine red background is an elegantly luxurious series of arabesques *(grotesques)*. Mural tapestries with ornamental decoration woven both in France and Italy were much appreciated during this period and remained popular until the eighteenth century.

In addition to Brussels the imperial regulation of 1544 limited the production of the great tapestry sets to Liège, Antwerp, Bruges, Audenarde, Alost, Enghien, Grammont, Ath, Lille and

Tristan and Isolde

This tapestry, whose cartoons date from the middle of the 16th century, illustrates the theme of Tristan and Isolde. Six hangings from the set are now in a private Austrian collection.

TRISTAN AND MORGAIN OR MORGAN. Brussels, mid-16th century. Woven in silk, gold and silver.

On the left, Tristan, wearing a helmet and armor, is preparing to enter a tournament. On the right, the fairy Morgain, King Arthur's sister, presents Tristan with a green shield representing a knight resting his feet on the head of a queen and king.

Brussels. Musée communal. Museum photo.

The Months with Grotesques ▶

Consisting of twelve pieces, this tapestry evokes the twelve months personified by divinities represented against a red background, with their symbols and signs of the zodiac, in the midst of a group of grotesque figures. The cartoons have been attributed to an artist of Raphael's entourage. The style of the figures and landscape, however, recalls the Flemish School. In 1574-1575 the weaver Joost van Herselle sold the tapestry to the Duke of Lorraine. It was then inherited by the treasury of the Austrian Empire. Several similar sets were woven at Brussels and at the Gobelins in Paris.

OCTOBER. Detail. 4.28 × 5.30 m. Brussels, third quarter of the 16th century. Woven in silk and gold.

October is symbolized by Mars depicted in the center of the composition with Scorpio on his left.

Vienna. Kunsthistorisches Museum. Museum photo.

OCTOBER.
SVB TVTELA MARTIS
CVM SIGNO SCORPII.

Scenes from The Book of Joshua
Border detail. Brussels, workshop of Marc Crétif, second quarter of the 16th century.
Children playing in the midst of flowers.
Vienna. Kunsthistorisches Museum.
Museum photo.

Tournai. The production of these workshops cannot be dismissed although it was not comparable with that of Brussels. During the sixteenth century Tournai gradually lost its importance, yet its workshops remained active until the eighteenth century, although we possess few sets woven after 1550. Charles de Croy, however, presented his church with a STORY OF ESAU woven by Jean Martin the Younger. Weavers were satisfied with producing pieces with armorial decoration or *verdures* designed in the early spirit.

The city of Antwerp was a warehouse and sales market rather than a center of production. Among the tapestries of definite Antwerp origin, we must mention a set of THE LABORS OF HERCULES (Munich) commissioned from Michel de Bos's workshop by the Duke of Bavaria for his small château at Dachau. During the second half of the sixteenth century Antwerp took advantage of the decline of Bruges and Ghent and became a world market monopolizing the sale of tapestries.

In 1555 a special building known as the *Pant* was constructed for the exhibition of tapestries to be sold as well as the raw material and looms used in the process of weaving. After Brussels, Enghien and Audenarde became the two centers where the weaving industry achieved its greatest development.

Enghien specialized in finely executed *verdures* with arabesques or garden scenes. Audenarde appears to have produced chiefly inexpensive hangings or *verdures* known as *Oudenarden*, representing rich foliage with wild beasts.

Italy: the workshops at Ferrara, Mantua and Florence

During the sixteenth century Italy ranked second to Flanders for her brilliant tapestry production. She not only created cartoons for other European countries but also produced tapestries, often turning to the aid of Flemish weavers. By the final quarter of the fifteenth century the Italian princes, enamored of art, gathered at their court a number of artists who could promptly fulfill their wishes. These princes founded workshops at Ferrara and Florence which assured Italy an important although sometimes neglected place in the history of tapestry.

In the fifteenth century Italy was already familiar with this art. Interesting tapestry examples include the set of THE PASSION (St. Mark's Cathedral, Venice) and an equally remarkable tapestry, THE MONTHS, woven at Vigevano about 1500 to decorate Gian Giacomo Trivulzio's château. The first prince to become a true patron of a tapestry workshop was Lionello d'Este, who summoned to Ferrara a Brussels weaver named Rinaldo di Gualtieri Boteram. In the second third of the sixteenth century, the head of the House of Este at Ferrara, Duke Ercole II, endeavored to infuse a fresh approach to tapestry among his collections and for this purpose he brought from Flanders two skilled weavers, Nicolas and Jean Karcher. Together with eight other Flemish masters, the two men created workshops which produced numerous pieces for the Este family, the Gonzaga of Mantua and the Medici of Florence. The weavers included the equally skilled Jan Rost. Gifted with outstanding technical ability and finding themselves in Italy, where they had occasion to study the cartoons of such great masters as Battista Dossi, these weavers produced sets of rare beauty.

The Labors of Hercules

One of a set of four, this tapestry is characteristic of a very common type in the 16th century woven in Audenarde, Grammont and Enghien, and known as à feuilles de choux. *The general décor consists of large rolled leaves including a few frolicking animals. The presence of a historiated subject among the* verdure *makes this tapestry an exceptional work.*

HERCULES AND ONE OF DIOMEDES' STALLIONS. 3.55 × 4.44 m. Audenarde, second half of the 16th century. Paris. Louvre. Photo Hachette.

In addition to an unusual artistic milieu, it is worth mentioning the favorable economic conditions which enabled Ferrara to make the first experiment in a workshop organized by a court, an experiment which was to be repeated in Florence by the Medici.

The masters of the School of Ferrara, the two Dosso brothers and Battista Dossi, who were in the service of Duke Ercole II, produced easel paintings as well as frescoes and cartoons for the tapestry workshops. It is to Battista Dossi that we are indebted for the cartoons of the pieces inspired by Ovid's *Metamorphoses* which are now in the Musée des Gobelins. Despite their poor condition, we can judge the fresh interpretation of the ancient myth. It is often difficult to know whether the tapestries woven in the Karcher workshops for the Gonzaga family of Mantua were made at Ferrara or at Mantua itself. THE STORY OF MOSES (cathedral of Milan) bears the arms of the Duke of Mantua which are found on two pieces illustrating children's games, the designs for which are by Giulio Romano for one (Poldi Pezzoli Museum, Milan) and by Giovanni da Udine for the other (cathedral of Milan). The tapestries produced in the Ferraran workshops are outstanding for the importance given to the decorative element, the *grotesques*, the vegetation, the landscape. But the duke's death soon followed by that of Jean Karcher proved a fatal blow to the activity of these workshops.

Following the example of the House of Este, the Grand Duke of Tuscany, Cosimo I (1569-1574), decided to estab-

Jeux d'Enfants
CUPIDS PLAYING IN A GARLAND OF FRUIT. Ferrara or Mantua (?), workshop of Jean and Nicolas Karcher, about 1545. Woven in silk.
Milan. Museo del Duomo. Museum photo.

The Story of Moses
THE BRONZE SERPENT. Ferrara or Mantua, workshop of Jean and Nicolas Karcher, about 1545. Woven in silk.
Milan. Museo del Duomo. Museum photo.

(Overleaf)
The Story of Joseph
JOSEPH SOLD BY HIS BROTHERS after Bronzino. Florence, workshop of Giovanni Rost, 1549. Rome. Quirinal Palace. Photo Secretariat General of the President of the Republic.

BRONZINO
FIORENTIN

THE BANQUET. 4.03 × 8.23 m. Florence, second half of the 16th century. Woven in silk.
The origin and subject of this tapestry have given rise to various theories. The latest is that of John Shearman who believes this composition to be derived from Vasari's Feast of Ahasuerus *at Arezzo* (1549), *suggesting an artist of Allori's circle as the one who designed the cartoons.*
Château d'Oiron. Dépôt du Service des Monuments historiques. Photo Hachette.

(Overleaf)

Tapestry of the Gallery of Fontainebleau
The six pieces of this tapestry copy the decoration of the Galerie des Réformes at Fontainebleau after Rosso and Primaticcio. These tapestries with the heraldic emblem of the salamander were ordered by Francis I who died in 1547 *and did not live to see their completion.*
DANAE after Primaticcio. Detail of the central medallion (also see p. 173). 3.23 × 6.25 m. Fontainebleau, 1540-1550. Woven in silk, gold and silver.
Vienna. Kunsthistorisches Museum. Photo Bildarchiv d'Öst. Nationalbibliothek.

lish in Florence a workshop worthy of competing with that of Ferrara. The *Arrazeria Medicea* was to last as long as the Medici, that is, until the eighteenth century. The two masters in charge of the new establishment were the Flemings Jan Rost and Nicolas Karcher. They began with an appreciable guaranty on the part of the Grand Duke, who promised to furnish them with a suitable building, to pay each man six hundred gold *écus* annually yet permit them to work for other clients and to pay them separately for any works executed for the House of Medici. In return the two Flemings agreed to install twenty-four looms and to furnish apprentices free of charge. Concluded at first for a period of three years, the contract was renewed until 1558.

This tradition of turning to Flemish masters was maintained until 1568, the year an Italian named Benedetto Squili was placed in charge of the workshops. The first tapestries were destined chiefly for the Medici needs. From the outset tapestry had a well-defined character, for it was essentially the masters of Florentine painting who supplied the cartoons. These painters were Mannerists. Deeply imbued with the art of Michelangelo, they were fond of complicated compositions designed in such a manner as to make the most of the nude body in action, as seen in THE STORY OF JOSEPH, twenty pieces composed for the Room of the Two Hundred. Tapestry was part of a grand art and every important painter of this generation turned to cartoon projects. Cosimo I was surrounded by a talented group including Pontormo, Bronzino, Salviati, Bachiacca and later Alessandro Allori. We must also mention Vasari, a man of many talents, who as early as 1555 was entrusted with the entire tapestry decoration of the Palazzo Vecchio in Florence. His writings reveal his personal conception of this art, for he considered the painter who furnished the cartoon of chief importance and relegated the weaver's role to that of mere execution. Thus he praised the manner in which "the hairs on a man's face are rendered as though by a paintbrush." Tapestry for him was a complement to fresco. He did not regard it as a mobile and temporary form of decoration but, on the contrary, as a set and rigid form of ornamentation. Long exhibited, the tapestries of this group are today in poor condition.

The Fontainebleau and other French workshops

The first royal tapestry workshop in France was established by Francis I. In contrast to the Netherlands, which had only private workshops, the one in France was to become a royal enterprise. The king was fond of tapestry and intended to follow the example set by Cosimo I by having works woven for his own residences. The building accounts *(comptes des bâtiments)* from 1540 to 1550 mention details relative to this subject. The workshop was probably established in the château itself under the Superintendant of the Royal Treasury, Babou de la Bourdaisière. The weavers from Paris and the Netherlands were under the direction of Jean and Pierre Le Briés and formed the personnel consisting of at least ten masters. The painter Babouin worked under the two court painters, Rosso and Primaticcio. The principal work wo-

Tapestry of the Gallery of Fontainebleau
The Death of Adonis after Rosso. Fontainebleau, 1540-1550. Woven in silk, gold and silver. Vienna. Kunsthistorisches Museum. Photo Bildarchiv d'Ost. Nationalbibliothek.

ven at the Fontainebleau workshop in a relatively short period is the fine set now in Vienna comprising six pieces made after the mural painting to decorate the window sides of the famous gallery in the château de Fontainebleau. It was not finished until after the death of Francis I and was sent to Vienna at an unknown date. Its essential novelty lies in the fact that not only frescoes but also the entire mural decoration with the stuccowork and reliefs have been interpreted in wool. Here for the first time tapestry was completely subordinated to painting and sculpture; even the upper part of the framework is treated in *trompe-l'œil.* The purely decorative framework acquires importance since it is greater than the central subject. The DIANA woven from the design by Primaticcio with its elegant play of lines is the most remarkable. The surface is divided by large groups of caryatids and creates a pleasant harmony between the plastic decoration and the central medallion which here acquires its full value. The calm and restful figure of Diana is in utter contrast to the complicated movements of Rosso's often violent figures as in THE DEATH OF ADONIS.

To this same workshop are attributed the *grotesque* compositions, the most famous being CYBELE and THE DEATH OF JOAB in the Musée des Gobelins. The design of the first recalls the fine arabesques by Du Cerceau and the style of the second a painter closely related to Niccolò dell'Abbate.

We know something about the workshop of a certain Parisian named Pierre Biasse, who was working at Fontainebleau from 1540 to 1550. In 1544 together with Jacques Langlois he agreed to execute a LIFE OF ST. MAMMÈS for Cardinal de Givry, bishop of Langres, for his cathedral; the cartoons are by

Jean Cousin the Elder (two tapestries in the cathedral of Langres and one in the Louvre).

Many attempts were made in Paris to create a favorable climate for the development of tapestry. In the early reign of Henri II a tapestry workshop was organized in the hospital of La Trinité, in the Rue St. Denis (1551). La Trinité included among its functions the instruction of orphans and abandoned children in various crafts. THE STORY OF DIANA which bears in the borders the initials of Henri II and of Diane de Poitiers, later replaced by the arms of the Genoese family Grillo, appears to have been a royal order and was doubtless woven in this workshop rather than in that of Fontainebleau. The set is now divided among the Château d'Anet, the Musée de Rouen and the Metropolitan Museum of Art.

The most skilled weaver was certainly Maurice Dubout or Dubourg, who was working at La Trinité. In 1584 he was commissioned by the church of Saint-Merry to supply a LIFE OF CHRIST (some pieces in the Musée de Cluny, others in the Musée des Gobelins). Wishing to infuse fresh life into French tapestry, Henri IV chose him to head the workshops and established him in Paris in an ancient building once belonging to the Jesuits.

Tapestry workshops in Germany

In the sixteenth century Germany produced an important number of tapestries, but though of much variety, they lacked unity, for the workshops remained unorganized. The art of tapestry followed two clearly defined tendencies. In the South and in the center of Germany where weaving had long been practiced, the very strong tradition turned its back to the new impetus introduced by the Renaissance. The themes were rigidly set and secular subjects always represented amorous or allegorical scenes with couples surrounded by banners set against a background of rinceaux. Other works of religious inspiration were woven in convents, including that of Walpurgis at Eichstadt, which soon became famous. These works represented saints, men or women, in an archaic and even popular style, but with a definite decorative effect as is evident in ST. WALBURGA AND HER NUNS (Munich).

Tapestry weavers who had fled the Netherlands because of religious persecution settled in northern and eastern Germany, which until then lacked workshops. Here in this Protestant country the art of tapestry acquired the character of German national teaching in the service of the new religion. Early in the century master weavers at Cologne, then at Cassel and Hamburg, created works whose character remained distinctly Flemish. Saxony also had several looms. The chief center was at Torgau, which produced the curious tapestry woven by Serger Brombeck about 1550, THE ALLEGORY OF THE REFORMATION. In this work both subject and style are related to the cycle of sixteenth-century Flemish painting and were influenced by the art of Cranach the Elder, the most important painter of the Reformation. Both the landscape background and the border retain a strong Flemish character.

ST. WALBURGA AND HER NUNS. Eichstätt, first third of the 16th century.
Munich. Bayerisches National Museum. Museum photo.

ALLEGORY OF THE REFORMATION. Left part of the composition. Torgau, workshop of Serger Bombeck, about 1550.
On the right, Luther kneeling.
Weimar. Schlossmuseum. Photo Louis Held.

Tapestry in northern Europe: Sweden, Denmark and Norway

From the middle of the sixteenth century Europe witnessed a constant emigration of Flemish weavers. A short-lived efflorescence existed in Sweden under Erik IV (1560-1568). Itinerant weavers from the Protestant cities of the northern Netherlands traveled from one château to another, from Gripsholm to Svartshö, from Kalmar to Stockholm to execute royal commissions. These weavers numbered not only Paul de Bucher but also Nils Eskilsson, who had produced the very important work THE STORY OF THE KINGS OF SWEDEN; the cartoon painter was Dominikus Verwilt of Antwerp. Having settled at Stockholm, the latter borrowed his subject from a work by the last Catholic bishop of Sweden, Johannes Magni, the *Historia de omnibus Gothorum Suedonumque regibus*. This excellent tapestry was woven with metal threads from 1561 to 1569. The pieces now in the Royal Collection at Stockholm reveal the hold of Flemish art and its influence on Swedish art in general. Under John III production declined and the royal workshop was closed; the Crown once again turned for its tapestry to foreign workshops.

In Denmark King Frederick II in his desire to decorate his château at Kronborg summoned Hans Knieper of Antwerp in 1577 to be court painter and cartoon designer. He also obtain-

THRONE TAPESTRY OF FREDERICK II, KING OF DENMARK. Cartoon by Hans Knieper. Elsinore, Denmark workshop of Hans Knieper, 1585.

The center of the composition displays the coat-of-arms of the Kingdom of Denmark surmounted by a crown. Four medallions representing scenes from antiquity stand out against a grotesque décor. This tapestry was removed by the Swedes as war booty after the siege of Kronborg in 1658-1659.

Stockholm. Nationalmuseum. Museum photo.

THE RIGHTEOUS MAN AND CHRISTIAN VIRTUE. 1.70 × 2.18 m. Nordtröndelag, Norway, about 1580. Woven in silk and gold.
This tapestry shows a righteous man on his deathbed, surrounded by the Christian virtues represented in the form of feminine figures. The fringe around the border is characteristic of Norwegian tapestry.
Oslo. Kunstindustrimuseet. Museum photo.

ed the services of the weaver Antonio de Cortes, and tapestry workshops were established at Elsinore. Knieper remained active until his death and his large cartoon designs included THE STORY OF DAVID and THE STORY OF THE OLD TESTAMENT. The set of KINGS woven from 1581 to 1584 for the great hall in the château at Kronborg (now in Copenhagen) represents the Danish sovereigns against a strongly detailed background treated in a characteristic Flemish manner. Knieper also executed the model of the tapestry for the royal throne (Stockholm Nationalmuseum), a tapestry woven in a very rich but largely ornamental decoration.

In Norway the art of tapestry retained a strong personal character which related it to popular art and a refusal to accept foreign influence. The works constantly represented the same themes such as HEROD'S FEAST; SOLOMON AND THE QUEEN OF SHEBA, ESTHER AND AHASUERUS and THE JUST MAN AND CHRISTIAN VIRTUE.

It is no problem to identify these pieces whose surface is entirely covered with landscape, flowers, objects and decoration, the stiff, angular outlines closely connected with each other. In their treatment these tapestries were medieval rather than Renaissance, and the themes were repeated with little change until the eighteenth century. Whereas the coastal regions of Telemark and Numedal were relatively receptive to foreign influence, Gudbranstal remained the center of this folklore art.

The Story of the Kings of Sweden
The cartoons for this tapestry are by Dominikus Verwilt of Antwerp.
KING SVENO. Detail of the king's head. The entire tapestry measures 3.30 × 2.97 m. Kalmar, Sweden, workshop of Nils Eskilsson, about 1560. Woven in silk, gold and silver.
Stockholm. Royal Palace. Photo National Furniture of Sweden.

Friderich. 2. Christian
des. 3. son,
So balde ins Regiment Ich tratt
An meins Hern vattern loblich stadt,
Bezwang Ich mein aufrürisch Landt,
Das Furstenthumb Dietmarsch genandt,
So meinem Stamb viel trotz und spott
Gar oft vorhin zugfuget hatt
Darnach mit Schweden kham In streitt.
Zu langem schwerem krieg geriett
Endtlich der Kayser sichs ahn nham
Franckreich, und Poln mitt dazu kham.
Der Churfurst auch auß Sachsenlandt
Versuchten handlung aller handt
Taten sampt ichs mit fleis do zu
Biß nach mein wiln wardt fried und Ruh
Ach Gott hinfurt zu meiner Zeitt
Gib gluck beschutz mein Lande und leutt
Christian, Erwehlter Koning zu
Dennemarcken, Friderichs des
anderen Sohn,
Mein Gluck stell ich in Gottes handt
Dem alle dinge sein bekandt,
Der wirdts schicken nach sein gefall,
Wies hernach mit mir werden soll,
Ist sein Gottlich will, dohin stelle
Das ich soll leben in der weldt
Woll er mich nemen in sein hutt,
Und fuegen zu, was nutz und gutt,
Des ich ihm fast vertrawen will
Und mich richten nach seinem ziell,
Wer sein sach setzt in Gottes gwalde
Dem gehet es wol, sey Jung oder alt.
Zu Gott allein

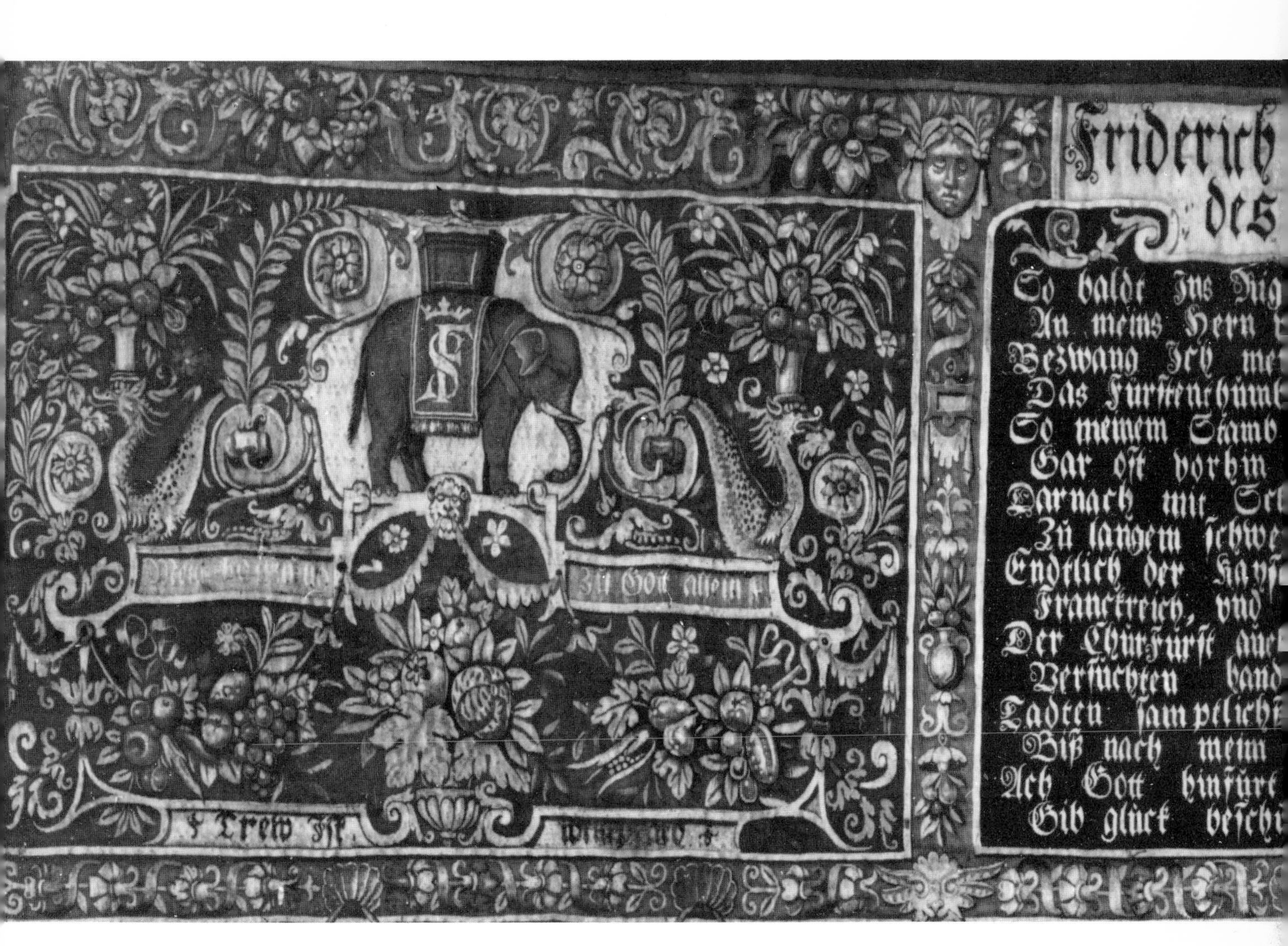

The Kings of Denmark
Hans Knieper of Flemish origin, painter to King Frederick II of Denmark at the Kronborg castle, designed the project of forty-two tapestries representing the kings who had ruled over Denmark from the time of Dan, supposedly a contemporary of King David, until the reign of Frederick II.

KING FREDERICK II AND HIS SON, CHRISTIAN. Height 3.98 m. Elsinore, Denmark, workshop of Hans Knieper, about 1584.
King Frederick is shown with his son, Christian, on his left, and his faithful dog on his right. In the background we see the castles of Fredericksberg and Kronborg.
Tapestry detail.
In the upper part, German verse relates the story of the kings.
Copenhagen. National Museum. Museum photo.

VI The seventeenth century — from Rubens to Le Brun

Cartoons by Rubens and his followers. - The tapestry dynasties in Flanders and the Netherlands. - Tapestry in France before the creation of the Gobelins. - The Gobelins factory under Le Brun. - The crisis of 1683-1694. - The Beauvais factory.

NE fact dominates the history of seventeenth-century tapestry: the emigration of the most skilled Flemish weavers. The civil and religious wars which ruined the Netherlands as early as the second half of the previous century created a situation unfavorable to the production of luxury goods. By 1591 an excellent Antwerp weaver, François Spierinck, was in charge of the Delft workshops. The Flemish weaver Daniel Pepersack, who had been summoned by the Duke of Mantua, established the workshop at Charleville. In 1603 Jan van der Biest of Enghien assumed the leadership of the Munich workshop and at about the same time also led the Brussels weavers working at Nancy. Of greater importance was the arrival in Paris, in 1602, of the Flemings Marc de Comans and François de La Planche, the first directors of those workshops destined to evolve into the great royal Gobelins factory. This proved an event of utmost importance, for Brussels lost the monopoly of fine tapestries and henceforth it was the French workshops—Gobelins, Beauvais, Aubusson—which set and created the tone in Europe.

Under the leadership of Charles Le Brun, court painter to Louis XIV, the Gobelins soon gained a prestige which continued to increase.

Cartoons by Rubens and his followers

What importance can be given to the work by Rubens in the field of tapestry? Certainly the models created by this great master of color and movement were in utter contrast to the traditional conception of tapestry. Rubens gave little thought to the weavers' requirements; the cartoons he supplied remained paintings in which the figures consist of multiple tonalities which, according

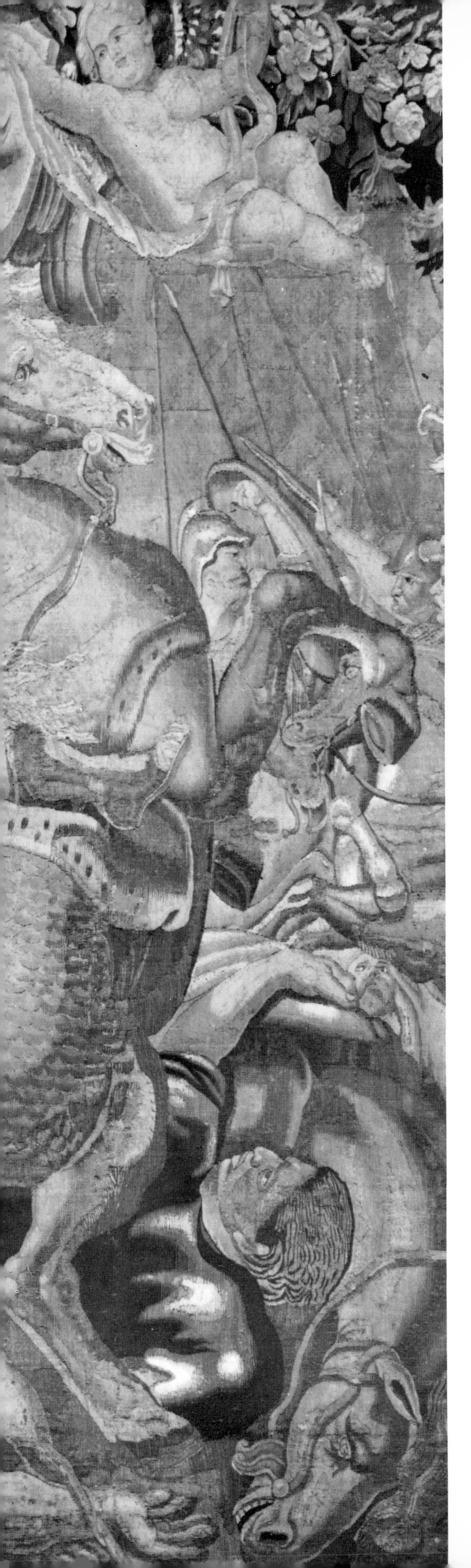

The Story of Decius Mus
Cartoons by Rubens.
The subjects of this tapestry are reproductions of eight paintings by Rubens in the Liechtenstein Gallery in Vienna. We know that the first version of The Story of Decius Mus *was woven as early as* 1618. *This set was repeated numerous times, with copies in Madrid, Stockholm, Vienna, Hamburg and elsewhere.*

THE DEATH OF DECIUS. 3 × 4.80 m. Brussels, about 1620-1625.
The subject represents the battle of Veseris in which the consul, Publius Decius Mus, gave his life for a Roman victory. This tapestry is among the earliest weavings. The border, not shown here, is characteristic of the one often used by Franz van den Hecke, who therefore may have executed the tapestry.
Brussels. Musées royaux d'Art et d'Histoire. Photo A.C.L.

The New Testament

This tapestry of the New Testament, comprising twenty-nine pieces, was ordered from Brussels by the Grand Master of the Order of Malta, Roman Perellos, on his election in 1700. It was designed to decorate the convent church of Saint-Jean de La Valette. Its twenty-nine subjects were borrowed from several tapestry sets after various paintings including the tapestry of The Apotheosis of the Eucharist *after Rubens.*

THE TRIUMPH OF DIVINE LOVE OR CHARITY after Rubens. 6.50 × 6.70 m. Brussels, workshop of Judocus de Vos, 1700. Woven in silk.

The first tapestry of The Apotheosis of the Eucharist *was commissioned from Rubens by Isabelle Claire Eugénie, daughter of Philip II, who was married in 1599 to Archduke Albert of Austria. In 1630 she presented the tapestry to the monastery of Las Señoras Religiosas Descalzas Reales, to which she was affectionately attached. This tapestry, still in the same monastery in Madrid, enjoyed much success and was woven numerous times, the copies including that of La Valette.*

La Valette. Church of Saint-Jean. Photo Police Laboratory, Malta.

to Van Puyvelde, "model the forms and even soften the silhouettes in order to include the figures in the atmosphere."

The tapestry weavers found themselves faced by difficult problems which they solved more or less successfully. For THE STORY OF ACHILLES (cartoons finished by Jacob Jordaens), the weavers Geraert van der Strecken, Franz van den Hecke and Franz Raes adopted the use of hard lines which did not exist in the original (Royal Palace at Turin and the Venetian Palace at Rome). On the other hand, in the set of DECIUS MUS (Liechtenstein Collection), the weavers Geubels and Raes attempted to equal the fineness and gradation of colors, but as a result diminished the splendid contrasts. In THE STORY OF CONSTANTINE (Philadelphia Museum of Art), ordered directly from Rubens by Louis XIII, the Paris workshops headed by Comans and La Planche exaggerated the chromatic force and created a violent effect which was further intensified by the gradation of colors in these tapestries which have changed in tone.

The great influence which Rubens exerted on the art of tapestry cannot be denied; for several generations the style of those painters who designed very *recherché* cartoons was marked by that of the Antwerp master. These tapestries correspond to the taste of the period for important compositions in which enthusiasm is combined with a decided sense of rhythm, reconciling dramatic power with exuberant detail. In THE STORY OF CONSTANTINE the figures and costumes are directly inspired by classical sculpture. We know that not only Peiresc, the classical scholar and friend of Rubens, but also Louis XIII's entourage admired such forms of historical accuracy. In a letter to the painter, he emphasized "the precision you have shown to detail, down to the nails of the shoes." This precision Le Brun was not to forget when he designed for the Gobelins the cartoons of the tapestry THE STORY OF ALEXANDER.

Rubens imposed a new vision; he repudiated all that was unessential and abolished narrative episodes and landscapes of purely decorative character which were strongly favored by Flemish artists. The pieces of various sets he designed are now for the most part dispersed in different collections. As a result, the grandiose effect attained by complete sets are sometimes overlooked. Nevertheless, we have an exception in THE APOTHEOSIS OF THE EUCHARIST whose subject was borrowed from the great struggle on the part of the Church against the heretics condemned by the Council of Trent. This tapestry is preserved intact in the convent of Las Descalzas Reales at Madrid for which it was woven. Instead of the traditional border, Rubens framed each scene with pilasters and columns. Using *trompe-l'œil* he sought to create the impression of a tapestry hanging in an architectonic ensemble and supported by cherubs.

Rubens's immediate followers continued this notion of an architectural frame instead of a border. After Rubens, Jacob Jordaens was the chief cartoon painter of the Flemish countries in the seventeenth century. In his work as a whole, he was more active in this area than Rubens. Indeed, his name is listed in the records of the Guild of St. Luke at Antwerp as a distemper painter *(water scilder)*. From 1635 to 1660 we find Jordaens working chiefly for weavers and his workshop produced important cartoons such as THE STORY OF PHILIP OF MACEDONIA, THE STORY OF ACHILLES, THE STORY OF ULYSSES and GIDEON. Although some tapes-

The New Testament
THE TRIUMPH OF THE CATHOLIC CHURCH after Rubens. Brussels, workshop of Judocus de Vos, 1700. Woven in silk.
Detail. The angel bearer of St. Peter's keys. La Valette. Church of Saint-Jean. Photo courtesy of the author.

Horsemanship
Cartoons by Jacob Jordaens (1593-1678). 4.10 × 5.08 m. Brussels, workshop of Everaert Leyniers, about 1650. Woven in silk.
This tapestry of eight pieces traces various scenes of horsemanship and stages of apprenticeship in the equestrian art which had enjoyed fresh favor under Manuel de Pluvinel, who died in 1620.
EXECUTION OF A PESADE. Detail of the right part. Vienna. Kunsthistorisches Museum. Photo Bildarchiv d'Ost. Nationalbibliothek.

tries no longer survive, we still have the cartoons or *modelli* as they were called.

The most characteristic tapestries of Jordaens's art are THE SCENES OF COUNTRY LIFE (the cartoons date from 1635), a set repeated several times, which praises the pleasures of country life, hunting, rich food and amorous games. In this same spirit the artist designed the PROVERBS which illustrate themes whose tradition often dates from antiquity. Flemish popular settings of the period furnished subjects full of verve for this painter who was admirably capable of translating the robust forms and the vibrant color effect. In a set such as the one entitled HORSEMANSHIP, Jordaens returned in a degree to traditional tapestry decoration and renewed the conception of the "decoration" proper to the art of tapestry. These eight pieces trace various stages in the equestrian art. During the Renaissance riding enjoyed a new vogue. From Italy the taste spread throughout the northern European countries and found one of its most enthusiastic practitioners in Antoine Plivinel, whose *Manège royal* certainly influenced Jordaens. Rubens's most famous followers contributed to restoring to the Flemish workshops some of their past reputation. These included Jean Bol, Josse de Momper, Denis and Louis van Alsloot, Louis de Vadderre, Antoine Sallaerts and above all Juste van Egmont, whose STORY OF ANTHONY AND CLEOPATRA was inspired by the style of Rubens.

Scenes from Country Life
Cartoons by Jacob Jordaens.
This tapestry, consisting of eight pieces, praises the pleasures of rural life.
THE MANAGER'S WIFE FEEDING THE POULTRY. Detail. Brussels, about 1635. Woven in silk. Vienna. Kunsthistorisches Museum. Photo Bildarchiv d'Öst. Nationalbibliothek.

The tapestry dynasties in Flanders and the Netherlands

The emigration of the weavers was to prove fatal to Flemish industry; the tapestry guild was upset, as was the government which was headed by Archduke Albert, who sought in vain to solve the crisis. The guild granted loans to the workers, the government exempted them from taxes and above all, in addition to the traditional Antwerp market, permitted the establishment of another tapestry market in Brussels known as the *Pant*.

Nevertheless, the tapestry craft was well implanted in Flanders and there still remained true weaving dynasties which for several generations contributed to the continuation of the art of weaving. Catherine van den Heynde, widow of Jacob Geubels, was among the tapestry weavers most favored by Archduke Albert. Within a period of eight years (1605-1613), she sold no less than thirty pieces. In 1607 Guillaume Toens furnished the archduke with a HISTORY OF CONSTANTINE. Martin Reynbouts was active at Brussels until 1615 and was succeeded by his son François, who died in 1648. The governor of the Netherlands bought several important sets from him, including THE BATTLES OF THE ARCHDUKE ALBERT. During the seventeenth century the Raes and Van den Hecke families were represented by numerous members. About 1676 François van den Hecke had one of the most active workshops in the country. No less important was the Leyniers family, including a dyer named Gaspard, who proved so skillful that in 1672 he was named dyer to the Governor of the Netherlands. Henri Reydams, who entered the profession in 1629, was succeeded by his son in 1671. The descendants of the Reydams in association with the Leyniers retained their workshops until the middle of the eighteenth century and certain tapestries often bear the combined names of both families. We must also mention the Le Clerck and Pannemaker families, who established a number of workshops in Flanders and in the neighboring countries, as well as the Leefdaele, the de Vos and the van der Borgtecht families. The list could be increased, for there are many tapestry documents dating from this period.

Special interest attaches to the workshops of François Spierinck who, having come from Antwerp, settled at Delft in 1591. His tapestries are outstanding for the fine execution of their weaving and for great refinement in the use of decorative elements. Spierinck executed various famous sets. The reputation of the Delft workshops was so important that their tapestries were exported to England, Denmark, Sweden and other countries. THE HISTORY OF SCIPIO was executed in 1610 for the English chamberlain, then in 1621 for Gustave Adolphus of Sweden, from cartoons by the painter Coquel. He also produced THE DESTRUCTION OF THE INVINCIBLE ARMADA, commissioned by Lord Howard for the English government, from the cartoons by Henrick Cornelisz Vroom. THE STORY OF FURIOUS ROLAND, now in the Poldi Pezzoli Museum in Milan, represents a more pleasant subject with graceful figures in a forest vibrating with color, knights, animals and architectural motifs, all treated with enchanting subtlety. Spierinck's assistant for more than ten years (1604-1615) was Karel von Mander, who established a new workshop of an outstanding artistic level, produc-

TRANSFER OF THE RELICS OF ST. AUGUSTINE. Bruges, 1637.
The processional scene is framed by St. Frigdianus, on the left, and St. Herculanus, on the right.
Bruges. Musée de la Chapelle du Saint-Sang. Photo A.C.L.

ing such sets as THE STORY OF ALEXANDER and THE STORY OF TROY. Spierinck's workshop was to continue after his death in 1630 under the direction of his sons Pieter and Aert.

The history of Delft tapestries was continued during the entire century with the workshops of Maximilien van der Gucht, who produced a number of decorative works (*verdures*, heraldic pieces) as well as the set of ENGLISH HUNTS and especially THE GREAT BATTLE OF NIEUPORT (Musées royaux d'Art et d'Histoire, Brussels) woven in 1648, an important historical tapestry with delightful landscapes.

Tapestry in France before the creation of the Gobelins

In the seventeenth century there was a change in values, for French tapestries acquired supremacy over those woven in the Flemish countries. In the development of the art of French tapestry, the role of Henri IV, who recognized the economic importance of this industry, was significant. In 1608 Girard Laurent and Maurice Dubout, first installed in a house once used by the Jesuits, settled in the Grande Galerie of the Louvre; the final occupants were doubtless attached to the royal Gobelins workshops in 1662. As for the workshop of La Trinité, which had been created by Henri II, it continued in existence until about 1638 when it appears to have been incorporated into the Gobelins by François de La Planche's followers. Among the final products of this workshop we can mention the rather mediocre STORY OF ST. CRÉPIN AND ST. CRÉPINIEN (Musée des Gobelins).

On the request of Henri IV, François de La Planche of Audenarde and Marc de Comans of Antwerp settled, in 1602, in the Faubourg Saint-Marcel, on the banks of the Bièvre, a tributary of the Seine which flowed nearby. Henri IV was anxious for France to have workshops worthy of competing with those of the Netherlands. In 1607 letters patent granted the two partners a number of privileges, including titles of nobility, the right to brew beer and the exclusive sale of tapestries in France. It is amusing to point out, as M. Weigert does, that "this famous clause authorizing them to brew beer for themselves and their workers" permits the conclusion that without beer the Gobelins might never have existed!

The death of François de La Planche ended the early partnership and his son Raphael opened another workshop in the Faubourg Saint-Germain in 1627. These two Paris workshops produced "Flemish style" tapestries whose origin is often difficult to distinguish, for they all bear the fleur-de-lis. The Parisian magistrates watched this influx of privileged Flemish workmen in the capital with displeasure. Moreover, they objected to the low-warp tapestry *(faite à la marche)* of the Flemish weavers as being inferior to high-warp tapestry. They finally won their point since, when the royal factory was created in 1662, three of the four workshops were working in high-warp under the direction of Jean Jans, Jean Lefebvre and Henri Laurent and only a single one in low-warp headed by Jean La Croix from the Faubourg Saint-Marcel.

Throughout the seventeenth century, French and Flemish weavers collaborated in order to achieve fine craftsmanship. From other viewpoints the Flemish contribution is worthy of note. The tapestry sets of PASTOR FIDO and GOMBAUT ET MACÉE were woven both at Brussels and Paris and it is difficult to say which was executed first. On the other hand, in 1622 the cartoons of THE STORY OF CONSTANTINE were ordered from Rubens by Louis XIII and numerous sets were executed in the Faubourg Saint-Marcel workshops with borders from various models. Towards the close of the first third of the seventeenth century the Paris workshops undertook the execution of a STORY OF PSYCHE woven from an ancient Brussels tapestry. Philippe de Champaigne, who was born in Brussels but settled in Paris at the age of ten, supplied several tapestry cartoons; his STORY OF ST. GERVAIS AND ST. PROTAIS was woven in the Louvre workshops. We are also indebted to him for two cartoons for THE LIFE OF THE VIRGIN, a tapestry commissioned by the abbot Le Masle for Notre-Dame of Paris. Executed from 1640 to 1657 in Paris at Pierre Damour's workshops, it is now in the cathedral of Strasbourg.

It is impossible to list every tapestry made in the Paris workshops, and we must therefore concentrate on those which are well known. The cartoons of the ARTEMISIA set, dating from the previous century, were based on a manuscript of 1562 relating the story of Catherine de' Medici. It represents the funeral honors rendered by the unconsolable Queen Artemisia to the memory of her husband Mausolus for whom she had erected the celebrated monument at Halicarnassus, a direct allusion to widowhood, first to Artemisia, then to Catherine herself. The text was by Nicolas Houel, a botanist, scholar, art patron and poet. In his dedicatory letter, he explained that he had imagined this "painting design" to be executed in tapestry: the designs are attributed to Antoine Caron and to other Fontainebleau artists and appear to have

The Story of Furious Roland

4.30 × 2.05 m. Brussels or Delft, workshop of François Spierinck, 1602. Woven in silk.

The Poldi Pezzoli Museum in Milan has two tapestries signed "F. Spierinck" and dated 1602. These bear the marks of both Brussels and Delft as well as Spierinck's monogram. We know that Spierinck settled in Delft in 1591 and remained there until 1610. The subjects of The Story of Furious Roland *have not been identified.*

Milan. Museo Poldi Pezzoli. Museum photo.

Scenes from the Martyrdom of St. Gervais and St. Protais

In 1645 the "Fabrique" of the parish of Saint-Germain in Paris asked the painters Philippe de Champaigne, Eustache Le Sueur and Sébastien Bourdon to design six tapestry cartoons to be exhibited on the church's feastday.

THE DECAPITATION OF ST. PROTAIS. Cartoon by Sébastien Bourdon. The entire tapestry measures 4.85 × 7.25 m. Paris, Galerie du Louvre, workshop of Jean Laurent, about 1645. Woven in silk. Detail on the left. The saint's head is presented by the executioner. Detail above. A soldier mistreats an aged woman.
Paris. Petit Palais. Photo Bulloz.

The Old Testament
Cartoon by Simon Vouet, about 1627.
Consisting of eight pieces, this tapestry was ordered by Louis XIII to decorate the Louvre palace.
THE DAUGHTER OF JEPHTHAH. 4.80 × 5.96 m.
Paris, workshop of the Louvre galleries, first half of the 17th century.
Jephthah, surrounded by mounted guards, tears his clothes on seeing his daughter, who throws herself before him. The arms of France are represented in the border.

◀ Detail, left. Young Negress and a dog.
Paris. Mobilier national. Photo Hachette.

been executed full size by Henri Lerambert.

A painter at the Valois court, Antoine Caron was also a clever composer and a brilliant narrator. Influenced by Flemish artists, he soon became fascinated by Italian art, especially by the elegant work of Niccolò dell'Abbate although he remained strongly French in his feeling and personality. The tapestries which have survived date from the seventeenth century but are still marked by Caron's style and charm. Indeed, the slender figures and their graceful balance have a strong Mannerist flavor. THE STORY OF ARTEMISIA enjoyed great favor and became, in the words of M. Ehrmann, "the bequest of the Valois dynasty to that of the Bourbons." These tapestries were woven a number of times during the reign of Henri IV's widow, who was proud of her Medici heritage, then in the reign of Anne of Austria during the minority of Louis XIV. Louis XIV's collections included as many as fifty-four examples.

During the reign of Louis XIII the great painters made contributions to the art of tapestry. On the advice of M. de Noyers, Superintendant of the Fine Arts, Poussin was summoned by the king to take charge of the decoration of the galleries in the Louvre and his tasks included the execution of tapestry cartoons which, however, proved fruitless. THE STORY OF MOSES, made after eight paintings by Poussin and two by Le Brun, were woven at the Gobelins at a much later date, about 1685.

During the first half of the seventeenth century Simon Vouet remained the undisputed master of French tapestry. In 1627 the king requested the service of the painter, who was then in Italy, "to decorate the royal residences and to aid the new tapestry workshops which His Majesty desires to see flourish." In 1627 Vouet returned to Paris, settled at the Louvre and worked on tapestry designs which were executed in distemper by other painters, including a number from Flanders. Among his pupils was J. V. Mole, a painter of outstanding talent for the landscapes he treated in an entirely Flemish manner. Shortly after Vouet's return to France, THE STORY OF THE OLD TESTAMENT was ordered from him by the king to decorate the Louvre palace.

The cartoons furnished by Vouet were generally made from works which he had painted to decorate Parisian

The Life of the Virgin

This tapestry of fourteen pieces was executed from 1638 to 1657 for Michel Le Masle, prior of Les Roches, canon and cantor of Notre-Dame Cathedral in Paris. He presented the tapestry to the cathedral to decorate the choir on feastdays. Cardinal de Richelieu undoubtedly had a hand in this enterprise, for his initials and arms are represented in each border as well as the arms of the abbé Le Masle. The tapestry was displayed in the cathedral until 1699. In 1739, however, it was given to the chapter of Notre-Dame de Strasbourg for the sum of ten thousand livres. The cartoons of The Life of the Virgin *were done by several artists, including Philippe de Champaigne, Charles Poërson and Jacques Stella. As for the tapestry itself, the source has not been identified. One piece is by a Brussels workshop; seven others, among those produced later, have the signature of the weaver Pierre Damour, who worked in Rheims until 1650, then in Paris.*
THE NATIVITY after Charles Poërson. Detail in the center of the composition. 4.75 × 5.43 m. Paris, workshop of Pierre Damour either in the Galerie du Louvre or in the cloister of Notre-Dame, before 1657. Strasbourg. Cathedral. Archives Photographiques.

Rinceaux ▶

Evoking the elements and the seasons, this tapestry consists of eight pieces. In the center of each composition is an animal symbolizing one of the elements or one of the seasons on a rinceaux background. The cartoons are perhaps by Charles Errard, who was inspired by the work of Raphael's pupil, Polidoro Caravaggio.
THE PEACOCK OR AIR. 4.30 × 3.47 m. Paris, workshop of Raphaël de La Planche, about 1650-1660. *In the center, in a medallion, a peacock is surrounded by small birds of every type. The general décor consists of large rinceaux with birds and squirrels.*
Paris. Mobilier national. Photo Hachette.

hôtels or châteaux. These are characterized by full, open compositions and rich Venetian coloring, as is evident in THE LABORS OF HERCULES, THE STORY OF RENAUD AND ARMIDA and THE LOVES OF THE GODS. These tapestries have characteristic large, rich borders which relate them to the works of the School of Fontainebleau or to those woven in Florentine workshops. They were based on the stucco frames which Jacques Sarrazin executed for Simon Vouet's paintings.

One of the last tapestries to be woven in the Paris workshops was the fine RINCEAUX which, in the inventory made in the seventeenth century, is attributed to the painter Polidoro Caldara known as Polydoro da Caravaggio, one of Raphael's pupils. The man responsible for these compositions appears to have been Charles Errard, a famous ornamentalist painter under Louis XIV, who introduced the Italianate style under Mazarin's government and whom the king, in 1642, made *peintre et architecte ordinaire avec logement au Louvre.* This appointment underscores the importance attached to the role of the French ornamentalist painters of the period who supplied the tapestry workshops with cartoons and who took their inspiration chiefly from the works of Italian painters of the previous century.

The development which Henri IV and his successors contributed to the tapestry industry favored the establishment of numerous workshops in the provinces. At Amiens and Tours, in addition to the privileges they had received at Paris, François de La Planche and Marc de Comans had other responsibilities which, however, were

THE BENEDICTION OF AN ABBESS. 3.52 × 3.16 m. Charleville, workshop of Daniel Pepersack, about 1628.
This tapestry represents the benediction of the abbess of Avenay, Benedicte de Gonzague. Her father. Charles de Gonzague, is probably the figure seen in the foreground, on the left, facing the viewer.
Paris. Mobilier national. Photo Hachette.

PORTIÈRE OF MARS after Charles Le Brun, about 1659-1660, 3.30 × 2.50 m. Gobelins, late 17th century. Woven in silk. ▶
This subject, for which Le Brun made an earlier composition for the Maincy workshop founded by Foquet, was often woven in the Gobelins workshop (sixty-seven tapestries).
Paris. Mobilier national.
Photo Visages de France.

relatively secondary. The workshop which the Duc d'Éperon established under the minority of Louis XIII in his Château de Cadillac was directly related to the one previously mentioned in the Faubourg Saint-Marcel, for the man in charge was Claude de la Pierre, who had been a weaver in these workshops. The duke installed him at Cadillac and later at Bordeaux. His chief tapestry is THE STORY OF HENRI III of which only fragments remain but which are of great documentary interest for the subjects represented.

From Charleville, where he had settled with the title of "tapestry weaver to the Duke of Mantua," who owned the principality, Daniel Pepersack was summoned to Rheims in 1629, where he executed for Archbishop Henri de Lorraine a set of tapestries of THE LIFE OF JESUS consisting of twenty-nine pieces after the cartoons by the painter Mergallet de Troyes. This tapestry was destined to replace the cathedral's THE LIFE OF THE VIRGIN, which had fallen into disfavor. Finally there are the important workshops which the superintendant Fouquet installed in the village of Maincy, near his Château de Vaux, in 1658. In 1660 Fouquet obtained from Louis XIV letters of patent conferring on Maincy the status of a privileged workshop for the weaving of high-warp tapestry. Headed by Charles Le Brun, who was soon to reveal his remarkable talent, Maincy produced the PORTIÈRES or door hangings with the arms of Fouquet, as well as THE MUSES, whose cartoons reproduced the paintings on the ceiling of the Château de Vaux. This workshop produced a STORY OF CONSTANTINE and a set of MELEAGER. But in 1661, after the fall of Fouquet, the workshop was closed. Charles Le Brun continued to work exclusively rof Louis XIV not only as the decorator of the royal châteaux but also as the director of the Gobelins factory.

The Gobelins factory under Le Brun— The crisis of 1683-1694

The year 1662 marks an outstanding date in the history of French decorative art, for it witnessed the creation of the Gobelins which for more than three centuries was to produce those splendid tapestries that have made the name "Gobelins" famous. On June 6, 1662, Louis XIV bought from Sieur Lelu the *hôtel* of the Gobelin family for the sum of 40,775 livres. This old Parisian family, which gave its name to the royal factory, was descended from a certain Philibert Gobelin, who died before 1510 and who during his lifetime was a merchant dyer of scarlet fabrics residing at Saint-Marcel-les-Paris. He practiced his art on the banks of the Bièvre which was said to have exceptional properties for dyeing purposes.

As early as the seventeenth century the tapestries woven at the Gobelins became famous and even today there is a tendency to use the word "Gobelins" for any tapestry with little concern for the date of execution and the workshop in which it was made. Here at the Gobelins the king's Controller General of Finances, Colbert, concentrated the high-warp and low-warp workshops which were scattered in various quarters of Paris. He wanted the new factory to be constructed for his special purpose. With this aim in mind, he had all the buildings rebuilt so well that the work necessitated several years' time.

Although the purchase of the Hôtel des Gobelins dates from the year 1662, the letters patent relating to the factory,

Les Enfants Jardiniers after Charles Le Brun.

The entrefenêtres of the tapestry, The Seasons, *after Le Brun, were the models of the four pieces of the* Enfants Jardiniers, *though certain details were changed.*

SUMMER. Cartoon by Sève the Younger after Charles Le Brun, about 1664. The entire tapestry measures 3.65 × 3.35 m. Gobelins, fourth tapestry, workshop of De La Croix, *père*, 1703-1704. Woven in silk and gold.

Two details. Child watering flowers. Following page, child playing with a bird.

Paris. Mobilier national. Photo Hachette.

which was given the title *Manufacture royale des meubles de la Couronne*, date from November 1667. During the interval, the original project was greatly enlarged. Instead of housing only the high-warp and low-warp looms, the Royal Factory had to provide complete furnishings for every royal residence. In other words, in addition to tapestry artists there were cabinet makers, goldsmiths and mosaic workers and every type of craftsman practicing his trade at Louis XIV's palace, especially at Versailles.

The letters patent of 1667 definitely regulated the organization within the factory. Privileges and exemptions similar to those which Henri IV had granted to the first Flemish weavers who had arrived in Paris were granted to the workmen in the Royal Factory. Sixty apprentices had to be trained in various factories. After six years of study and four in the service of their employer, they received the title of master. The workers were installed with their families in the outbuildings of the *hôtel* or in surrounding houses, thus forming in this isolated quarter of Paris a unique community. The edict ended with the clause absolutely forbidding any foreign tapestry to be introduced into France under penalty of confiscation and fine. The method of payment adopted under Henri IV was retained; the tapestry heads worked for themselves and the king paid them for their tapestries according to an established special rate. The raw material (wool, silk, gold and silver threads known as *étoffes*) was furnished by the king. A dyeing laboratory stood near the workshops; it was meant solely for wool and was headed by the Fleming Josse van den Kerchove. In addition to working for the court, the weavers were free to accept commissions from private individuals.

The first tapestry workshops created at the Gobelins in 1662 were four in number, three of high-warp and one of low-warp. At the head of the first workshop producing high-warp tapestries was Jean Jans, a native of Bruges or Audenarde, who was succeeded by his son in 1668.

The four workshops numbered some two hundred and fifty workers, not counting apprentices. When he took charge, Le Brun devoted all his energy to the triumph of French royal art which was entirely devoted to celebrating the glory of Louis XIV. Differing from Rubens, Le Brun respected the traditional technique. The sole change he introduced was to place the workshop heads under the authority of a man who was "capable and intelligent in the art of painting to make tapestry designs and to execute them correctly." For the cartoons, Le Brun surrounded himself with a host of painters, some fifty of whom are known to us, chiefly Baudrin Yvart, who had already worked with him at Maincy, Louis Licherie, Verdier Testelin, Houasse, de Sève, Monnoyer, Noël and Charles-Antoine Coypel, the Boullogne and Poërson. They were divided into groups with a leader for each team. Each man had his own specialty, such as architectural motifs, decoration or landscapes.

Le Brun's paintings acquired a slightly different form once converted

(Overleaf)

The Story of Alexander after Charles Le Brun. ▶
This tapestry comprising twelve pieces — Le Brun painted the first subject, The Family of Darius, *in 1661 — was very famous. It was not only copied several times at the Gobelins but also by the Brussels and Aubusson workshops.*
THE TRIUMPH OF ALEXANDER. Cartoon painted by Testelin after Charles Le Brun's composition. 4.73 × 8 m. Gobelins, first tapestry, workshop of Jean Jans, *père*, 1664-1680. Woven in silk and gold.
Alexander in his chariot making his triumphal entry into Babylon, whose hanging gardens are depicted in the background.
Paris. Musée des Gobelins. Photo Hachette.

into tapestry; the vigorous rendering of the different planes and above all a certain effect of simplification resulted in their classical aspect which greatly differed from the paintings which were in a Baroque spirit.

Louis XIV marked the fall of Fouquet, resulting from financial speculations, by confiscating the looms in the Maincy workshop. He also confiscated the tapestries which had been executed. The first task given to the Gobelins consisted of finishing these works. THE ELEMENTS and the set of THE SEASONS were among the new tapestries offered by Le Brun as models for the Gobelins. This was followed by LES ENFANTS JARDINIERS, a tapestry which may be considered a return to the famous theme of the JEUX D'ENFANTS often seen in sixteenth-century tapestry. In all these works we find a balanced composition: a foreground of figures and accessories in a *verdure* background treated in the pure tapestry tradition without *trompe-l'œil* effect.

Le Brun's most famous work is no doubt THE STORY OF THE KING which was ordered by Louis XIV himself in accordance with a tradition already established by other sovereigns. From 1663 to 1673 fourteen paintings were executed to trace the happy period of the reign; the first episode was to be THE CAPTURE OF DOLE on February 16, 1668. Conceived as the king's apotheosis, this tapestry represents one of the most successful of classic art, with battle scenes and interiors revealing the same monumental spirit. The colors are splendid and well distributed. Le Brun's chief assistant on this set was Van der Meulen, who left a number of preparatory drawings and water colors with scenes of cities, landscapes and battles.

Not only did Le Brun provide the cartoons for THE STORY OF THE KING but he also followed the progress of the weaving down to the final days of his life. The first set was woven with a range of a hundred and twenty colors selected by Colbert himself. THE MONTHS OR THE ROYAL HOUSES represent the king's diversions. By returning to the theme of THE MONTHS Le Brun infused the subject with much charm. Yet the tapestries which best suited his character are doubtless those of THE STORY OF ALEXANDER. As a painter of battle scenes, Le Brun proved to be the successor of Giulio Romano. Addressing the members of the Academy, the painter Bourbon praised the great skill with which Le Brun was able to mingle and combine his "multitudes" and use light to "form groups and separate them from others." In spite of the apparent confusion there is much narrative clarity. As for THE TRIUMPH OF ALEXANDER it has retained a definite mural character. The scene is designed as a frieze with no attempt to create illusion of depth, for the background is filled with terraces representing the Hanging Gardens of Babylon. The whole design takes on a massive quality suitable for evoking the solemnity of the event.

From 1683 to 1694, however, the Gobelins underwent a crisis with the result that in the early eighteenth century there was a change in tapestry style. The origin can be traced to the rivalry between Le Brun and Mignard. Each was patronized by a minister, Colbert and Louvois respectively, who

◀ **The Months or The Royal Houses**
after Charles Le Brun (twelve pieces).
ENTREFENÊTRE: THE NEW CHATEAU OF SAINT-GERMAIN. Detail in the background. Cartoon painted by Van der Meulen after the composition by Le Brun. 3.15 × 2.52 m. Gobelins, workshop of Mozin, about 1680. Woven in silk and gold.
The king accompanied by the queen rides on horseback before the Château de Saint-Germain.
Paris. Mobilier national. Photo Hachette.

The Story of the King after Charles Le Brun (fourteen pieces).

THE KING VISITING THE GOBELINS FACTORY (October 15, 1667). 5.10 × 7 m. Gobelins, first tapestry, workshop of Jean Jans, *fils*, 1673-1680. Woven in silk and gold.

In a room of the Gobelins, the king accompanied by Colbert admires various objects of art, furniture, paintings, tapestries and silver work which the Gobelins artists present to him.

Paris. Mobilier national. Photo Hachette.

The Ancient Indies after Albert van der Eckhout (eight pieces).

Rewoven numerous times, this tapestry was made after the paintings presented to Louis XIV by Prince Maurice de Nassau. Albert van der Eckhout and Frans Post, who accompanied the prince on his expedition to Brazil and Africa, painted on the spot "documentary" pictures which were used as cartoons for the Gobelins weavers.

THE DAPPLED HORSE OR THE INDIAN ON HORSEBACK. 4.70 × 3.60 m. Gobelins, second tapestry, workshop of De la Croix, 1689. Woven in silk.

Paris. Mobilier national. Photo Hachette.

The Ancient Indies
THE ELEPHANT OR THE HORSE ISABELLA. 4.70 × 4.85 m. Gobelins, second tapestry, workshop of Mozin, 1690. Woven in silk.
Paris. Mobilier national. Photo Hachette.

themselves were rivals. Colbert died in 1683 and the king named Louvois to replace him. Although Le Brun still remained titular director of the Gobelins, M. de la Chapelle Besse was actually in charge of the workshops. The financial situation of the royal treasury necessitated an economical policy—the weaving of THE STORY OF THE KING was suspended, for example, since it contained too many gold threads—and there was no inclination to order new cartoons. Louvois decided to have woven a whole series of tapestries which were copies made from those of the Brussels workshop belonging to the Crown furnishings. Among these were THE ACTS OF THE APOSTLES after Raphael, FRUCTUS BELLI, THE STORY OF SCIPIO and THE HUNTS OF THE EMPEROR MAXIMILIAN I after Van Orley. The fine TRIUMPHS OF THE GODS, also known as THE ARABESQUES OF RAPHAEL, inspired Noël Coypel to execute a series of compositions whose style heralds the æsthetic change which marked the close of the seventeenth century. To this scarcity of cartoons we are indebted for an exceptional work which for more than a century was to prove the great success of the Gobelins factory. This was THE ANCIENT INDIES whose history is rather curious.

This tapestry was executed from eight large paintings which had been given to Louis XV by Prince Maurice de Nassau. These represented exotic Indian figures, animals and plants painted by two Dutchmen, Frans Post and Albert van der Eckhout, who had accompanied the prince in his colonial expedition for the Dutch East Indies Company in South America and Africa. Exoticism triumphed as the Gobelins artists interpreted in tapestry a profusion of "Indian" plants and animals, many of which were undoubtedly based on live models furnished by the famous menagerie which Louis XIV had established at Versailles.

Le Brun died in 1690 and was succeeded by Mignard, then aged seventy, who introduced an artistic change and at the request of Philippe d'Orléans decided to reproduce the paintings he had executed in the so-called Saint-Cloud Gallery. Mignard remained only a short time, for in 1694 the financial situation was so poor that the workshops had to be closed for five years.

The Beauvais factory

The Royal Beauvais factory was created shortly after that of the Gobelins. On August 5, 1664, letters patent were issued by the king to Louis Hinart, a Parisian tapestry merchant, granting him numerous privileges and authorizing him to establish tapestry workshops "similar to those in Flanders." Activity at the Gobelins was in fact completely devoted to royal orders and it was to satisfy wealthy members of the nobility and of the bourgeoisie that Colbert had decided to turn to Hinart. Until the Revolution, the Beauvais factory remained a private enterprise with royal patronage, yet it was obliged to exist on the sale of its tapestries. Although in the beginning several weavers had come from Aubusson and others from Paris, the majority were of Flemish origin, from Antwerp, Brussels, and Audenarde, and in 1665 they totalled as many as one hundred and twenty-seven.

Despite royal aid, the new factory found it difficult to prosper as the result of negligence on the part of Louis Hinart and his son. Its real rise did not begin until 1684 under the fine management of Philippe Behagle, a merchant tapestry-weaver of Audenarde

Les Portes de Mer

Derived from the Verdures with Birds, *the* Portes de Mer, *the models of which had been supplied by the painters Kerchove and Campion, were woven from the end of the 17th century until 1737.*

The whole tapestry measures 2.76 × 4.11 m. Beauvais, end of the 17th century.

This was part of a tapestry of four pieces and known as the "Chevalier d'Allone," a sea captain (1668-1707). *It was woven with the coat-of-arms of his family and offered by the king in memory of his exploits.*

Detail of the lower part of one hanging.

Private collection. Photo Hachette.

The Conquests of the King of Sweden
The four pieces comprising the tapestry were woven after the cartoons by Jean-Baptiste Martin inspired by the paintings of the Swedish artist Lemke (1631-1671). *The borders are by Berain. These tapestries commemorate the victories which Charles XI, who became King of Sweden in* 1660, *had gained over the Danes.*
The Battle of Landskrona (July, 1677) 5.34 × 4.04 m. Beauvais, 1699.
Stockholm. Royal Palace. Photo Swedish National Furniture.

Grotesques
These decorative compositions with small figures reminiscent of the grotteschi *painted by Raphael were woven from before* 1694 *until* 1730. *The sketches were probably furnished by Jean I. Berain, "dessinateur de la Chambre et du Cabinet du Roi." The cartoons are by Jean-Baptiste Monnoyer.*
The Rope Dancer and the Dromedary. 3.35 × 5.10 m. Beauvais, about 1689.
Large border with arabesques and Chinese figures. Detail. Peacock and vase of flowers.
Paris. Mobilier national. Photo Visages de France.

who later settled at Tournai. When the Gobelins closed in 1694, the Beauvais factory was rich enough to receive some of the workers dismissed from the Paris factory. During the early years of its activity, Beauvais borrowed its models from Flemish traditions and wove landscapes with small figures, such as Jeux d'Enfants, whose compositions were probably by Jacques Fouquières, a pupil of Rubens and a landscape artist, as well as others by Damoiselet, who was working at Versailles and Marly. A Wedding in Picardy, bought by Louis XIV, was mentioned in the accounts of 1670. For more than forty years, that is, until 1737, Beauvais produced *verdures* based on models such as the Verdures with Birds and Les Ports de Mer by the painters Kerchove and Campion.

From 1684 to 1704 Behagle's workshops wove a number of important sets, chiefly The Conquests of Louis the Great based on another tapestry on the same subject with allegorical additions woven by Behagle at Tournai. This set was obviously inspired by The Story of Louis XIV woven at the Gobelins. Beauvais created copies of the famous Acts of the Apostles which is said to be the work of the Gobelins weavers who were received at Beauvais while the factory was temporarily closed from 1694 to 1699. Under Behagle, Beauvais executed also The Adventures of Telemachus after Arnault, The Story of Achilles, and a set of four tapestries ordered by the King of Sweden to commemorate his victory over the Danes. The cartoons were painted by Martin des Batailles after the works of the Swedish painter Lemke. Berain's work was limited to the border models perfected by Louis-Guy de Vernansal. Only The Battle of Landskrona was woven in the Beauvais factory (1699); the other tapestries were woven in Behagle's Paris workshops.

But the most successful tapestries were the FIRST CHINESE SET and the GROTESQUES. The FIRST CHINESE SET was originally executed by Behagle for the Duc du Maine after the cartoons by "four illustrious painters," three of whom are known: Jean-Baptiste Monnoyer, Belin de Fontenay and Louis-Guy de Vernansal. The subject, repeated several times until 1731, was probably inspired by the reports of the Jesuits after their journey to China. On his return to France, the Jesuit Bouvet presented, in 1697, a work entitled *Portrait historique de l'empereur de Chine* in which the emperor is presented somewhat as a Sun King of China. Here, perhaps, is the origin of the themes represented in this work which in a delightful Europeanized manner evokes the court of the Chinese monarch at Peking.

The decorative compositions by Jean I. Berain and J.-B. Monnoyer, familiarly known as GROTESQUES, enjoyed even greater success and were woven until 1730. It is also to Berain, *dessinateur de la chambre et du cabinet du roi*, that we are indebted for the famous MARINE TRIUMPHS with the arms of the Count of Toulouse which are now the property of the Bank of France. As M. Weigert points out, "Their sumptuousness is reminiscent of the settings which Berain devised for the operas of Lulli, in his capacity as designer to the Royal Academy of Music."

Marine Triumphs
This set of four panels, with the arms of the Count of Toulouse, was ordered in 1690 by Mme. de Montespan; the cartoons were designed by Jean I. Berain.
THE TRIUMPH OF VENUS. 4.35 × 3.35 m. Paris and Beauvais, workshop of Philippe Behagle, late 17th century. Woven in silk.
The composition is arranged in an impressive architectural setting inspired by opera décors.
Detail of the architecture decorated with sea shells.
Paris. Banque de France. Photo Bulloz.

(Overleaf)

First Chinese Set
This tapestry was undoubtedly woven for the first time by Philippe Behagle at the end of the 17th century after the cartoons of "four celebrated painters," three of whom are familiar: Jean-Baptiste Monnoyer, Belin de Fontenay and Louis-Guy de Vernansal. It corresponds to the taste of the period for "chinoiseries" and was repeated several times until 1731.
PINEAPPLE HARVEST. 3.51 × 2.78 m. Beauvais, about 1725.
Munich. Residenzmuseum. Photo Hachette.

VII French workshops in the eighteenth century

Oudry, artistic director of the Gobelins, makes tapestry subservient to painting. - The great traditional sets woven at the Gobelins. - New tapestries: the "alentours." The Beauvais factory. - The Aubusson and Felletin workshops. - Workshops in Lorraine: Nancy, Lunéville and La Malgrange. - Secondary workshops in northern and eastern France.

ITH the creation of the Royal Gobelins factory, France became the leading country in the production of tapestry and held this supremacy down to the present day. Actually, the art of tapestry changed more during that period than in any other. To weave works after the cartoons by Raphael and Rubens, the weavers had always enjoyed much liberty for the process of turning the cartoon into a tapestry. Le Brun himself had left the Gobelins weavers a free hand. The eighteenth century marked a definite step toward the subservience of tapestry to painting. This æsthetic change followed the general taste for "decorative" rather than "monumental" art. The Regency witnessed a change in the interior decoration of palaces; the apartments were altered and their dimensions diminished. As a result, tapestries became smaller; they were now hung in salons to be viewed at a closer distance and served as a precious background for rare *bibelots*. Their ornamental scale was consequently different.

On the other hand, what tapestry lost in force and breadth, it gained in decoration. There is no denying the great charm of THE STORY OF DON QUIXOTE or the decorative value of Boucher's compositions such as THE CHINESE TAPESTRY and THE LOVES OF THE GODS.

Oudry, artistic director of the Gobelins, makes tapestry subservient to painting

After remaining closed for five years, the Gobelins reopened in 1699. The Manufacture royale des Meubles de la Couronne practically ceased to exist and only the high-warp and low-warp workshops once again began to function. The directors' authority was limited to administrative questions, but artistic directors were needed. The first man to fulfill this function was

The Story of Don Quixote
Consisting of twenty-eight subjects, this tapestry enjoyed enormous success in the 18th century; from 1714 *to* 1794 *nine sets were woven at the Gobelins. The models for the paintings were by Charles-Antoine Coypel* (1694-1752), *who was named Painter to the King in* 1747. *Several painters collaborated on the various* alentours *designed to accompany these subjects.*
DON QUIXOTE IS SERVED BY THE DUCHESS' LADIES. Seventh tapestry. 3.68 × 5.16 m. Gobelins, workshop of Neilson, 1776-1779. Woven in silk.
Coypel's cartoon dates from 1723. *The model of the* alentour *with crimson background was painted by Belin de Fontenay and Claude III Audran. The corners of the border contain the initials of the Duc de Penthièvre. This tapestry along with three others of the same set were sold to the duke in* 1787. Paris. Mobilier national. Photo Visages de France.

Robert de Cotte, the king's chief architect, who in 1733 was succeeded by Jean-Baptiste Oudry, followed by François Boucher from 1755 to 1770. These two masters were destined to exercise great influence not only on the choice of models but also in technical matters. Oudry and Boucher really thought more as easel-picture painters than as cartoon designers and the weavers soon found themselves obliged to render the infinite nuances of oil painting in the works of these two painters. The weavers succeeded in their task, but tapestry lost its essential, independent, decorative character to become the field of skilled copyists.

Already at the Beauvais factory Oudry had insisted that the weavers deliver a literal reproduction of his models. He renewed his requirements at the Gobelins and aroused the hostility of the middlemen and workshop heads, who were anxious to retain their liberty of execution. "Give your work," wrote Oudry, "all the spirit and intelligence of the paintings in which lies the secret of achieving tapestries of outstanding beauty." The workshop heads replied, "To paint well and to execute tapestries are completely different.... In the Crown's furniture-repository there are ancient mural tapestries executed under middlemen alone, and so far as color and tone are concerned, they are greater than those found in the paintings." Oudry, however, had the last word. The order was given by M. Tournehem, then repeated to M. de Marigny and M. d'Angiviller to follow the colors of the models in the strictest manner and to imitate the effects of oil painting.

The death of Jean-Baptiste Oudry in 1755 did not put an end to this disagreement; there was an increased number of dyes indispensable to reproduce the color scheme and gradations of color imposed by the cartoons. Thanks to chemical methods, it became easy to create an infinite range of colored zones. To the one hundred and twenty woolen colors chosen by Colbert because of their solidity, we must add hundreds of new tints necessary to translate a painting with all its slight nuances and subtle gradations. The use of evanescent tints *(petits teints)* later resulted in real catastrophes. A tapestry such as THE STORY OF JASON is now discolored and the background in a similar work by Oudry is completely faded. This taste for imitating painting was to continue until the early nineteenth century.

The great traditional sets woven at the Gobelins

The first half of the eighteenth century witnessed the continuation of the great religious and mythological sets in the manner of Le Brun's colossal compositions. A set of THE OLD TESTAMENT comprising eight pieces after Charles-Antoine Coypel was begun in 1710. As a complement to this set, a NEW TESTAMENT was woven to designs by Jean Jouvenet and Jean Restout. This was followed by an ILIAD after Charles-Antoine Coypel, a STORY OF MARK ANTHONY after Natoire and THE STORY OF THESEUS after Carle van Loo. The cartoons of THE ANCIENT INDIES were renewed by François Desportes and gained continued success as THE NEW INDIES.

But the sets with figures which achieved the greatest success were doubtless the ones designed by Jean-François de Troy, director of the French Academy at Rome. The seven pieces of his STORY OF ESTHER were woven fifteen times to the point where Jean-François de Troy received a new

The Hunts of Louis XV
The cartoons for this set of nine pieces are by Jean-Baptiste Oudry (1686-1755). *Two sets were executed, one for Compiègne, delivered in* 1748 *(workshop of Monmerqué), and the other, purchased by the Infante Don Philippe of Parma, is now in the Pitti Palace, Florence (workshop of Audran).*
THE DEATH OF THE STAG IN THE SAINT-JEAN POND. Detail of the left section. The entire tapestry, without border, measures 3.80 × 5 m. Gobelins, workshop of Monmerqué, 1743-1745. Woven in silk. Paris. Mobilier national. On exhibit in the Musée de Compiègne. Photo Hachette.

The Loves of the Gods
The subjects of this tapestry were painted between 1762 and 1764 by François Boucher.

VENUS AT THE FORGE OF VULCAN. 3 × 10 m. Gobelins, workshop of Neilson, 1766-1771. Woven in silk.

Detail of the central medallion.

This tapestry, whose alentour *was designed by Maurice Jacques* (1764), *was part of a mural tapestry commissioned by the Count of Coventry for his residence of Croome Court in Worcester.*

Metropolitan Museum of Art. Gift of Samuel H. Kress Foundation. Museum photo.

commission for The Story of Jason. Perhaps today these pieces appear pompous, but those which still have their fine coloring evoke the sumptuousness of Venetian painting, thanks to the importance given to decoration and costumes. The Story of Jason was taken from Ovid's *Metamorphoses* and comprises seven pieces which relate how Jason found the Golden Fleece and the unfortunate fate of his wife Creusa, who was determined to gain her revenge on jealous Medea. One of these tapestries was used in 1770 to decorate the pavilion erected at Strasbourg, in the midst of an island on the Rhine, to receive Archduchess Marie-Antoinette on her entry into France. Goethe, then a law student at Strasbourg, had an occasion to visit this pavilion and was greatly shocked by the subject chosen to receive the future Queen of France. "The great blunder committed in the great hall drove me to distraction," he wrote in his *Memoirs*. "Disregarding those who could hear me, I cried out: 'How can we allow a young queen, who is about to set foot into her new territories, to witness such a horrible example of marriage?' "

Following his ancestor's example, Louis XV ordered the Gobelins to weave The New History of the King. It was under this title or that of The Story of Louis XV that the workshop accounts from 1731 to 1734 list two mural tapestries, The Turkish Embassy after Charles Parrocel (only two pieces were executed) and the more familiar one of The Hunts of Louis XV after Jean-Baptiste Oudry. Style and execution had developed at the Gobelins and the very spirit of this work is far removed from that of The Story of the King woven in the previous century. Indeed, The New Story of the King evokes neither an important military feat nor a grandiose ceremony. The figure of the king surrounded by a large group of hunters is merely a pretext to represent delightful hunting scenes in the forests of Compiègne and Fontainebleau. The set comprises nine pieces executed after Oudry's work which was painted from 1734 to 1745. His delightful sketches are now in the Musée Nissim de Camondo, Paris. The paintings themselves were installed by Louis-Philippe in the hunting apartments of the palace at Fontainebleau. In these compositions, the chief subject is not the hunters with their carefully delineated costumes, escorted by the excited dogs in the foreground, but the majestic forest which lends its splendor to this form of royal diversion. Oudry masterfully rendered the magnificence of the trees and the background of forest masses.

The Hunts of Louis XV aroused the enthusiasm of contemporaries; two sets of tapestries were woven as early as 1742. Both sets had a border designed by Pierre-Josse Perrot in the style of this period, that is, consisting of a reproduction of a gilt-carved frame. One set bears in the center the arms of France and in the corners the king's initials (Château de Compiègne), the other, which was bought by Louis XV's son-in-law, the Infante Don Philip of Parma, bears the latter's arms (Palazzo Pitti, Florence). Some of these pieces have more or less successfully withstood the effects of time and the credit lies with Oudry, who certainly did not desire posterity to see discolored figures on a faded background, for it was he who said that coloring "was the chief beauty of tapestry."

Russian Games
The six cartoons for this tapestry are by Jean-Baptiste Le Prince who, after a long stay in Russia, launched the Russian fashion. Thirteen tapestries were woven from 1769 *to* 1791.
Bird Hunting. Central part without border. 2.87 × 3.72 m. Beauvais, 1771-1772.
Paris. Mobilier national. Photo Bulloz.

New tapestries: the *alentours*

After remaining closed for five years, the Gobelins factory reopened in 1699. Jules Hardouin-Mansart, then Superintendant of the Royal Buildings, commissioned from Claude III Audran a new set of THE PORTIÈRES OF THE GODS which enjoyed much success and was woven several times throughout the eighteenth century, the number totaling two hundred and twelve pieces. Claude III Audran had another opportunity of adapting his talent to tapestry requirements in THE GROTESQUE MONTHS which inaugurated at the Gobelins the æsthetics of the eighteenth century. Since 1699 Audran had been engaged in decorating the château of the Grand Dauphin, son of Louis XIV, at Meudon. The building accounts of 1709 mention that the models of THE GROTESQUE MONTHS were executed at the Gobelins *pour le nouveau bâtiment de Monseigneur à Meudon.* Since 1707 Antoine Watteau had been one of Audran's assistants and he probably took part in the execution of the tapestry for which François Desportes designed numerous animals. Officially the Gobelins wove this tapestry only once. The MONTHS were destined to hang without interruption one next to another. The three tapestries are divided into bands about two feet wide which are separated by rich borders decorated with silver thread representing shells between dolphins and the initials of the Grand Dauphin. The god or goddess symbolizing a month is depicted beneath a portico in the midst of a delightful decoration of attributes, Cupids, animals and flowers. Designed to be integrated into a panel decoration, these tapestries were directly inspired by Berain's creations at the Beauvais factory and correspond to the taste then favored by French society.

This love of decoration and fantasy can be seen in a far more original manner in another set after Charles-Antoine Coypel. His subject, THE STORY OF DON QUIXOTE, was then popular. Every tapestry workshop in Europe—Gobelins, Beauvais, Aubusson, Brussels, Madrid, Naples—soon produced a DON QUIXOTE set after the cartoons by various painters. Nine times (1714-1794) the Gobelins set, which comprised twenty-eight scenes, was set to the loom, with variations in the coloring and in the *alentours* (a type of tapestry surrounded by decoration) imagined with much talent by Blain de Fontenay, Claude III Audran and Louis Tessier. These mural tapestries mark the triumph of *trompe-l'œil:* the central subject is eclipsed by the surrounding decoration which represents garlands of flowers, architectural motifs and attributes against a crimson or yellow background in imitation of damask fabrics. The central scene is designed as a painting bordered by an imitation gilt-carved frame. After the success of THE STORY OF DON QUIXOTE, the *alentours* reappeared at the Gobelins with THE SCENES OF OPERA, TRAGEDY AND COMEDY, after the designs painted by Coypel from 1744 to 1752, which was woven for the Queen of Poland, Marie-Josèphe. The *alentours* were the work of Jean-Marc Ladey, Chevillon and Tessier. Those designed by Maurice Jacques about 1758 offered a new model and were to complete the scenes representing the loves

The Story of Psyche
François Boucher (1703-1770).
PSYCHE LED BY ZEPHYR INTO THE PALACE OF LOVE.
3.68 × 6.45 m. Beauvais, 1741. Woven in silk.
Detail. The followers of Psyche.
Washington, D.C. The Corcoran Gallery of Art.
Photo Hachette.

of the gods painted by François Boucher for the tapestry THE GODS.

In fact, Boucher had a workshop at the Gobelins from 1749. After Oudry's death in 1755, he was appointed factory superintendent to the immense satisfaction of the workshop heads, who were jealous of the success achieved by the Beauvais factory. They hoped that by offering new models, Boucher would help them to obtain advantageous offers. Prior to the year 1755 Boucher had executed for the Gobelins two large compositions, SUNRISE and SUNSET, as well as a set of twenty paintings for the armchairs and *bergères* destined for Mme. de Pompadour. Together with Carle van Loo, Pierre and Vien, he contributed to the achievement of THE LOVES OF THE GODS (1758). Finally the painter was able to begin work on the composition of THE GODS in collaboration with Maurice Jacques for the *alentours*. The execution of this set responded to the desire on the part of Neilson, contractor for the Gobelins low-warp workshops, to produce sets for private clients in less time and therefore at a lower price.

Thanks to an idea by Soufflot, director of the factory, a solution was found and on September 10, 1762, Maurice Jacques presented decorative compositions which could include Boucher's medallions of 1758. Owing to the surprising variety of decorative subjects and their design, it was no problem to increase or decrease the size of a tapestry. Moreover, Jacques had produced a project in color representing a royal apartment as it ought to be, tapestries covering the walls and the bed, the armchair and the sofa. Orders soon flowed in and for years Neilson's looms were busily engaged in weaving variations of Boucher's tapestries. The first sets

◀ **The Turkish Costume**
Tapestry of four pieces after Amédée van Loo.
The Sultana Ordering from the Odalisques.
Height 3.20 without border. Gobelins, workshop of Audran, 1781-1784. Woven in silk.
Compiègne. Château. Photo Hachette.

The Iliad
Jean-Baptiste Deshays, who entered the Academy of Painting in 1759 with a painting inspired by the Iliad, designed the six cartoons for this tapestry. It was woven three times between 1761 and 1769.
Agamemnon Refusing to Return Chryseis to Her Father. Song I, 22-32. Dimensions 3.16 × 3.76 m. Beauvais, second half of the 18th century.
Border with the arms of France and Navarre.
New York. French and Company. Photo Hachette.

with corresponding seat covers were made for English lords. In 1767 Nelson wrote in reference to one of them that "it is in a new taste yet to appear in France." All these tapestries reveal slight differences and when a series was finally woven for the king (1772-1776) the *alentours* proved to be more complicated. Jacques had produced new designs for them in 1770 and that same year Tessier had made others with a blue damask background which he changed to yellow in 1779. The weaving continued successfully, even during the Revolution, until 1806.

There is no doubt that a number of practical economic reasons contributed to the fashion for the set of The Gods, but these so-called *alentours* continued to an extent the tradition of late medieval *verdure* tapestry. They could be used on a wall as a single piece and thus regained their original function as a continuous decoration. The medallions with clear colors and graceful forms stood out against a red background which was not violent and the general effect proved to be magnificent. Already chair models supplied by Boucher had been woven at the Gobelins, while those by Jacques with their beribboned flowers against a damask background enjoyed equal popularity. Their weaving was done at the same time as the reproductions of the portraits of Louis XV, the queen, the future Louis XVI, the Empress Maria Theresa, Joseph II and many others. Although "technical masterpieces," these works reveal a total misunderstanding of the art of tapestry which had become subservient to painting. We must also mention The Turkish Costume (1772-1776) after Amédée van Loo from the "Scenes of the Levant" paintings destined for Mme. de Pompadour's bedroom in the Château de Bellevue. This set still retains a certain charm with its touch of exoticism. The Seasons after Callet (1773-1791) is, on the other hand, an example of the taste of the period for antiquity and the vogue for the new style "in the Greek manner" during the reign of Louis XVI.

The Beauvais factory

During the first quarter of the eighteenth century work at the Beauvais factory, as at the Gobelins, proceeded at a slower pace. From the death of Behagle in 1704 to the appointment, in 1726, of Jean-Baptiste Oudry as official painter, the factory continued to decline. As a competent artist and an equally competent administrator, Oudry enabled the workshops to regain their prosperity and established the factory's reputation. While re-establishing the school of design and increasing the number of workers, he endeavored to execute works responding to the taste of contemporary clients. From 1726 to 1734 he furnished the models of three tapestries, THE NEW HUNTS in six subjects and four scenes, COUNTRY PLEASURES, and four scenes inspired by Molière's comedies.

The year 1734 marked the beginning of an important productive period for the factory under its new director Nicolas Besnier, who had been appointed to replace Mérou. For more than twenty years the Oudry-Besnier association proved successful and the painter's activity did not slacken. In addition to the subjects already mentioned, he supplied fresh designs inspired by Ovid's *Metamorphoses* and followed these in 1735 with ten FINE VERDURES designated by the name of the animal which characterizes each one. In 1736 the Beauvais factory produced THE FABLES OF LA FONTAINE and their success was so great that the set continued to be rewoven. All these subjects reveal Oudry's taste for landscapes and animals. The artist also executed models of furniture accessories and the demand continued to increase. Moreover, he did not hesitate to turn for assistance to other well-known artists. Although Charles-Antoine Coypel had furnished the Gobelins with a STORY OF DON QUIXOTE, Charles Natoire painted for the Beauvais factory ten scenes inspired by the same subject. This STORY OF DON QUIXOTE, commissioned in 1735 for M. de Durfort, now hangs in the archbishop's palace at Aix-en-Provence.

The artist who contributed most to assure the reputation of the Beauvais factory was François Boucher who, in 1756, succeeded Oudry as the factory painter. The brilliant qualities of the king's chief painter placed him in the front ranks of the decorators of his time. The six tapestries consisting of forty-five compositions which he executed are among the most original Beauvais models. In 1736 Boucher painted his VILLAGE FESTIVITIES in the Italian style followed by a STORY OF PSYCHE (1741) which was much appreciated abroad and of which there remain numerous compositions in various collections. In 1743 Boucher did a Chinese set (known as the SECOND CHINESE SET) which differed greatly from the one woven in the seventeenth century (Musée de Besançon). The designs were by Jean-Joseph Dumons of Tulle, the king's painter at Aubusson from 1713 to 1754. THE LIVES OF THE GODS, woven beginning in 1749, were followed in 1752 by FRAGMENTS OF OPERA. We are also indebted to him for THE NOBLE PASTORAL woven in some fifteen tapestries of various compositions between 1755 and 1778. Boucher's cartoons enriched both the Beauvais and Gobelins factories and enjoyed great success. The very nature of his easy and elegant talent was well suited to the decoration, offering no difficulty in translating the mother-of-pearl flesh and the delicate gray clouds which were a far cry from the range of traditional colors. Fascinated by this delightful art, the weavers did not hesitate to use evanescent colors which in a number of cases changed considerably in tone after the passage of many years.

In 1737 there was talk of ordering from the Beauvais factory a JASON AND MEDEA in imitation of the one woven in the Gobelins, as had already been the case of THE STORY OF DON QUIXOTE. This project, however, was never carried out. Voltaire even thought of having several episodes of his epic poem *Henriade* made into tapestry, but the price deterred him. Thus the Oudry-Besnier association proved a very prosperous one and several pieces bear the signatures of both directors. Whereas tapestry formerly remained in shops awaiting clients, orders now flowed in and the weavers could hardly satisfy requirements. Popular tapestries were rewoven as many as ten or twelve times, for every important person not only at the French court but also at foreign ones wanted to decorate his *hôtel* and château with a *verdure* after Oudry's designs or with a *scène galante* after Boucher.

During Behagle's administration, Louis XIV had paid a visit to the factory. Louis XV followed the example and rendered the same honor to the painter of THE ROYAL HUNTS. He went to Beauvais and visited the workshops or, in Voltaire's words, "Oudry's kingdom."

In January, 1754, after Besnier's death, the direction of the royal factory passed into the hands of André-Charlemagne Charron, a relation of the principal tax collector of the Paris region. Oudry died in 1755 and was succeeded by the landscape painter Juliard. He in turn was succeeded by Jean-Joseph Dumons, then in 1777 by Camousse. Although none equalled Oudry's talent and activity, the reputation of the Beauvais factory was so great that its success lasted until the Revolution. Taste changed and brought a demand for novelty. Boucher's pleasant mythology became more emphatic with THE ILIAD by his son-in-law Deshays, who began a set of cartoons inspired by Honoré d'Urfé's pastoral romance *L'Astrée*.

About 1763, on his return after a long stay in Russia, the painter Jean-Baptiste Le Prince launched the fashion for Russian themes based on his oil paintings and engravings, and Charron commissioned from him a set of six pieces entitled RUSSIAN GAMES. The sets designed by François Casanova, COUNTRY PASTIMES, BOHEMIANS, and MILITARY CONVOYS, brought to the art of tapestry a distinctly naturalistic and picturesque note. In accordance with established custom, all these mural tapestries by Le Prince and Casanova were sold with chair upholstery, whose backs had reproductions of several figures or groups of the tapestry, whereas the seats themselves were merely covered with *verdures*.

The factory continued to prosper under Charron's skillful administration until 1780, when he was succeeded by Menou who served until 1793. In 1780 Jean-Baptiste Huet produced his models of THE PASTORAL WITH BLUE DRAPERIES AND ARABESQUES, decorative tapestries borrowed from compositions by Boucher represented against a light background framed by flower-decorated draperies. But the new mode insisted upon heroic subjects and at the close of the century the return of academism was crowned by such tapestries as Lavallée Poussin's CONQUEST OF THE INDIES and Lagrenée's ARTS AND SCIENCES as well as compositions by Desoria and Monsiau. At the beginning of the Revolution, the Beauvais factory continued to function normally; it remained closed only a few months

Second Chinese Set

Several of the nine sketches by François Boucher for this tapestry consisting of six pieces are now in the Musée de Besançon. The cartoons were painted by Jean-Joseph Dumons of Tulle, Painter to the King at Aubusson.

FISHING. 3 × 4 m. Beauvais, 1758. Woven in silk.

The tapestry with its arms of France and Navarre was presented by Louis XIV to the Count de Moltke, Grand Marshal of the Danish court. It was placed in the Amalienborg Castle in Copenhagen which became the royal residence in 1794.

Copenhagen. Amalienborg Castle. Photo Hachette.

The Loves of the Gods

The nine cartoons by François Boucher for this tapestry are similar to those by the Gobelins (see pages 232-233). They were woven from 1749 to 1772, some as many as seven times.

THE RAPE OF EUROPA. Detail of the central part. The whole tapestry measures 3.70 × 4.75 m. Beauvais, 1764. Woven in silk.

The tapestry was woven for the palace of Prince Henry, brother of Frederick the Great.

Berlin. Charlottenburg Palace. Photo Steinkopf.

Les Verdures d'Anglards-de-Salers
This set of ten tapestries may have been woven for the lords of Montelar, whose nearby Château d'Anglards dominates the valley of Le Falgoux. The tapestries bear the arms of this family.
COMBAT BETWEEN A LION AND DOGS. Detail. Aubusson, second half of the 16th century. Anglards-de-Salers, Cantal. Mairie. Photo Imbault.

THE PAGODA. 2.85 × 5.84 m. Aubusson, workshop of Dorléac, 18th century. Paris. Mobilier national. Photo Visages de France. ▶

and on *13 Prairial, an II* (June 1, 1794) the Committee for Agriculture and Art ordered the factory to be reopened. The enterprise ceased to be private and henceforth was annexed by the State, like the Gobelins and the Savonnerie, the famous carpet factory created by Colbert. Ever since that date these three great weaving factories have remained national enterprises.

The Aubusson and Felletin factories

Since the Middle Ages the art of weaving was practiced at Aubusson and Felletin in that historic region of central France known as La Marche. These two centers had family workshops consisting of the father aided by his sons, a few apprentices and often one or two workmen. Their tapestries were destined for the bourgeoisie and were therefore woven on low-warp looms with wool for the warp and weft. Like the Flemings with whom these Aubusson weaving families appear to be related, they produced biblical and mythological subjects as well as *verdures*. One of the finest of these tapestries dating from the second half of the sixteenth century is the VERDURES D'ANGLARD-DE-SALERS in which animals, fabulous or real, are represented frisking in a setting of large floral designs with volutes.

Eager to patronize the art of tapestry, Henri IV helped to develop the weaving art in central France. The royal edict of 1601 forbade the importation of any tapestry with figures or *verdures*; this decision proved advantageous to the Marche industry now free of Flemish competition. About the year 1637 Aubusson enjoyed great prosperity; the town itself numbered some two thousand workers, including apprentices. The regulation established by Colbert brought additional progress; the letters patent of 1665 conferred on the workshops the title of royal factory and organized apprenticeship, workmanship and the verification of pieces by important juries. The middlemen *(entrepreneurs)* had to weave on each piece the Aubusson factory mark which was often abbreviated to MRD or MRDB (Manufacture royale Daubusson or Du Buisson) followed by the manufacturer's initials; the same regulation prescribed blue-galloon borders.

Similar letters patent were sent to Felletin in 1689 ordering brown-galloon borders for the tapestries woven there. This formality, however, was not always respected. In addition, the king promised to send a competent painter for the tapestry cartoons as well as a master dyer for the wool. The Aubusson weavers waited in vain for the arrival of these men and it was not until the reign of Louis XV that the administrative regulations proved effective for Aubusson (1732) and Felletin (1737). Finally, the king's painter arrived in the person of Jean-Joseph Dumons, a native of Tulle, followed by Juliard, Ranson and Lagrenée. They organized a school of design and soon instructed these Marche weavers in the art of designing cartoons. As for the dyer promised for Aubusson, this proved to be Sieur Fimazeau of the Gobelins. The workshops were carefully inspected and silk spinning was created.

Aubusson entered into relations with the Beauvais factory, which supplied it with cartoons, and with the Gobelins, where some of the Marche workers were hired while waiting to return to their province. Manufacturers established shops in Paris in the Rue de Buci and in the Rue de la Huchette.

The eighteenth century proved a brilliant period for Aubusson. In 1743 workshops were founded for the production of carpets "in the Turkish manner," encouraged by royal orders. A decided development took place. Alongside the small workshops, a certain number achieved remarkable growth, thanks to the technical and commercial ability of such men as Grellet, Picon, Furzaud, Fourié, Vergne and their families. The sets satisfied current taste, with their country scenes and landscapes filled with attractive shepherds and delightful shepherdesses forming the principal themes, but as in the previous century there was a return to the royal factory cartoons. These included THE HUNTS OF LOUIS XV and THE FABLES OF LA FONTAINE after Oudry in multiple compositions, followed by those of the COUNTRY DIVERSIONS and the CHINESE SCENES after Boucher although they were set to the loom with innumerable interpolated variations.

These sets reveal the liberties taken by the weavers in their interpretation of the models by adding or omitting several

The Story of Daphnis and Chloë

The first set of tapestries after the cartoons by Étienne Jeaurat (1699-1789) were woven at the Gobelins. The subjects were later reproduced at Aubusson.

GRAPE GATHERING WHERE DAPHNIS AND CHLOE ARE ADMIRED. 2.10 × 3.21 m. Aubusson, mid-18th century.

Victoria and Albert Museum. Museum photo. Crown copyright.

figures of the composition according to the dimensions of the required tapestry. The works of Boucher were familiar to the Aubusson weavers, thanks to engravings, notably by Huquier. The persistent vogue for this Far Eastern world led to the production of the CHINESE LANDSCAPES by the ornamentalist Jean Pillement. After 1770 there was the influence of Ranson's style; he had done much work at Aubusson and produced decorative tapestries with trophies, arabesques and flowers in addition to furniture tapestry. At the close of the century, however, the weaving industry found itself in serious commercial difficulty. The Revolution dealt it a heavy blow and forced the Aubusson and Felletin workshops to cease activity.

Workshops in Lorraine: Nancy, Lunéville, and La Malgrange

Weavers from Brussels had been working at Nancy since the seventeenth century, but the Thirty Years' War and the general state of poverty resulted in the disappearance of almost every loom. After the peace of Ryswick (1697), which restored the sovereignty of Lorraine and Bar to Duke Leopold, the latter shortly after his arrival named a native of Nancy, Charles Mité, as "tapestry artist of his *hôtel*." Mité was first engaged in restoring the beautiful court tapestries, after which he began to weave one after the Lorraine painter Herbel representing THE VICTORIES OF CHARLES V, Leopold's father, celebrating his triumphs over the Turks (1683-1688). The workshops themselves were established in the buildings of the ducal palace. To this tapestry, which was finished in 1710, we must add a copy, woven that same year, of THE TWELVE MONTHS with slight variations, made at Brussels by Joost van Herselle and which was part of the duke's furniture repository. Mité's enterprise was to prove even more important with the achievement of another set devoted to THE STORY OF CHARLES V. The cartoons were requested from the French painters J.-B. Martin, who specialized in battle scenes, and Jacques Guyon for the landscapes and "distances." Since there were many Gobelins weavers, the workmanship was excellent. The large tapestry was woven in less than eight years by the Nancy workshop (1710-1718) and reveals the same qualities as the best Gobelins and Beauvais works.

Shortly afterward Mité fell into disagreement with his personnel and the workshops declined. Two weavers, F. Josse Bacor and Sigisbert Mengin, established themselves at Lunéville with rather limited material and personnel. This workshop became known as the Nouvelle Fabrique de Portières. The two PORTRAITS OF DUKE LEOPOLD woven by Bacor in this style were followed by six PORTIÈRES WITH THE ARMS OF DUKE LEOPOLD AND HIS WIFE. A disagreement soon separated the two weavers. Mengin established a low-warp workshop at Nancy in 1722, while Bacor transferred his workshops to La Malgrange, just outside Nancy. In 1737, following the duke's departure, the workshop was closed. The art of high- and low-warp tapestry in Lorraine was now closely linked with the prince's initiative.

Secondary workshops in northern and eastern France

In 1667, the art of tapestry, after vegetating for many years, enjoyed a new period of splendor at Lille. A low-warp workshop was founded in that city by Georges Blomaert in 1680, but he left it in 1684 to become the director of the Beauvais factory. He was replaced by François Pannemaker and his son André, descendants of the famous Brussels family. The Pannemakers wove numerous tapestries for the *hôtels* at Lille and in the city's surroundings in competition with those by the weaver Jean Le Melter, who was also established in the city. The Lille production was much influenced by Flemish tapestry and the majority of the weaving was devoted to Teniers-like compositions known as "Tesnières." After the death of Guillaume Warniers, Melter's son-in-law, in 1738, the Lille workshops were overtaken by a sluggishness from which they never recovered despite the attempts made in 1780 by Étienne Deyrolles.

The art of tapestry was practiced in northern France at Valenciennes, Torcy, Cambrai and in the east at Strasbourg in the workshops of Jean-Joseph Lamiral, who was at the head of the factory from 1743 to 1751 under the patronage of Cardinal de Rohan.

The Story of Charles V of Lorraine

The tapestries devoted to the victories of Charles V of Lorraine were executed by order of Duke Leopold of Lorraine to perpetuate the memory of his father's heroic exploits. The cartoons for the tapestry comprise nineteen pieces painted by Jean-Baptiste Durup (1709-1746), *Jean-Louis Guyon* (1672-1736), *Jean-Baptiste Martin* (1659-1735) *and Claude Jacquard* (1685-1736).

THE BATTLE OF KAHLENBERG AND THE RELIEF OF VIENNA. Detail showing the background. The entire tapestry measures 3.60 × 5.60 m. Lorraine, workshop of La Malgrange, 1724, directed by Josse Bacor. Woven in silk.

Vienna. Kunsthistorisches Museum. Museum photo.

Portière with Turkish Trophies. Two series of portières were woven on Bacor's and Mengin's looms in Lunéville, totaling twenty tapestries. One of the series has a yellow background, the other red. 3.98 × 3.08 m. Lorraine. Lunéville, about 1720.

Two eagles, with a Cross of Lorraine at their necks, support the alliance arms of Duke Leopold of Lorraine and Elisabeth Charlotte d'Orléans. They are joined by the collar of the Order of the Golden Fleece. Below, heaped trophies recall the victories gained by Charles V of Lorraine. In the border, in imitation of a wooden frame, are the Cross of Lorraine and the lilies of France. The background is red.

Vienna. Kunsthistorisches Museum. Bildarchiv d'Öst. Nationalbibliothek.

VIII Tapestry outside of France in the seventeenth and eighteenth centuries

The Netherlands and the Nordic countries. - Germany. - Italy. - England. - Russia and Poland. - Spain and Portugal. - Peruvian tapestries after the Spanish conquest. - Far Eastern tapestries.

IN the sixteenth century the heads of the houses of Este and Medici had established their own workshops for the purpose of producing on their own estates the tapestries needed to decorate their palaces. This example was followed in many countries. During the seventeenth and eighteenth centuries the ruling princes favored the development of tapestry workshops, whose production contributed to the outstanding embellishment of their residences. The creation of the royal Gobelins factory by Louis XIV increased this tendency; in imitation of the Sun King, sovereigns turned to the art of tapestry to evoke and perpetuate the memory of their exploits. The first master weavers summoned to these princely courts were Flemish, but they were soon replaced by Frenchmen whose skill was common knowledge everywhere and who taught their art to local weavers.

Thanks to the compositions designed by such artists as Jean-François de Troy and Charles-Antoine Coypel, France exerted a great influence on the art of tapestry.

In Spain, however, Goya's tapestries were quite different from those woven in France. Nevertheless, as in the case of Oudry, tapestry for Goya was the reproduction of a painting.

Whereas in the Far East the art of tapestry was in no way influenced by Western art, in Peru, after the Spanish Conquest, woven work revealed a continuing vitality that was receptive to European contributions.

The Netherlands and the Nordic countries

In Flanders, which suffered from wars and invasions, conditions were scarcely propitious to the development of tapestry. As a result, weavers emigrated from Tournai, Enghien, Tourcoing, and Alost. Moreover, the taste in Brussels turned from tapestry decoration to the use of painted leatherwork in imitation

Country Scenes

The cartoons for this set are by David Teniers's pupil, Lambert de Hondt, who was born in Malines. He settled in Munich and died in that city in 1667 after enjoying much success there. The tapestry was woven in several workshops and has various borders.

FORAGING. Brussels, workshop of Gaspard van der Borght, called A. Castro, early 18th century. Munich. Bayerisches National Museum. Museum photo.

of Cordovan leather made at Malines. Nevertheless, the Brussels workshops retained a certain prestige and foreign clients were still important. In the early eighteenth century the Grand Master of the Order of Malta commissioned from Judocus de Vos a STORY OF THE NEW TESTAMENT to hang in the church of Saint-Jean La Valette. Although large sets such as THE STORY OF THE DUCHY OF BRABANT for the Brussels council hall and MYTHOLOGICAL SUBJECTS for that of Ghent continued the tradition of great Flemish mural tapestries with allegorical subjects, a change in taste occurred with a definite predilection for *genre* and country scenes inspired by the paintings of David Teniers the Younger. These represent popular scenes and were woven in various sizes according to the dimensions of the walls to be covered. The same was also true of the tapestries with battle subjects in the style of Wouverman and Pegna.

On the other hand, the French style exerted a definite influence on the cartoon painters. THE STORY OF ALEXANDER after the cartoons by Le Brun, then quite familiar from engravings, was repeated several times. The COUNTRY SCENES after the cartoons by Lambert de Hondt recall the military episodes of THE STORY OF THE KING. The garden decoration by Le Nôtre, the architectural motifs in imitation of those at Versailles, the figures treated after the fashion of Mignard are all found in many Brussels tapestries dating from the eighteenth century. French literature itself oriented the choice of subjects, and THE STORY OF TELEMACHUS, from the adventure narrative by Fénelon, inspired a mural tapestry which was made by Urbain Leyniers.

In Denmark Christian V attempted to create a tapestry workshop by summoning, in 1684, a weaver named Bernt van der Eichen, probably a native of Audenarde. But after producing a set entitled THE STORY OF ALEXANDER and another called THE WAR OF SCANY, the workshops ceased activity in 1700. In 1735 Queen Sofia Magdalena summoned to Copenhagen the French tapestry weaver François Léger and commissioned him to furnish the decoration of the royal castle of Christianborg and of Hirschholm. He was aided by other French weavers, including Pierre Duru, who later worked at Stockholm, where after 1744 he produced furniture covers.

Germany

Germany was among the first countries to receive Flemish weavers. At the close of the sixteenth century Boldewin of Brussels was working in the center of Wolfenbüttel, in Lower Saxony. About 1600 Joost II van Herselle, in the Hamburg region, produced quality works such as THE STORY OF SCIPIO and THE STORY OF OCTAVIUS AUGUSTUS. But French influence gradually gained the upper hand, and in 1617 an Aubusson weaver named Marrot, who had produced THE EXPLOITS OF PRINCE PHILIP, settled in the center of Cassel. After the Revocation of the Edict of Nantes in 1685, more and more French weavers emigrated to the countries of northern and eastern Europe.

These dispersed tapestry attempts, whose success was relatively short-lived, were followed in the seventeenth and eighteenth centuries by an efflorescence of the textile art favored by an entirely different outlook. The nobles who built their châteaux after French and Italian models often bought Brussels,

The Story of the Duchy of Brabant
THE ABDICATION OF CHARLES V IN 1555. Detail of the right section. Brussels, workshop of Henri Reydams and Urbain Leyniers, 1717-1718.
Prince Philip kneels before the emperor. The Regent of the Low Countries, Mary of Hungary, turns to the left as though uninterested in the scene.
Brussels. Musée communal. Museum photo.

(Overleaf)
The Story of Telemachus ▶
This set represents five scenes from Fénelon's novel, Les Aventures de Télémaque.
THE YOUNG HERO DINES WITH CALYPSO. 3.71 × 5.76 m. Brussels, workshop of Reydams and Leyniers, about 1725.
Telemachus and faithful Mentor are received by Calypso.
Vienna. Kunsthistorisches Museum. Photo E. Meyer.

Aubusson or Beauvais tapestries to decorate the interiors, but the wealthiest princes had their own workshops, thanks to the presence of foreign weavers. Naturally, these workshops existed only so long as the prince, a lover of the fine arts, was present to commission the work from them and follow its execution.

The most ardent tapestry patron in southern Germany was certainly Maximilian of Bavaria. For his new residence in Munich, the duke desired a great number of tapestries. He first turned unsuccessfully to the Frankenthal masters, then in 1604 he summoned Hans van der Biest of Enghien. The latter soon arrived with his workers, who were natives of Brussels. The first Munich workshop lasted until 1615 and there is no question of the excellence of the tapestries produced. Van der Biest's son-in-law, Van den Bosch, and Lucas van Neuenhofer outdid each other in skill. The decoration of the new residence was entrusted to two Flemish painters, Frederick Sustris and Peter Candidus, who had studied at Florence under Vasari. They supplied the designs for five tapestry sets which were woven at the workshop, GROTESQUES, THE MONTHS, THE SEASONS, THE DAYS and finally the principal work, THE STORY OF OTTO OF WITTELSBACH, a monumental glorification of the ruling family. Here we can see that Candidus, an artist of Flemish origin, took special interest in the presentation of pomp and ceremony; armor and trophies represented in the borders stand out in red and gold and are in opposition to the clear colors of the important subjects. A second workshop was established at Munich about 1718, thanks to the initiative of the Prince Elector, Maximilian Emanuel, who summoned to the city a dozen weavers, this time French. These included Jean-Louis and Louis-François Vavoque, who had deserted the Gobelins. They executed THE STORY OF THE HOUSE OF WITTELSBACH, finished in 1726, but the quality was inferior to Van der Biest's tapestry. About 1765, following a crisis, the Parisian Jacques Sentigny was summoned to take charge of the workshop. He was soon assisted by the master Chedeville and from 1766 to 1775 they produced a set of THE FOUR SEASONS after the cartoons by Christian Winck which had been inspired by French creations dating from a slightly earlier period.

The Revocation of the Edict of Nantes obliged many Aubusson weavers to emigrate to Germany, where they were well received by the Grand Elector in Berlin. In 1686 Pierre Mercier established a workshop whose production was destined chiefly to enrich the prince's châteaux and palaces at Berlin and Potsdam. After some rather simple work such as furniture covers, Mercier began an important set of THE EXPLOITS OF THE GRAND ELECTOR. Finished in 1699, this set appears to have been inspired by THE STORY OF LOUIS XIV, executed at the Gobelins, but the result is not comparable. Mercier was replaced by his nephew Jean II Barraband, but the death of the Grand Elector, who became King of Prussia as Frederick I, proved a fatal blow to the workshop which ceased production. Meanwhile, in 1714 Mercier went to the court of Frederick Augustus of Saxony and Poland.

Barraband produced tapestries "in

The Months
The cartoons for the twelve pieces that constitute this set are by Peter de Witte, called Petrus Candidus, and represent labor in the fields.
MAY. Detail of the right section. Munich, workshop of Hans van der Biest, 1604-1615. Woven in silk and gold.
Munich. Bayerische National Museum. Museum photo.

MENSIS V
HIC DECVS HYBLÆVM, FLORES, ET APRICA VOLVPTAS;
LVDIT IN OSTRINO FESTA PVELLA SATO.

GERMANICI IMPERII MAIESTATEM ADVERS
GRÆCORVM ARTES ET FACTIOSOS ALIOS
MINISQVE REPVLSOS ASSERIT AN. MCL

The Story of Otto of Wittelsbach
The tapestry cartoons were commissioned from Peter Candidus, who was summoned from Florence to Munich by Maximilian, Duke of Bavaria, who wanted to honor the memory of Otto the Great, creator of Wittelsbach, Count Palatine of Bavaria in 1156, *representative of Frederick Barbarossa in Italy in* 1159, *and Duke of Bavaria from* 1180 *until his death in* 1183.
RECEPTION OF THE GREEK AMBASSADORS. Munich, workshop of Hans van der Biest, 1611. Woven in silk and gold.

Following pages: Otto of Wittelsbach's horse. The saber of one of the Greek ambassadors. Munich. Bayerisches National Museum. Museum photo.

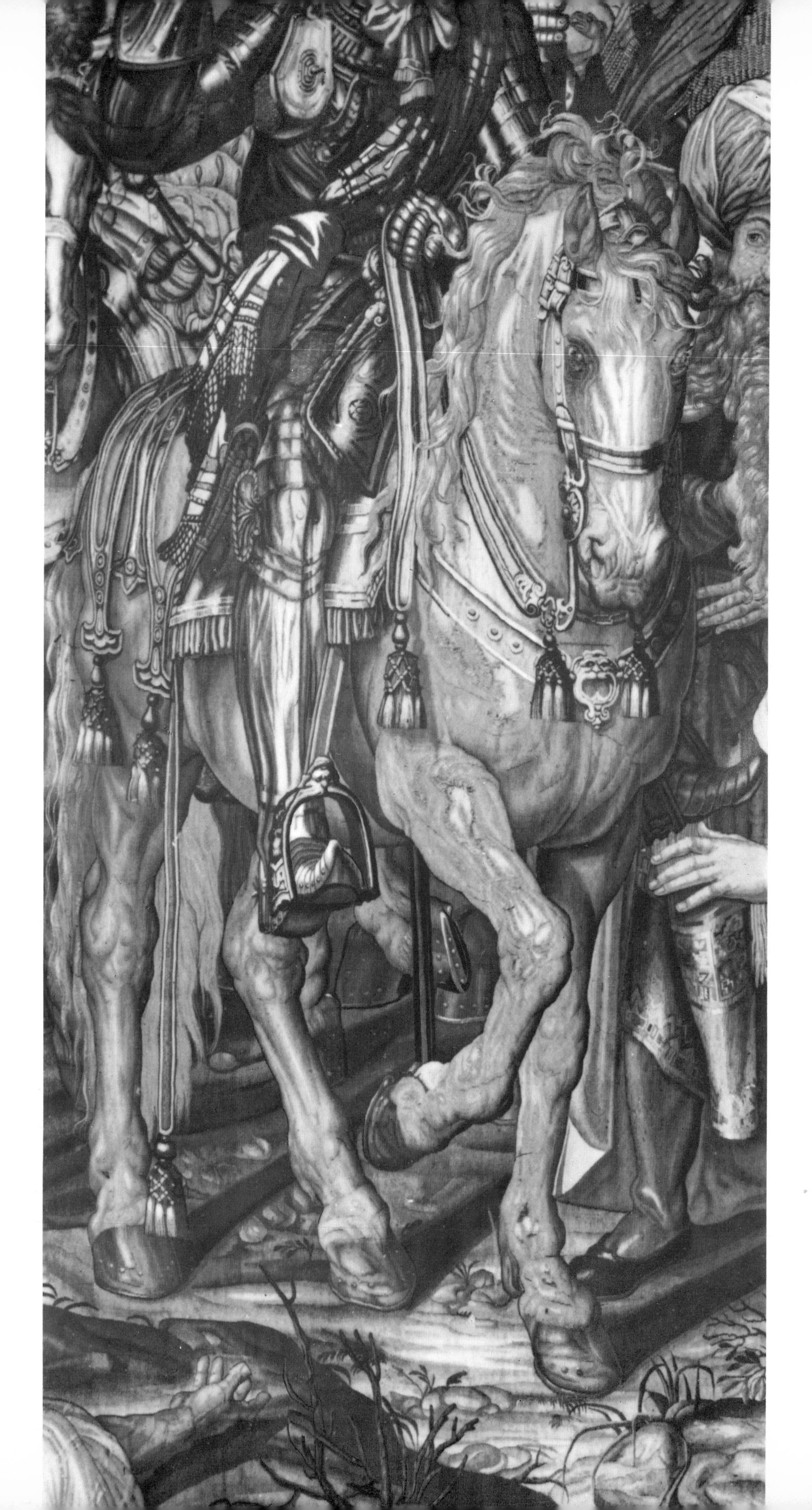

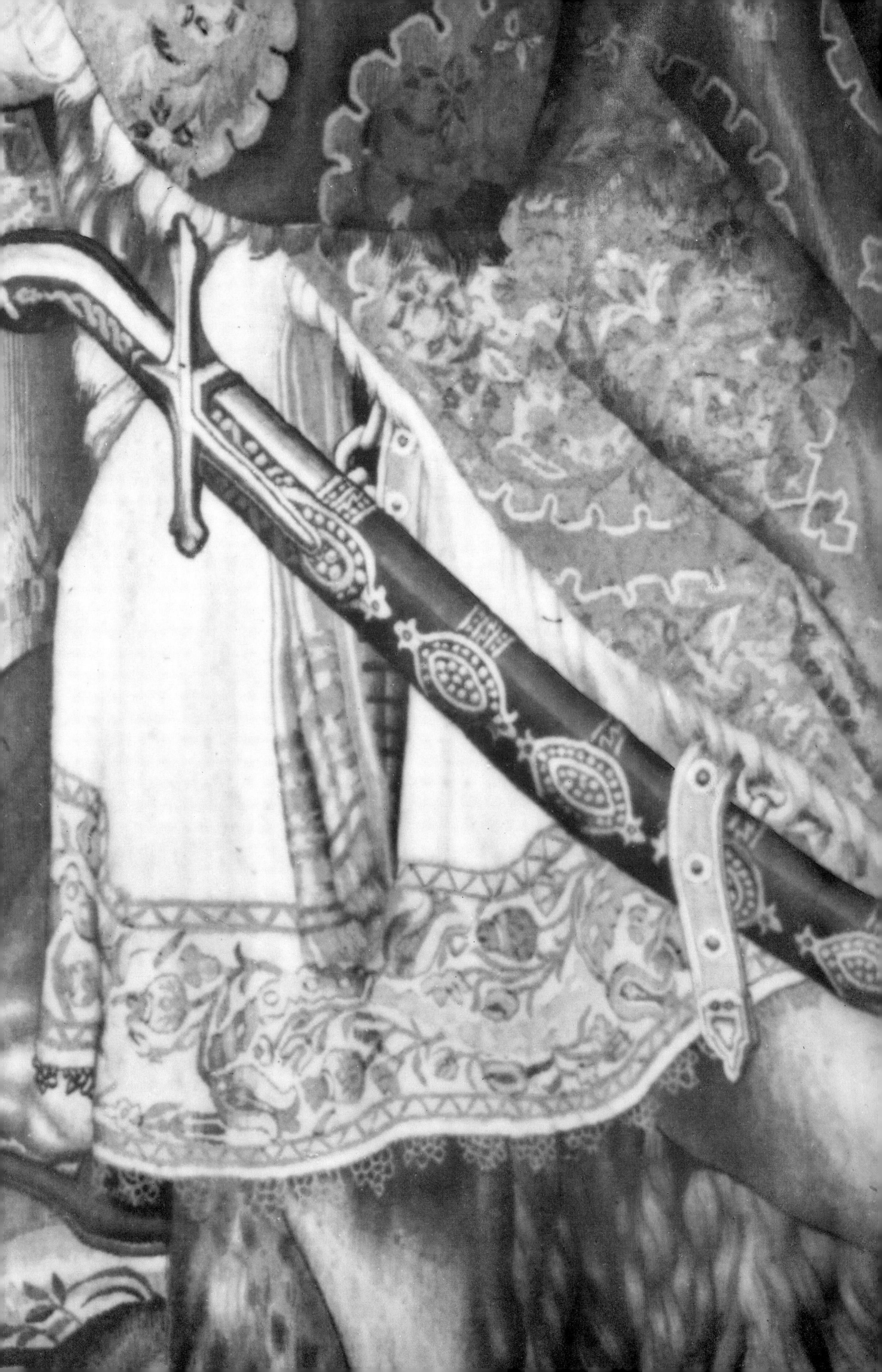

the French style," especially a set of GROTESQUES ON A YELLOW BACKGROUND after the model by Berain and Monnoyer, also a Chinese set after the cartoons by Vernansal and Blain de Fontenay. In 1720 Barraband entered into partnership with the Frenchman Charles Vigne, who continued the Berlin enterprise until 1786. The models were doubtless inspired by engravings from the works of Watteau, Lancret and Boucher, as is evident in THE ITALIAN COMEDY now in the Château of Charlottenburg.

In 1714 Mercier was summoned by King Frederick Augustus and settled at Dresden. After weaving several small pieces, he undertook THE HISTORY OF AUGUSTUS THE STRONG, two pieces evoking the king's journey to France. Mercier died in 1729 and the work was continued by his assistant Jacques Nermot. In 1720 the bishop-princes of the House of Schönborn founded a workshop at Würzburg after summoning the Flemish weaver Johann Thomas, who was soon replaced by his pupil André Pirot, a native of Frankfurt. From 1738 to 1749 he worked on THE VENETIAN CARNIVAL set after the cartoons by the court painter Johann Rudolf Biss. Although the design is rather attractive, the colors have become murky and the pastel tones are hidden by shades of gray.

A panorama of German tapestry would be incomplete if we failed to mention the workshops founded by two families from Aubusson: the Deschazeaux family at Erlangen and the Peux family at Schwabach.

The Story of the House of Wittelsbach
CORONATION SCENE. Munich, workshop of Jean-Louis and Louis-François Vavoque, 1726.
Otto of Bavaria is crowned King of Hungary at Albe Royal in 1305 by bishops and important lords of his kingdom.
Munich. Bayerisches National Museum. Photo Bavarian Museums.

Italy

At the head of the workshops established at Rome from 1630 to 1635 by Cardinal Barberini, nephew of Pope Urban VIII, was the Frenchman Jacques de La Rivière (Giacomo della Riviera), assisted by two weavers, Antoine who was also French, and Michael who was Flemish. In 1625 the papal legate Cardinal Barberini had been sent to the French court to negotiate the Valteline affair. On the eve of his departure he received the seven tapestries of THE STORY OF CONSTANTINE which Louis XIII had ordered from La Planche's workshop after the cartoons by Rubens. On his return the cardinal conceived the project of opening workshops in Rome.

The earliest documents which mention the drawings of a tapestry entitled THE CHATEAUX date from 1627. The cardinal took a passionate interest in everything that concerned the art of tapestry and was informed of all that was happening in the European workshops as well as the technical methods applied. He decided to complete the Rubens set which he had received with other tapestries to be woven in the Roman workshops. The designs were requested from Pietro da Cortona, who painted five compositions lacking in the set by Rubens with various subjects except the piece called THE APPEARANCE OF THE MONOGRAM OF CHRIST. This half-Italian and half-French tapestry was destined to decorate a complete room, probably, as David Dubon says, the large salon of the Palazzo Barberini. In addition to tapestries, it consists of overdoors, a canopy decoration and *portières* woven in linen, silk and gold by La Rivière from 1630 to 1641.

This manner of decorating an entire room with tapestries introduced a fashion which became current in every other country in the eighteenth century. At Rome the habit was acquired as early as the seventeenth century and the mural tapestries which followed THE LIFE OF URBAN VII and JEUX D'ENFANTS had very small panels forming a "set" with the principal one. La Rivière died and was succeeded by his brother-in-law Gaspare Rocci, who finished THE LIFE OF CHRIST after the cartoons by Pietro da Cortona and Romanelli (St. Patrick's Cathedral, New York). The cardinal's death in 1679 led to the closing of the workshops.

Early in the following century Pope Clement XI organized another workshop in the convent of San Michele a Ripa (1710). In charge of the workshop was the Frenchman Jean Simonet, assisted by the painter Procaccini. But there was little artistic impulse and the

The Venetian Carnival
The cartoons for this tapestry of five pieces are by the court painter Johann Rudolf Biss. They recall the cartoons of the First Chinese Set *woven in Beauvais and those of the* Comédie italienne *woven in Berlin by Charles Vigne.*
HARLEQUIN'S ENTRY INTO VENICE. Würzburg, workshop of André Pirot, 1740-1745. Woven in silk.
Opposite page: Detail of the clever bear holding a fox.
Würzburg. Residenzmuseum. Photo Gundermann.

(Overleaf)

The Story of Constantine
The cartoons for this Story of Constantine *were ordered from Rubens by Louis XIII and reached Paris in 1622. The first set woven in the Paris workshops of Philippe Maecht and Hans Taye was offered to Cardinal Francesco Barberini, papal-legate of his uncle Pope Urban VIII, on the occasion of his visit to the French capital. The set of seventeen pieces was shipped to Rome in 1625. Cardinal Barberini founded his own factory in Rome in 1627. Among the first assignments given to this workshop was the weaving of the tapestries meant to complete Rubens's work. The cartoons were requested from Pietro da Cortona, who designed five pieces, plus the portières and the overdoors as well as a canopy. This tapestry set decorated the grand salon of the Barberini Palace in Rome.*
THE CAMPAIGN AGAINST LICINIUS. Naval battle after Pietro da Cortona. 4.90 × 6.90 m. Rome, Barberini factory, workshop of Giacomo della Riviera, 1635. Woven in silk and silver.
The bees represented in the border are the emblems of the Barberini family.
Philadelphia Museum of Art. Photo A. J. Wyatt.

The Story of Constantine
CONSTANTINE FIGHTING THE LION after Pietro da Cortona. 4.90 × 2.80 m. Rome, Barberini factory, workshop of Giacomo della Riviera, 1637. Woven in silk, gold and silver.
Philadelphia Museum of Art. Photo A. J. Wyatt.

latter left Rome for Spain to head the Santa Isabella workshop. A fresh attempt was made by Benedict XIV, but it met little success and the workshop established in Piazza Santa Maria in Transtevere produced few tapestries.

Under the Medici the art of tapestry once again assumed importance during the reign of Ferdinand II (1621-1670). The head of the workshop was the French master Pierre Lefèvre, who had established a workshop in the Grande Galerie of the Louvre. He had settled in Florence in 1659 and worked there until his death in 1667. He principally produced reproductions of paintings by Michelangelo, Raphael and Andrea del Sarto as well as THE SEASONS woven with Bernardin van Hasselt (1642-1643). The Medici workshop, however, died out in 1737. One of the last works to be woven was THE FOUR PARTS OF THE WORLD after the cartoons by Giovanni Sagrestani, who tried to reproduce the light tones and chromatic range of oil painting. François II of Lorraine, who succeeded the Medici, made an attempt to establish workshops at Poggio Imperiale under the direction of the painter Lorenzo Corsini, but his initiative met with failure.

In 1738, the year after the closing of the Medici workshop, the ruler of the House of Savoy, Charles Emmanuel III, engaged the skilled Victor Demignot and placed him in charge of a low-warp workshop. The sovereign wanted the workshop to produce tapestries which would decorate the Royal Palace at Turin, whose renovation had been active since 1730. The court painter Claude Beaumont supplied a number of models for important mythological and epic sets after the fashion of the compositions by Jean-François de Troy, including THE STORY OF ALEXANDER, THE STORY OF CÆSAR, THE STORY OF CYRUS and THE STORY OF HANNIBAL. Other tapestries with an essentially decorative character were also woven and included SEASCAPES, ARCHITECTURAL SCENES and COUNTRY SCENES. In 1754 the high-warp workshops were removed in favor of the low-warp ones; the weavers worked chiefly after the cartoons of a Lyons painter named Laurent Pecheux, who after 1766 replaced Claude Beaumont as workshop painter. In 1784 François Demignot, Victor's son, was succeeded by Antoine Bruno, who remained at the head of the workshop until it was closed in 1832.

Like the Turin workshop, that of Naples was largely the result of the closing of the Medici workshop. In 1737 some of the weavers were transferred to the Naples workshop which Charles III wanted to establish at San Carlo delle Mortelle in order to produce tapestry sets for his royal residences. The Florentine Domenico del Rosso was named director and retained this post until 1761. Most of the subjects were taken from the Gobelins repertory. The first to be woven was THE ELEMENTS after Le Brun (1754-1759), followed by a DON QUIXOTE after Coypel which was executed at Naples from 1758 to 1761. In addition, there were overdoors and five new cartoons by various artists. The Neapolitans accentuated in these compositions the caricatural character of French tapestry designs but rather successfully expressed the decoration of the *alentours*. At the close of the century other works were devoted to celebrating the merits of Charles III (1794-1795). The fall of the monarchy brought an end to the workshop.

(Overleaf)
The Four Seasons ▶
The subjects were inspired by drawings made by Martin de Vos.
SPRING. 3.25 × 3.80 m. England, Sheldon factory, 1611.
Hatfield House. Photo Precision, St. Albans.

England

Many texts confirm that the art of weaving existed in medieval England, but the finest tapestries of this period came from Flanders, for the great collections of Henry VII, Cardinal Wolsey and Henry VIII were almost entirely imported. It was not until the middle of the sixteenth century that England began to have organized workshops. The first important one was that of William Sheldon, who established his at Bercheston in Warwickshire. The director was Richard Hickes, who had come from Holland, followed by his son Ralph. The tapestries executed were not only designed as mural decoration but also as useful objects, including cushions, then very popular and used for benches and stools. The most curious works consist of a set of maps of different counties in England, one of which is now in the Bodleian Library, Oxford, and bears the date 1588. These geographical maps or those representing town plans woven in tapestry correspond to the taste of the period and several such tapestries had already been woven in Flanders, indicating the influence of Flemish art on English tapestry. These maps have very rich borders filled with figures alternating with bowers based on heavy Brussels models. Yet a distinct English style finally emerged, with a tendency toward graphic design and a pleasing treatment of forms. These characteristics are revealed in the final Shelton sets such as THE FOUR SEASONS, woven in 1611 (Hatfield House). This style is similar to that of the *petit point* tapestries on canvas which were greatly developed in England.

Following the example of Henri IV in France, James I founded the famous Stuart workshop at Mortlake. In 1619 the master weaver Philippe de Maecht was asked to leave Paris for Mortlake. Francis Cleyn, a native of Rostock, was engaged as the new workshop's painter. Soon the Mortlake looms rivaled those at Paris and became famous. Sir Francis Crane was made director and the head of the workshop was a Brussels weaver named Josse Ampe. The weavers themselves were some fifty in number and chiefly from Flanders and France.

The Mortlake workshops first produced ancient classical scenes. The first to be set to the loom was THE STORY OF VENUS AND VULCAN; the cartoons by an Italian painter were doubtless bought at Brussels, where they had been used in the sixteenth century. About 1630, on Rubens's advice, Charles I bought at Brussels seven of the famous cartoons by Raphael of THE ACTS OF THE APOSTLES which Pierre d'Alost had used as models for the famous tapestries ordered by Pope Leo X. Three of these ten cartoons were lost together with the models of the borders framing the sixteenth-century mural tapestry. According to Jules Guiffrey, it was Van Dyck, court painter to Charles I, who designed the splendid models for the borders which frame THE ACTS OF THE APOSTLES now in the Mobilier National. Woven in wool and silk this first set was a remarkable achievement. Mazarin bought it from the possessions of Charles I and left it to Louis XIV.

During the fifteen years of its existence, activity at the Mortlake workshop never slackened, for it also produced the original HERO AND LEANDER representing the famous story of the lovers celebrated by Christopher Marlowe at the end of the sixteenth century. This set, whose models are attributed to the painter Francis Cleyn, has a graceful

design and much charm in the rendering of the faces. The figures reveal all the customary nobility and elegance of the lords and ladies of the English aristocracy who chose Van Dyck as their favorite portrait painter. In 1636 Sir Francis Crane died in Paris after an operation. At that date the king owed a rather important sum to Mortlake for various mural tapestries, and after a petition addressed to him, Mortlake, with its one hundred and forty workers, found itself in difficult circumstances.

Prior to the death of Charles I several important tapestries, such as THE FIVE SENSES and CHILDREN PLAYING, were woven. After the execution of Charles I in 1649 the workshop was seized together with other Crown property. Yet work continued during the Civil War and under Cromwell the Mortlake weavers executed an important tapestry after Mantegna's cartoons for THE TRIUMPH OF CÆSAR. After the restoration of the Stuarts, Charles II followed his father's example by patronizing the workshop and in 1662 Sir Sackville Crow was named director with an annual subsidy of one thousand pounds. The prosperity of Mortlake appeared to have died out, its popularity eclipsed by the fame of the Gobelins factory in France. Yet during this period the workshop produced VERDURES, HUNTS and HORSES and above all a tapestry representing THE NAVAL BATTLE OF SOLEBAY (1672) in which

The Four Parts of the World
The cartoons were executed in 1715 by Giovanni Sagrestani for the figures, Stefano Papi for the border, and Girolamo Cortes for the landscape.
ASIA. Detail. 3.55 × 5.70 m. Florence, Medici factory, workshop of Victor Demignot, Leonardo Bernini and Gaetano Bruschi, 1719. Florence. Bardini Museum. Photo Italfoto.

The Acts of the Apostles
The cartoons by Raphael were woven in many workshops *(see p. 142).*
St. Peter and St. John Healing the Paralytic at the Temple Gate. 4.20 × 6.45 m. England, Mortlake factory, about 1630. Woven in silk and gold.
This tapestry, the third to be executed, was purchased, in 1659, by Colbert from the abbé Le Normant. It later became part of the King of France's garde-meuble. *The border models may have been designed by Van Dyck.*
Paris. Mobilier National. Photo Hachette.

The Story of Hero and Leander
The models for this tapestry, originally consisting of six pieces, are attributed to the painter François Cleyn, who worked at the Mortlake factory for several years.
THE MEETING OF HERO AND LEANDER BEFORE THE TEMPLE OF CYTHERA. Detail. England, Mortlake factory, 1628-1630. Woven in silk, gold and silver.
This tapestry was probably made for Charles I. In the upper border are the arms of England. After the English monarch's execution, it was sold and soon thereafter was acquired by Swedish collections.
Stockholm. Royal Palace. Photo Swedish National Furniture.

(Overleaf)
The Naval Battle of Solebay ▶
Originally this tapestry consisted of six pieces. It represents the battle of Solebay in 1672 in which the English and Allied fleets, commanded by the Duke of York and the Count d'Estrées, fought the Dutch fleet under De Ruyter. The cartoons are attributed to the Dutch painter Willem van de Velde. Two of these tapestries were partly woven at Mortlake and partly at Hatton Gardens.
THE ENGLISH FLEET ENGAGES IN COMBAT. 3.95 × 6.05 m. England, Mortlake factory, workshop of Francis and Thomas Poyntz, about 1685. Woven in silk.
Middlesex. Hampton Court. Reproduced by gracious permission of Her Majesty the Queen. Photo Ministry of Public Building and Works.

English, French and Dutch fleets took part. This tapestry, bearing the signature of Francis Poyntz, the last director at Mortlake, now hangs in Hampton Court.

By hiring most of the Mortlake weavers, other workshops were created. In the early eighteenth century John Vanderbanck established one in the Soho quarter of London and produced the best tapestries with Chinese decoration or "in the Indian style." Small, with narrow borders and well suited to English interiors, these tapestries enjoyed great success. Another Soho weaver was Joshua Morris who, about 1725, produced a fine group of tapestries with arabesque decoration. Later Paul Saunders tried to infuse fresh life into these workshops (1758-1770).

Russia and Poland

In a desire to celebrate the great events of the Russian court and escape foreign influence, Peter the Great determined to establish a tapestry workshop at St. Petersburg. The splendid tapestries which the King of France had offered to the Russian ambassador, Prince Dolgorouki, probably led the Tsar to decide to turn directly to the Gobelins for the workmen necessary. In April 1716, in agreement with the superintendent of the royal factory, the Duc d'Antin, the first group of weavers, including J.-B. Leblond, left for Russia. They were followed six months later by another group, including Jean Behagle, son of the Beauvais middleman Philippe, a wool dyer and a silk dyer.

The Russian workshop was modeled after the Gobelins factory, but results were disappointing, especially owing to technical difficulties. Weaving of the

THE MARTYRDOM OF ST. STANISLAS. Cracow, workshop of F. Glaize, 1758.
This tapestry was part of a series of five antependia ordered by Bishop Zaluski and based on designs by the painter Taddeo Konicz. They were meant to decorate the church of Saint-Stanislas-of-the-Poles in Rome, but after the bishop's death they remained unfinished.
Cracow. Czartoriski Museum. Photo Malinowski.

PORTRAIT OF PETER THE GREAT. Russia, St. Petersburg workshop, about 1720. ▶
Stockholm. Nationalmuseum. Museum photo.

set known as GREAT RUSSIA was terminated after the production of the first piece, THE BATTLE OF POLTAVA (1719-1723) after the cartoons by the court painter Caravaque. By 1723 the majority of the French weavers had left Russia. The works they had executed included a copy of the INDIES woven from the tapestry the Tsar had brought with him following his stay in Paris. The French weavers, however, had had sufficient time to train local workmen, and during the ensuing years, the workshop was active again under the technical direction of two Russian masters, Ivan Koboliakov, director of high-warp weaving, and Mikhail Atmanov, director of low-warp weaving. The tapestries executed solely by local workmen were the VERDURES and GROTESQUES with their characteristic yellow and brown.

The interest shown by the Tsarina Anna Ivanovna led to fresh interest in the art of tapestry and once again French weavers were summoned to Russia. They executed copies of Flemish tapestries as well as THE STORY OF DIANA after Toussaint Dubreuil and THE NEW INDIES after Desportes. In 1766 the new director, Dimitri Lobkov, foresaw the possibility of giving new prestige to the workshops and engaged other weavers, including Rondet of the Gobelins and Esprit Serre from Stockholm. Nevertheless, the tapestry devoted to the Tsarina Petrovna was not finished until after her death in 1771. After the short reign of Peter III, the ascension of Catherine the Great marked a new period of prosperity. The technical quality proved satisfactory, but new cartoons were lacking: copies of Gobelins or Beauvais tapestries alternated with works which were reproductions of paintings by Carle van Loo, Murillo and J.-B. Pierre. Financial difficulties finally caused the workshop to close in 1854.

About 1743 the French painter François Glaize, who was probably summoned by Bishop Stanislas Costka Zaluski, settled in Warsaw, where he produced tapestries with religious subjects based on famous paintings such as Van Dyck's "Crucifixion" (Antwerp). At Cracow he executed tapestries commissioned by the church of St. Stanislas of the Poles at Rome after the cartoons by Taddeo Konicz. Other workshops were established in Poland to satisfy the requirements of the nobility, including the Sokolov workshop, which wove tapestries for the Oginski family, but these workshops were secondary.

Spain and Portugal

When, in the sixteenth century, Charles V, ruler of the Netherlands, became king of Spain, he showed little interest in establishing tapestry workshops in Spain, accustomed as he was to order directly from the Flemish workshops, especially from those in Brussels, whose productions were appreciated throughout Europe. This policy was continued by his successor Philip II, but in 1562 he summoned the weaver Pietro Guiterrez from Salamanca to Madrid to restore his rich tapestry collections. Guiterrez established in the Calle Santa Isabella a workshop which was probably the original whose interior was represented by Velasquez in his famous painting "The Weavers."

In 1624 the archival documents mention the activity of a Brussels weaver named Frans Tons, who was working in New Castille for the Duke of Pastra-

The Hunts
Representing seven hunting scenes, this tapestry was probably woven for Philip V.
HORSES MAKING A HALT. Madrid, Royal Tapestry Factory, workshop of Van der Goten, 1723.
Spanish National Patrimony. Spanish Ambassador to Paris. Photo Hachette.

The Story of Don Quixote
Woven after the cartoons by Procaccini and Sani, this tapestry consists of three pieces which were made between 1727 and 1760, in the Spanish factories, with various borders. Two details of the tapestry illustrate chapters 25 and 26 of Cervantes' Don Quixote. *The Knight of La Mancha, Don Quixote, withdraws to the Sierra Morena to do penance in honor of his lady, Dulcinea. He sends his faithful squire Sancho Panza to inform his lady of his follies on her behalf, but Sancho's ass is stolen and he borrows his master's faithful horse Rocinante. Sancho takes tree branches with him and drops them while en route to mark his return fourney. On the left, we see Sancho on Rocinante, while Don Quixote, on the right, is engaged in his follies for Dulcinea.*
Madrid, Royal Tapestry Factory, workshop of Van der Goten, about 1730.
Spanish National Patrimony. Spanish Ambassador to Paris. Photo Hachette.

na. Spain, however, had to await the ascension of a Frenchman, Philip V (1700-1746), for tapestry workshops worthy of the name. Following the example set by Louis XIV, early in his reign Philip V established a workshop in his new estates, but he encountered strong opposition on the part of France who feared the loss of certain commercial outlets. Louis XIV's grandson had to summon weavers from Flanders. Jacob van der Goten of Antwerp, his wife and four sons reached Madrid in 1721 and settled in the Casa del Abreviador known as the Santa Barbara workshop. The low-warp weaver was Van der Goten. The king, anxious to improve production, established a high-warp workshop in 1731 under the direction of Van der Goten's son. When the sovereigns returned to Madrid the workshops were set up in the Calle della Santa Barbara, then in the Calle Santa Isabella.

During this early period of activity, an artistic director was lacking and the first works proved disappointing. Numerous copies were made from famous paintings by Raphael and Guido Reni, in addition to very Flemish or Teniers-like scenes or military ones after the fashion of Wouverman, differing little from contemporary works at Brussels and Antwerp. The most attractive set was undoubtedly that of the HUNTS (1723-1724), seven pieces whose borders bear the arms of Philip V. Michel-Ange Houasse did the designs for the ST. JOHN THE BAPTIST IN THE DESERT and began a STORY OF TELEMACHUS. The most significant tapestry, however, was that of DON QUIXOTE. In the eighteenth century the exploits of the "mad hidalgo" were the subject of tapestries woven in some of the most important workshops. The cartoons were by the Italian painter Procaccini, the pupil of Maratta, summoned to Madrid probably on the request of Cardinal Alberoni, who held an important position at the Spanish court. In 1721 Procaccini was made "chief painter of the chamber" and became the architect of the royal Château of Ildefonso. He furnished the first drawings *(petits-patrons)* and his pupil Sani executed the cartoons in full size. Three sets of DON QUIXOTE were woven with various borders. Actually these tapestries reveal great misunderstanding of technique; the composition is poor, and we still find a strong Flemish note in the profusion of men and animals.

After the death of both Houasse and Procaccini, production stagnated. There was a lack of painters and old mural tapestries from the royal furniture repository were copied, including THE STORY OF CYRUS from Van Tiegen's and Leyniers's workshop, and THE CONQUEST OF TUNIS, the famous set which was woven by Pannemaker and finished in 1743. This set differed from the first by its emphasis on detail taken to the extreme and the whole work is completely unrelated to the Renaissance spirit. Overdoors were added representing combats against the Turks.

A fresh impetus was given to the art of tapestry by the ascension of Ferdinand VI in 1746. The court painter was then Louis-Michel van Loo. Cartoons inspired by Teniers were woven for the Escorial and the Buen Retiro. They were without borders and destined to be embedded in the panelling. In a similar manner, large Biblical sets were woven such as THE STORY OF JOSEPH and THE STORY OF DAVID after the works by Corrado Giaquinto who, in 1752, became *pintor de camera.* Preparation for the new château at Madrid under Charles III established an important program for the weavers and a large tapestry decoration was executed for the state chamber after the cartoons by José del Castillo. Finished in 1770, these works, woven with many gold threads, were in the taste of contemporary Gobelins and Beauvais tapestries. Another royal set in the Pompeian style was woven for the king, who much admired Roman antiquity. José del Castillo's cartoons mingled garlands, rinceaux and cameos against a purple red background in imitation of the paintings at Herculaneum. All these different works proved the great prosperity of these workshops.

In 1762 Anton Raffael Mengs was placed in charge of the Santa Barbara workshop and the accounts from 1776 to 1790 list the painters who had been summoned to provide tapestry cartoons: José del Castillo, 16 cartoons; Antonio Gonzalez Velasquez, 23; Mariano Nani, 14; Giles Andres de Aguirra, 11; Ramon Bayeu, 20; Antonio Barbazza, 6; José de Sales, 1; Francisco Goya, 30; a total of 121 cartoons representing considerable material for the workshops and which cost no less than 357,981 reales.

Towards the close of the century the most original works were those by Bayeu and above all by Goya. Bayeu freed himself from copies and compositions in imitation of Teniers and interpreted various episodes in the life of the Spanish people in a very lively manner. But he was surpassed by his son-in-law Goya who, thanks to his protection, entered the Santa Barbara workshop as a cartoon painter. The first order included LUNCH ON THE BANKS OF THE MANZANARES and THE DANCE NEAR SAN ANTONIO DE LA FLORIDA. Goya's work met with great success, and

Life in Madrid after Francisco Goya.
EL CACHARRERO (FAIENCE MERCHANT). 3.75 × 2.60 m. Madrid, Santa Barbara Factory, about 1794. Spanish National Patrimony. Spanish Ambassador to Paris. Photo Hachette.

from 1771 to 1791 he was commissioned to design forty-five large cartoons and others of smaller dimensions for the overdoors destined to decorate the Infante's chamber as well as the royal one in the Escorial. These paintings, for paintings they were with delicate nuances, proved difficult to execute in tapestry and were the subject of frequent discussions between Goya and Cornelis van der Goten, the workshop's technical director. In Goya's opinion, the cartoons were poorly executed and the tapestries lacked finesse, the shadows being too heavy and compact and devoid of the delicacy of the Gobelins work. As for their subjects, these tapestries revealed a definite break with tradition. The subjects were taken from Spanish life and represented joyful groups of men and women, dances and games, all interpreted in a lively spirit with a taste for the picturesque and much variety of color. After all, Goya was influenced by the great Venetian colorist Tiepolo.

The establishment of the Tavira workshops in southern Portugal dates from the eighteenth century. At the end of the year 1776 two tapestry weavers, one a Frenchman from Aubusson named Pierre-Léonard Mergoux, and the other a Portuguese named Pedro Theotonio Hector, installed eight looms, whose work recalled the production at Aubusson. Some examples can still be seen at Tavira and Lisbon.

Peruvian tapestries after the Spanish Conquest

The conquest of Peru by Pizarro and his band of adventurers began in 1530. The great Incan empire was rapidly shaken but to some extent its culture remained. A fresh impetus was given to the art of tapestry, thanks to the importation from Spain of large looms. The works reveal in a rather curious manner a European influence mingled with Indian traditions. Under the Habsburgs, then the rulers of Spain, the tapestries often bore the two-headed eagle, the emblem of the Habsburg dynasty. For more than a century under the Bourbons (1700-1825) the French style proved fashionable and the fleurs-de-lis appeared along with motifs of classic inspiration such as baskets and garlands of flowers.

Peruvian Tapestry. Detail of the central section. 1.85 × 1.65 m. Peru, 17th century.
The décor of this tapestry was inspired by Spanish art but still reveals a slight influence of native art.
Boston Museum of Fine Arts. Museum photo.

Far Eastern tapestries

During the Ming dynasty (1368-1644) there were several kinds of *k'o-ssu*. Some were extremely fine in texture and inspired by the style of famous paintings; they were mounted on *kakemonos* and are often studied with the paintings themselves. In general, the landscapes are monochrome. This form of art partially suggests reality with much stylization of subjects and aerial effects to create an atmospheric mood. These *k'o-ssu* represent rocks and plants, doves on branches of blossoming apple trees or figures such as the portrait of T'ung-Fang, the friend of the gods who was so clever that he succeeded in stealing the peaches of longevity.

Only in the nineteenth century did highlights in paintings become increasingly common and this taste followed the decline of the art of weaving. Other *k'o-ssu* were destined exclusively for decorative purposes and included costumes and furniture objects (cushions, seat covers, screens, mural tapestries). They are distinguished from the first by heavy weaving and were often executed with gold threads; they have the same lively colors as we find in Ming porcelain. The decorative repertory of these tapestries was borrowed from Chinese flora and from an often imaginary flora. The subject of a late Ming panel in the Metropolitan Museum, THE FENG HUANG IN A ROCK GARDEN, is related to the legend of the hundred birds so often represented in Chinese art. The *feng huang* (a kind of phœnix) is a bird that resembles a five-colored rooster and, like the dragon, the king of the animals, the *feng huang* is king of the birds. A symbol of happiness, it brings peace to the world. During the course of centuries the name gradually became associated with the

K'o-ssu or Chinese tapestry.
T'UNG FUNG STEALING THE PEACHES OF LONGEVITY. 1.17 × 0.61 m. China, Ming period (1368-1644). Woven in silk.
Metropolitan Museum of Art. Museum photo.

THE FENG HUANG (PHŒNIX) IN A ROCK GARDEN. Detail. The whole tapestry measures 2.20 × 1.75 m. China, late Ming period. Woven in silk and gold.

Here we see the lower part of the tapestry. Above, on the right, is part of the body of the feng huang, *a kind of rooster in five colors, who is head of the birds and the symbol of happiness. He flies above the blue rocks in the midst of flowering trees and is surrounded by every type of bird.*

Metropolitan Museum of Art. Museum photo.

THE FENG HUANG. 3 × 2 m. China, K'ang-shi period, 1662-1722. Woven in silk and gold, heightened with painting.

This k'o-ssu *was part of a pair. The yellow background of both indicates that they were woven for the empress to decorate the palace. Five* feng huang *are depicted flying in a cloudy sky in which a few birds are playing with one another. A magnolia tree, bamboo and peonies in soft tones are also represented.*

Metropolitan Museum of Art. Museum photo.

person of the empress. Here we see it flying above blue rocks in the midst of trees in blossom surrounded by all kinds of birds, including peacocks, cranes, golden pheasants and mandarin ducks equally heavy in symbolism.

It is interesting to compare this work with another *k'o-ssu* in the same museum which dates from the reign of K'ang shi (1662-1722). During this period taste became more delicate and the color of Chinese porcelain known as *famille verte* and *famille jaune* became lighter. This *k'o-ssu* represents five *feng huang* of refined tones against a light yellow background in the midst of branches of magnolia trees in blossom. We know that yellow was the color reserved for the empress and are therefore certain that these *k'o-ssu* were woven for her imperial palace. Chinese art motifs and colors of this period were directly related to philosophical and religious beliefs.

The art of tapestry was doubtless imported from China into Japan at the close of the fifteenth century or beginning of the sixteenth. The technique of Japanese tapestry known as *tsuzure nishiki* (polychrome tapestry) is similar to low-warp tapestry, but instead of using a comb for the weft, the Japanese used their serrated fingernails. This polychrome tapestry differed only slightly from *k'o-ssu* by an aspect of the sides which were more in relief, thanks to the use of a heavy cotton warp covered with silk, gold or silver threads. The development of *tsuzure* reached its height in the early seventeenth century and during the entire eighteenth. During this period rich brocades also were produced. These polychrome tapestries were used for bonzes' robes as well as for panels in which to wrap gifts and only rarely for decorative purposes.

THE FEAST OF THE DRAGON. Detail. The whole tapestry measures 0.55 × 1.20 m. China, Ming period. Woven in silk.

This k'o-ssu *is part of a series of four panels meant to decorate a reception room. The subject represents the Dragon Procession, one of the chief Chinese festivals, held annually on the fifth month in memory of the minister Ch'u Yuan, statesman and celebrated poet, who committed suicide by throwing himself into the Mi-Lo River in 295 B.C. The ceremony simulates the search in the river for the minister's body, using boats in the form of dragons, and ends in a propitiatory rite destined to reconcile the soul of death by throwing rice into the river.*

Victoria and Albert Museum. Museum photo. Crown copyright.

(Overleaf)

TSUZURE: HORSES. 0.70 × 0.65 m. Japan, late 18th century. Woven in silk and gold.

A group of horses is represented on a light blue background.

Lyons. Musée historique des tissus. Photo Studios Associés.

IX Tapestry in the nineteenth and twentieth centuries — decline and revival

Decline of the art of tapestry in France. - First attempts at revival. - Jean Lurçat and his work. - The renaissance of French tapestry. - Contemporary tendencies. - Modern tapestry outside of France.

HE nineteenth century was a period of decline for the art of tapestry. This was due chiefly to the lack of interest shown by artists in the proper technique of weaving. Tapestry was used to reproduce paintings by famous masters and at the close of the century the Goncourt brothers wrote, "Tapestries are better than painting: they seem to be the dream." This sentence well sums up the state of mind of those who were contemporaries of the Goncourts. But in the years prior to 1900 artists turned to fresh sources of inspiration. Gauguin and the Nabis turned to an art which then appeared rather rudimentary but which drew attention to craftsmanship and to crude popular looms. Artists began to take interest in ceramics, stained glass and the metal arts, and tapestry aroused fresh curiosity.

The earliest attempts were made in England and the first name is that of William Morris and his Merton Abbey enterprise, followed by that of the Scherrebek workshop in northern Germany. The great renaissance of contemporary tapestry is no result of chance; it is the outgrowth of a logical initiative not only on the part of artists but also on that of artisans and even manufacturers. Everyone recognizes the great role of the late Jean Lurçat in arousing fresh interest in tapestry both in his native France and abroad. In contemporary architecture tapestry has regained its traditional role.

Decline of the art of tapestry in France

During the turbulent period of the Revolution the Gobelins and Beauvais factories managed to survive. In 1789 a radical change took place at the Gobelins. Instead of the piecework system the weavers were to be paid per day or per year. This change perhaps led to a slower output, yet it had the merit of preserving the existence of the factory itself, since all the ruined middlemen were on the point of abandoning their workshops.

The Revolution sought to purge the works woven at the Gobelins and Beauvais factories and on November 30, 1793, several tapestries with feudal or counter-revolutionary emblems were burned at the foot of a tree of liberty in the courtyard of the Gobelins. Shortly afterward a jury of artists was formed to choose among the factory's models and destroy those whose subjects they considered to be incompatible with revolutionary morals and customs. We still have the *procès-verbaux* of these sessions which reveal how strongly the decorative role of tapestry escaped the judges entirely. During the final years of the monarchy Boucher's models were already in disfavor. Louis XVI had ordered a HISTORY OF FRANCE after Barthélemy Suvée, Durameau and Ménageot, as well as a set whose subjects, taken from THE LIFE OF HENRI IV, had been painted by Vincent. These models were replaced by contemporary paintings, whose subjects this time had been borrowed from Greek and Roman history. Meanwhile competition was open and the candidates turned for inspiration to the great heroic scenes and acts of the Revolution. The situation was then critical and tapestry weavers were not paid regularly, the majority having joined the Republican armies.

The Directory decided to benefit by the unproductive treasure consisting of ancient royal tapestries. Those heightened with gold and silver had been melted down for their precious metal. As a result sixteen of the finest sets, or one hundred and eighty pieces, were destroyed.

When the Empire was established in 1804, the factory was considered among the general attributions of the Emperor's household and its fate was definitely established. A director (Guillaumot) was named as well as a drawing teacher as inspector, a workshop director and another for the dyes, with a chief worker and two fellow workers, a man in charge of the high-warp workshop with its sixty weavers and six apprentices, and another in charge of the low-warp workshop with its twenty-eight weavers and two apprentices. Finally there were five *rentrayeurs* or fine-drawers.

Unfortunately, the choice of models was inspired by the preoccupations which had guided the jury created by the Revolution. The weavers were reduced to executing copies of paintings, military subjects replacing revolutionary ones. Napoleon turned to the idea favored by Louis XIV of an art of apotheosis and ordered a tapestry set devoted to his reign, including THE PASSAGE OF THE ST. BERNARD by David, NAPOLEON ISSUING ORDERS ON THE MORNING OF THE BATTLE OF AUSTERLITZ by Carle Vernet, THE PRELIMINARY PEACE OF LEOBEN by Lethière, NAPOLEON RECEIVES THE ARMY DEPUTIES AFTER HIS CORONATION after Serangeli and NAPOLEON RECEIVING THE KEYS TO VIENNA after Girodet.

The Restoration, however, interrupted the Emperor's project, and on the return of the Bourbons many of these large pieces were unfinished. The first works to be ordered by the King of France were the PORTRAITS OF LOUIS XVI AND MARIE-ANTOINETTE. These were followed by THE STORY OF FRANCE after Rouget, THE BATTLE OF TOLOSA after Horace Vernet and tapestries with religious subjects such as THE LIFE OF ST. BRUNO by Le Sueur and THE MARTYRDOM OF ST. STEPHEN after Abel

Napoleonic Subjects

Napoleon Receives the Army Deputies After His Coronation (December 8, 1804). 3.30 × 1.95 m. Gobelins, begun in November 1809, interrupted in May 1814, then resumed on April 6, 1815, and definitely suspended on June 30, 1815. Woven in silk.

This unfinished tapestry was executed after a painting ordered by the emperor in 1806 from Serangeli. The painting is today in the Musée historique, Versailles. The scene occurs in the Louvre, in the Salle des Antiques. On the finished fragment we see Napoleon followed by his brother Joseph and Murat. On the right, Louis Bonaparte faces the emperor; on the left is a Mameluke.

Paris. Mobilier national. Photo Visages de France.

Pujol. The July Monarchy saw the execution of THE LIFE OF CATHERINE DE' MEDICI after Rubens which is no doubt the most interesting set of tapestries made during the entire century.

This fashion for "painting tapestry" continued throughout the nineteenth century and the first years of the twentieth. Beginning in 1824 the famous chemist Chevreul was in charge of the dyeing laboratory at the Gobelins. He achieved seventy-two ranges of two hundred tones each or 14,400 woolen tones. Moreover, the weavers acquired the habit of twisting two threads of different colors in order to obtain a third nuance with no thought to age and the inevitable "disharmonies" to follow. Thus the weaver could produce in tapestry form any painting whatever; but the results are far from conclusive when we examine the tapestries of this period. The tones are gray, dull and without effect; the almost unlimited chromatic range of colors has robbed the tapestry of all character. Nevertheless, during the entire nineteenth century, there was no weakening in production at the Gobelins and Beauvais factories. Associated with Beauvais since 1861 under the direction of the painter Badin, the Gobelins executed, in addition to copies of portraits by Winterhalter, works which were entirely decorative in character. The tapestry of the FIVE SENSES after Dieterlé, Paul Baudry, Chabal Dussurgey and Lambert was woven for the recently restored grand salon of the Elysées Palace. These works rather resemble the PORTIÈRES by Audran. The Empress Eugénie was especially fond of the light style of the eighteenth century. It is regrettable that Delacroix was never given an opportunity of turning to the problems of the art of tapestry.

After the Commune, which left the factory half destroyed, the Gobelins resumed activity in June 1871. Already there was a marked concern to give tapestry its true decorative character. The Third Republic ordered many tapestries to be used as decoration in the nation's palaces and public edifices. The efforts were commendable but the achievements questionable (the mural tapestry for the circular hall of the Opera buffet after Mazerolles, the tapestry known as POEMS OR APOLLO after Galland for the Elysées Palace, eight VERDURES for the grand staircase of the Senate after the work of various artists,

SELENE after Jules Machard. 3.65 × 2.63 m.
Gobelins, 1877. Woven in silk.
Paris. Mobilier national. Visages de France.

tapestries for the so-called "Mazarin's Chamber" at the Bibliothèque nationale, others for the chief chamber of the Palace of Justice at Rennes), all representing a considerable expenditure of time. Also worth mentioning is THE MERMAID AND THE POET after Gustave Moreau, a work highly praised by critics but whose colors have now acquired the dull, gray tone of tapestries of the period. Jean-Paul Laurens designed a STORY OF JOAN OF ARC, but discussions with Puvis de Chavannes met with failure.

In the early years of this century the national factories were anything but idle. The Gobelins director, Gustave Geffroy (1905-1926), tried to infuse fresh life into the establishment by turning to variously trained painters. THE SALVATION OF PARIS by Willette, the first tapestry devoted to the cities of France, was soon followed by Raffaëlli's BRITTANY. But the most interesting works are THE FOUR SEASONS after Jules Chéret, woven between 1909 and 1914, with its matching tapestry furniture; THE FAIRYTALES by Jean Veber, woven between 1913 and 1923; and certain tapestries by Bracquemond (father and son) executed in a rather personal style

Poems, also known as Apollo
After Pierre-Victor Galland.
Entrefenêtre: Marble vase. 2.50 × 1.60 m. Gobelins, 1886-1888. Woven in silk.
Paris. Mobilier national. Visages de France.

BASKET OF FRUIT after Moncomble. 0.42 × 0.66 m. Beauvais, 1831. Woven in silk.
Paris. Mobilier national. Photo Visages de France.

and similar to the requirements of decorative art. These attempts or experiments continued until the outbreak of the Second World War, but the origins of a renewal of the art of tapestry are to be found neither in the compositions by Daragnès nor in those by Paul Vera.

Beauvais continued to specialize in the execution of furniture accessories. In fact, the factory's talent lay in the dyers' hands.

The situation was even more serious at Aubusson. Forced to sell their output, the manufacturers returned to the eternal eighteenth-century reproductions of tapestries produced by Boucher and Oudry, woven and adapted to clients' requirements.

ANGELI LAUDANTES. Figures designed by Edward Burne-Jones. Border and background by H. Dearle. 2.25 × 2 m. England, workshop of William Morris & Company, 1894.
Victoria and Albert Museum. Museum photo. Crown copyright.

First attempts at revival

During the nineteenth century the general style of non-French tapestry followed more or less the same tendencies in France, but neither Brussels, London, Rome nor Vienna had workshops comparable to those in France. Some attempts were made to give Belgium new workshops. The Comte des Cantons de Montblanc founded a low-warp workshop at Ingelmunster and in 1856 he took as partners the Braquenié brothers, who established at Malines another workshop supported by the Belgian government and the municipal administrators. The large room of the Brussels Town Hall was decorated with a set of panels representing, after paintings by the local artist Geets, THE HEADS OF THE ANCIENT GUILDS, almost every head being a portrait. Other tapestries reproducing scenes taken from THE HISTORY OF FLANDERS were woven for the palace of the Belgian Senate, but these also were merely copies of paintings.

More interesting were the attempts made in England by William Morris. In 1861 he founded, with the help of his Pre-Raphaelite associates Burne-Jones, Rossetti, Ford Madox Brown and Philip Webb, the firm of Morris, Marshall, Faulkner and Company. In 1877 it was installed at Red Lion Square, but was later enlarged and transferred to Merton Abbey, near Wimbledon. Morris's researches included not only tapestry but also the decorative arts (stained glass, furniture, metal, jewelry, embroidery, stamped leather). He much admired medieval tapestry and sought to revive the spirit in his own work by turning to a limited number of colors and doing away with perspective effects. Although clearly inspired by late fifteenth-century tapestry, sets such as

SWANS after Otto Eckmann. German, workshop of Scherrebek, 1896.
Hamburg. Museum für Kunst und Gewerbe. Museum photo.

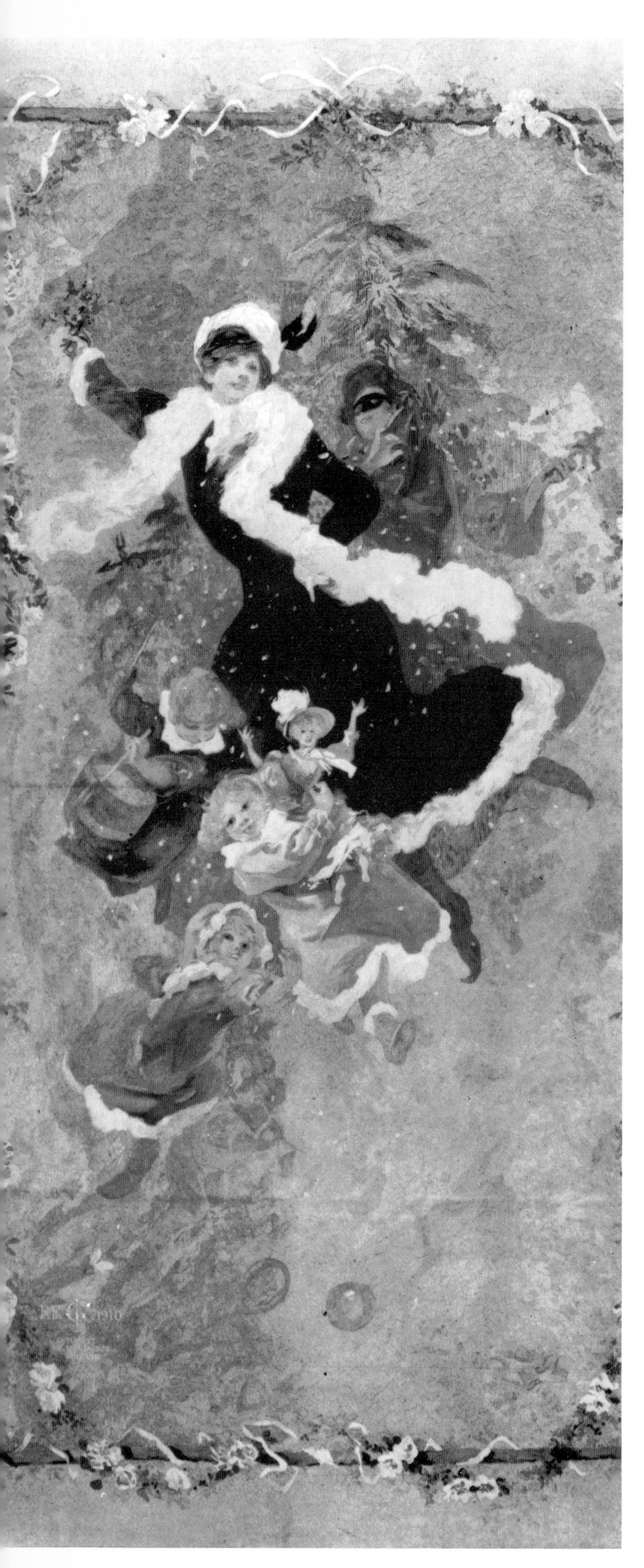

ANGELI LAUDANTES and THE FOREST are nevertheless original works.

Burne-Jones painted the models of the figures which were then reproduced by Henry Dearle, the chief designer. The general conception of the tapestry and the accompanying text in verse woven into the work itself were supplied by William Morris. When he died in 1896 Merton Abbey continued to exist and produced work until 1940. The most outstanding set is doubtless the SAINT GEORGE commissioned by Eton in 1922 to decorate the Lower Chapel. This set of four pieces after the designs by Mrs. Akers Douglas appears almost as a pastiche of early sixteenth-century Brussels tapestries commissioned from the famous Pannemaker family. More than fifty years before Lurçat, William Morris inaugurated a great movement in favor of the decorative arts, yet his tapestries are marked by both a medieval and a romantic spirit, far removed from the conceptions of modern art.

The art of tapestry was not unknown in the United States. In 1908 Albert Herter established a workshop in New York. He himself was a painter and his enterprise had much in common with that of William Morris in England. He often designed the cartoons which he executed himself and he turned for inspiration to Late Gothic tapestries woven in Flanders. In 1893 William Baumgarten established a fac-

The Four Seasons after Jules Chéret.
HOLLY OR WINTER. 2.78 × 1.58 m. Gobelins, 1910-1911. Woven in silk.
This tapestry was a part of a salon consisting not only of four tapestries but also of an ensemble of chairs. Much admired during the period, they were rewoven from 1911 to 1913 and offered by the French President to the Russian Tsar.
Paris. Mobilier national. Photo Visages de France. © SPADEM 1967.

tory at Williamsbridge, New York, with Foussadier, a native of Aubusson, as workshop head. The workshops were similar to those of the Gobelins and situated near the Bronx River, whose dyeing properties were similar to those of the Bièvre in Paris. At first inspired by eighteenth-century tapestry, production became more interesting when the painter Lorentz Kleister of Norwegian origin arrived in New York in 1900 and began to produce designs for the Baumgarten brothers. Finally in 1913 Kleister established his own firm known as Edgewater Looms in New Jersey which lasted until 1933.

In Germany the Berlin tapestry-artist Ziesch, who had been taught the art at the Gobelins, established a factory in 1879 in Berlin, but the tapestries produced were in the conventional taste of the period. It was not until the close of the century that a new spirit appeared. The *Jugendstil* was in fact at the origin of all the modern inspirations of German art as well as a renewal of mural tapestry. Under the impetus of a Swedish movement in favor of artisanal work, young weavers settled at Scherrebek (1896-1903) in North Schleswig, and the work they produced was well noticed at the International Exposition held in 1900. Made from designs by Otto Eckmann, Hans Christiansen, Alfred Mohrbutter, Otto Ubbelohde, August Endell, Henrich Vogeler and Walter Leistikow, these tapestries were woven according to the requirements of the material, which was wool. We must not overlook the experiments by the German Expressionists Franz

Guilds after W. Geets (1838-1919).
LES BRASSEURS. Belgium, workshops of Braquenie et Cie, Malines, 1878-1879.
Brussels. Musée communal. Museum photo.

Marc, August Macke and Ernst Ludwig Kirchner, who were interested in the decorative possibilities of tapestries. The works which they themselves wove were small in size and not destined for the public.

Throughout Europe there developed an increasing and renewed interest in tapestry which became integrated into the international movement known as Art Nouveau. Norway was represented by the work of Frida Hansen and, above all, that of Gerhard Munthe (1849-1929) which revealed the close affinities of Norwegian tapestry art and popular tapestry. Munthe returned to the use of vegetal coloring and his cartoons are composed of distinctly delimited monochrome surfaces with no concern to model the figures, the subjects being illustrations of Nordic folklore. The success of these compositions, however, was not enduring and the majority of these works are today in rather poor condition. At Budapest, Noemi de Ferenczy (1890-1958) wove her cartoons herself. For inspiration she turned to medieval art, for example, the stained-glass windows of Chartres cathedral. In Poland the first attempts to renew the art of tapestry were made early in the century by the Cracow Society of Polish Applied Arts. In Czechoslovakia it was Marie Teuntzerova, a pupil of William Morris and John Ruskin, who in her Judric Hradec workshop created the most personal works.

France appears to have been last in rediscovering an interest in the technical tradition of the art of weaving. About 1890, however, Maillol and his wife had their own workshop at Banyuls, where the sculptor was born. He sought to renew artisanal discipline with real love of purity, producing harmonious and peaceful works, though his interest

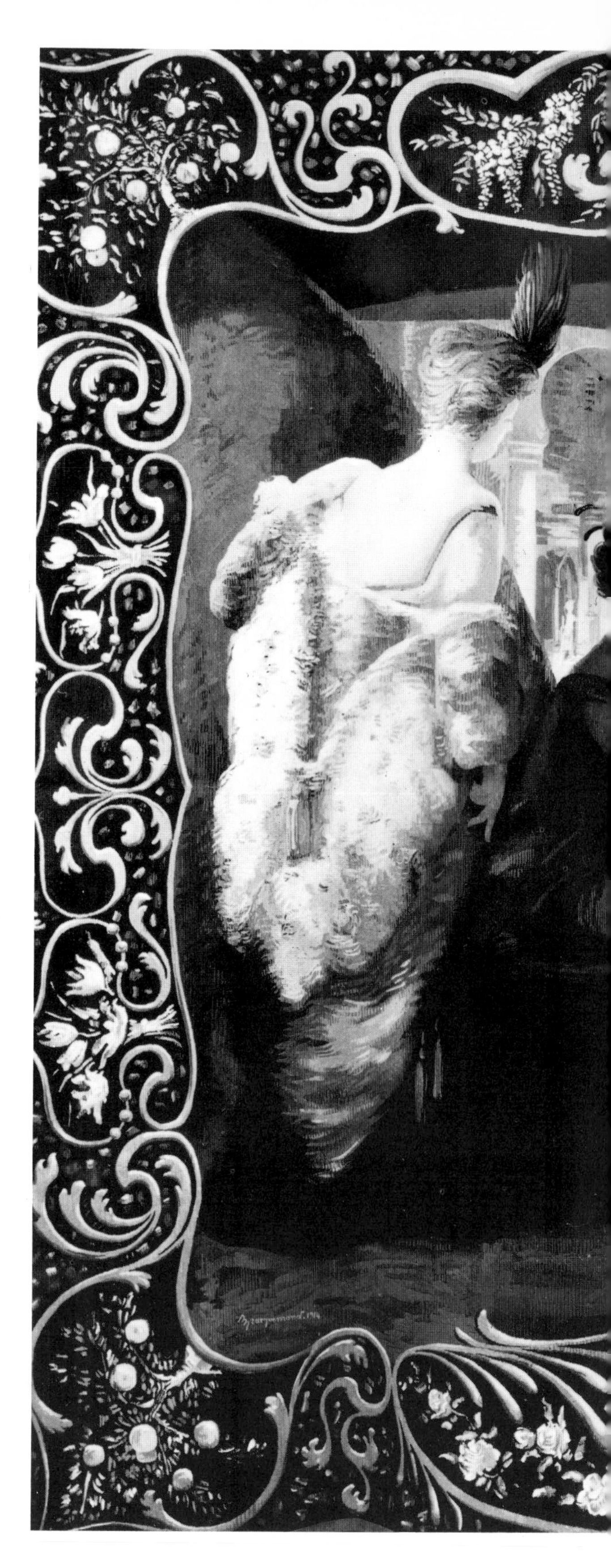

LA LOGE after Pierre Bracquemond.
2.84 × 2.77 m. Gobelins, 1923-1925. Woven in silk. The date of the cartoon is 1914.
Paris. Mobilier national. Photo Visages de France. Rights reserved ADAGP 1967.

soon turned to other activities. In 1895, Ranson, one of the founders of the Nabi movement, had his wife execute on canvas the tapestry entitled WOMEN IN WHITE (Musée d'Art moderne).

The year 1932 witnessed the experiment by Mme. Cuttoli, who requested the Aubusson weavers to execute a painting by Rouault, LES FLEURS DU MAL, followed by works by Picasso, Dufy, Braque, Matisse, Léger, Coutaud, Miro, Marcoussis, Derain and Lurçat. Although the style was new, the spirit was not, especially since some of these "tapestry paintings" were exhibited in a frame and under glass. The only painters to produce real cartoons were Coutaud and Lurçat. Yet by offering works woven from important paintings, Mme. Cuttoli's initiative had the merit of posing the problem and emphasizing the interest.

Jean Lurçat and his work

In 1932 Jean Lurçat took part in Mme. Cuttoli's experiment by supplying a cartoon. We can almost say that Lurçat devoted his entire life to the renewal of the art of tapestry, and if today this art enjoys great favor not only in France but also throughout the world, the credit lies with this artist. The very personality of this poet-painter was attractive in itself and we must unreservedly admire his obstinate and persevering efforts to give tapestry its former mural character. Lurçat had in fact made Dufy's statement his own: "No painter ought to imagine that he is going to create a useful tapestry work without devoting his entire life to it."

Since 1915 Lurçat had turned to the real problems of weaving technique and rediscovered its specific æsthetics. By fingering the woolen threads the

The Rooster and Its Shadow after Jean Lurçat. 2 × 1.50 m. Aubusson. Paris. La Demeure. Photo Pic. Rights reserved ADAGP, 1967.

young man enjoyed direct contact with this material which pleased him for its warm and resilient qualities. His earliest works, small and made on canvas, included GREEN GIRLS and EVENING IN GRENADA (1917). They soon increased in size. SUMMER, measuring 20 square meters, and SNOW, which measures 18, were both made in the Hennebert workshop at Toulon. During this period Lurçat did a number of paintings in oil and in gouache which he exhibited in France and in the United States. In these small paintings with their predominating ochre color, he represented a dry ground with its sun-scorched horizon, all in utter contrast to the green tapestries he was destined to produce ten years later.

From 1930 to 1937 he devoted all his intelligence and tenacity to the art of tapestry. Thanks to Mme. Cuttoli, his STORM was woven at Aubusson (1933). The first Gobelins order dates from the year 1936. This was THE ILLUSIONS OF ICARUS (3×5.34 m.) followed in 1937 by FORESTS (2.60×4 m.). Lurçat's first stay at Aubusson dates from 1937 when he met François Tabard, a tapestry master, and became interested in the latter's researches carried out with the aid of the Creuse painter Jorrand. Two groups, painters and artisans, entered into contact and it is thanks to this collaboration of artist and weaver that the tapestry renaissance finally began to take form. A trip to Angers in 1938 revealed to Lurçat the great APOCALYPSE tapestry known as "The Sistine Chapel of Wool." The event proved an emotional shock and revealed to him the immense possibilities of mural tapestry. When war broke out in 1939, the state factories, Gobelins and Beauvais, withdrew to

DAWN after Marc Saint-Saëns (the cartoon dates from 1948). 2.40 × 1.12 m. Aubusson. Paris. Photo La Demeure. © SPADEM 1967.

The Four Elements after Marcel Gromaire.
WATER (the cartoon dates from 1944). 3.53 × 4.91 m. Gobelins, 1944-1948.
Paris. Mobilier national. Photo Visages de France. © SPADEM 1967.

Aubusson, whose administrator, Guillaume Jeanneau, summoned Lurçat, Gromaire and Pierre Dureuil and asked them to make important designs to be woven on the Aubusson looms. Like Gromaire, Lurçat settled at Aubusson and has given us an account of the difficult war period which he spent in the tapestry workshops, where he acquired a perfect understanding of the art.

In 1946 the great exhibition entitled "French Tapestry from the Middle Ages to the Present Day" was held in Paris. It offered the public, at first surprised, then enthusiastic, an opportunity to see Lurçat's work and that of the cartoon painters who, at his request, had been responsible for the renewal of contemporary tapestry. For twenty years Lurçat continued to speak, write and work to spread the basic ideas of this art. He himself said: "When attacking the wall, the essential thing is never to have any confusion between easel-picture painting and architectural tapestry; their techniques are contradictory and their æsthetics above all dissimilar."

Lurçat's reform consisted essentially of a return to the medieval tradition: mural composition, banishing diminishing perspective and the modeling suitable to the technique of painting, recourse to a limited number of strong colors, the "complete tones" resulting in an economy of means, distinct design free of vagueness, and finally completely doing away with the horizon line by situating the viewpoint very high. The border is also abandoned: the sole natural frame of the tapestry is its own architectural integrity.

Lurçat produced an impressive number of tapestries. They are chiefly characterized by their large dimensions. THE APOCALYPSE OF ASSY, woven in 1947 for the choir of Notre-Dame-de-Toute-Grâce, measures 4.15 × 12.10 m., and WINE measures 4.10 × 10.50 m. (Musée du Vin, Beaune). In 1957 he began the first pieces of an enormous mural tapestry which would have measured 500 square meters. First entitled THE JOY OF LIVING, it is now known as THE SONG OF THE WORLD.

Lurçat had his own personal style, a blend of imagination and poetry. The world he represented is a dream in colors, a world of plants, animals and suns in which men and beasts develop in the midst of a colored paradise. For Lurçat beauty was never gratuitous, and a work of art was always much more than a work of art. In his *Lurçat* (1957), Claude Roy wrote: "The paradox of his development is that art (in appearance the most decorative and airy) has brought him back to men and earth, making his tapestries into large plastic correspondences of the society in which he lives and truths which he has slowly conquered." In the center of sumptuous flora, enlivened by a superb bestiary, sits enthroned the king of the creation, namely man, himself rooted to the sources of nature, surrounded by extraordinary animals invented by Lurçat and constantly renewed, including the snow lamprey, the Anzeinez marmot, the oak medusa, the moon carp, the striped bull-calf, the Castille dragon fly, and above all the sun cock. This cock, so often reproduced in his work, was created after a morning encounter with a rooster in front of the artist's studio: it became the *astropatte*, the *coq pêcheur*, the *coq dentelle*, the *coq et les planches*, *blue crimson*, *coquarlequin*, *solergot*, *dingo*, future peacock and warrior.

One of the reasons for the proliferation and complexity of Lurçat's finest tapestries is their poetical origin. "I laid out my circle and suddenly had the impression that I was controlling the world, and that is why I almost always introduce into it water and fire." He linked the various reigns of nature and

man as but an element of this complex world with its interpenetrating vegetables, minerals and animals. The world is not formed of separate elements; each being is stone, foliage, fish.

But all these plastic discoveries have meaning and are imposed by the subject. It is in the enormous tapestry of THE SONG OF THE WORLD that Lurçat best expressed himself with THE GREAT THREAT, THE MAN OF HIROSHIMA, THE GREAT CHARNEL HOUSE, THE END OF EVERYTHING, MAN IN GLORY OF PEACE, WATER AND FIRE, CHAMPAGNE, THE CONQUEST OF SPACE, POETRY and ORNAMENTOS SAGRADOS.

The renaissance of French tapestry

Technique is an indispensable tool, but it is merely a point of departure. Curiously, the acceptance of the painters' authority, which had such a bad effect on eighteenth-century tapestry, largely contributed to tapestry's renaissance. The beginnings of this renewal stem from the Aubusson workshops, which understood the necessity of turning to contemporary painters for a tapestry rebirth. Aided by Tabard, Lurçat continued his new researches at Aubusson in collaboration with other artists such as Gromaire and Dubreuil and

SIGNS OF THE SKY after Jean Picart le Doux (the cartoon dates from 1961). 3.06 × 5.26 m. Gobelins, 1962.
Inscription taken from Exil *by Saint-John Perse: "... et puis vinrent les neiges, les premières neiges de l'absence sur les grands lés tissés du songe et du réel."*
Paris. Mobilier national. Photo Visages de France. Rights reserved ADAGP 1967.

◀ JUNE after Dom Robert (the cartoon dates from 1966). 1.98 × 2.52 m. Aubusson, workshop of Tabard.
Paris. La Demeure. Photo P.-L. Buer.

finally, especially after the Liberation, a number of young painters were fascinated by his work and turned enthusiastically to him for guidance. Led by Denise Majorel the "Association des peintres-cartonniers" was founded in 1947 with Lurçat as president and as vice-presidents Marc Saint-Saëns and Jean Picart Le Doux.

At the head of the "Compagnie des Arts français," Jacques Adnet directed a small group of artists. After a short period, dominated by Lurçat's influence, the cartoon painters soon revealed their own personalities; the strong character of each artist dates from this period. Under the "School of Lurçat," we can group a certain number of artists, whose works, at least at the beginning, are related to those of the master. In such tapestries as THE MINOTAUR and ORPHEUS, Marc Saint-Saëns reveals a rather harsh realism, whereas other tapestries such as DANCE and THE TUMBLERS have a more personal lyricism. Jean Picart Le Doux has a sense of stylized graphism and in a sensitive, discreet manner turns to well-balanced compositions such as STILL LIFE WITH THE FOUNTAIN and GENESIS. The theme of his tapestries is nature or some symbol which remains ever of contemporary interest.

The Benedictine monk Dom Robert is still one of Lurçat's rivals, and in his En Calcat monastery, in the Tarn, he works at illustrated manuscripts and illustrations of the Holy Scriptures. In 1941 Lurçat visited him in his monastery and orientated him towards the art of tapestry. Gifted with much poetical fantasy, his spirit is that of a "mystery teller." Inspired by Persian illuminated manuscripts and by St. Francis's *Fioretti*, he represents beasts and flowers with pleasant naïveté. This love of nature and animals is found again in other cartoon painters, whose strong and healthy country taste appears to have the imprint of the soil. Savin, for example, gave the Gobelins a series of MONTHS whose iconography is related to field work and country festivities. A similar feeling of rural poetry is expressed in Perrot's tapestries. The artist is quite familiar with the desolate fauna of his country and designs large tapestries overloaded with birds and animals. HOMAGE TO AUDUBON and SOLOGNE are closed fields for flitting insects and birds.

Other artists benefited by Lurçat's technical reform, but in a very personal manner they respect the whole classic conception of tapestry. THE TAPESTRY OF THE THEATER (OPERA AND BALLET) composed by Brianchon represents figures in the noble taste of the seventeenth century, whereas a sad humor often marked by Surrealism is evident in works by Slavik, Coutaud, Guignebert and Lagrange (after an interruption of several years, this painter returned to cartoons). How many other names must be listed, each with his own character, who turned to the problems of tapestry: Hilaire, Dominguez, Cavaillés, Bezombes, Dayez, Despierre, Fumeron, Hieronimus, Poirier.

Important artists turned to the art of tapestry as a parttime occupation, one might say, rather than as their usual means of expression, and the works woven completely reflect their way of painting or engraving. At Lurçat's request Gromaire turned to tapestry and together with him as early as 1939 shared in the renaissance of this art at Aubusson. EARTH ,which was followed by WATER in 1944, was woven before the war at the Gobelins, but each piece reveals that he has understood how much tapestry owes to strong values and he therefore worked by contrasts. In 1939 the cartoon designs of THE FOUR SEASONS were executed at Aubusson and were finished only after the Liberation.

Like Dufy, Matisse was interested in tapestry. With surprising boldness, the painter composed the two cartoon designs of his POLYNESIA in cut-up paper of three colors: two blue and one white. The final works entitled THE SKY and THE EARTH evoke memories of a voyage to the South Sea Islands.

After the war, the great architect Le Corbusier designed numerous cartoons in a very personal style; he recognized in tapestry what he called "Muralnomad" or "The Nomad's Mural," the faithful work of modern man. The tapestries executed for the Chandigarh Court of Justice in India (1954) played an acoustical role in the

Polynesia, two tapestries after Henri Matisse (the cartoons date from 1946).
THE SEA. 2 × 3.10 m. Beauvais, 1962.
Paris. Mobilier national. Photo Bulloz. © SPADEM 1967.

THREE WOMEN AGAINST A WHITE BACKGROUND after Le Corbusier (the cartoon dates from 1950). 2.20 × 3 m. Aubusson, workshop of Picaud. Paris. La Demeure. Photo J.-P. Sudre.

room. In October 1956 the Tokyo Theater gave him a space measuring 230 square meters to cover with tapestry. Braque, Léger, Chastel, Cocteau, Lanskoy and Lapicque designed cartoons which reveal an astonishing diversity of talent and much variety in their conception of the art of tapestry.

Contemporary tendencies

The style of French tapestry has been considerably modified since the general movement led by Lurçat. Development occurred rapidly and the works created in 1950 have fallen by the wayside, so to speak, and are almost out of fashion. By 1967 the general tendency of French tapestry had become abstract decoration. As early as 1957 Jean Cassou wrote: "Every abstract artist is making or is going to make tapestries, that is, objects of decorative use. For the majority of the public, this is the sole justification of abstract art, its way out and final place. For the abstract artists themselves, deep within themselves and in the exercise of their vocation, it is possible that they will formulate something else after their own fashion and in function of the principles of their school and of its basic intentions."

In spite of this, the works these men have produced are excellent, for the unreal (abstract) motifs become part of the woolen substance and tones. For certain artists such as Picasso, Manessier, Soulages, Giloili, Zadkine, Piaubert and Beaudin, tapestry is little more than the transposition of their paintings with the imprint of their own strong character. Others are painters but also tapestry artists at heart with an intimate understanding of wool and of all its possibilities. There is no denying the success of their work, for the play of colors acquires a greater value, thanks to the material suitable to wool which offers an additional element of beauty to the work executed in tapestry.

Henri-Georges Adam, who died in the summer of 1967, was not only a designer, engraver and sculptor but also a cartoon painter. In a systematic manner he used black and white and no

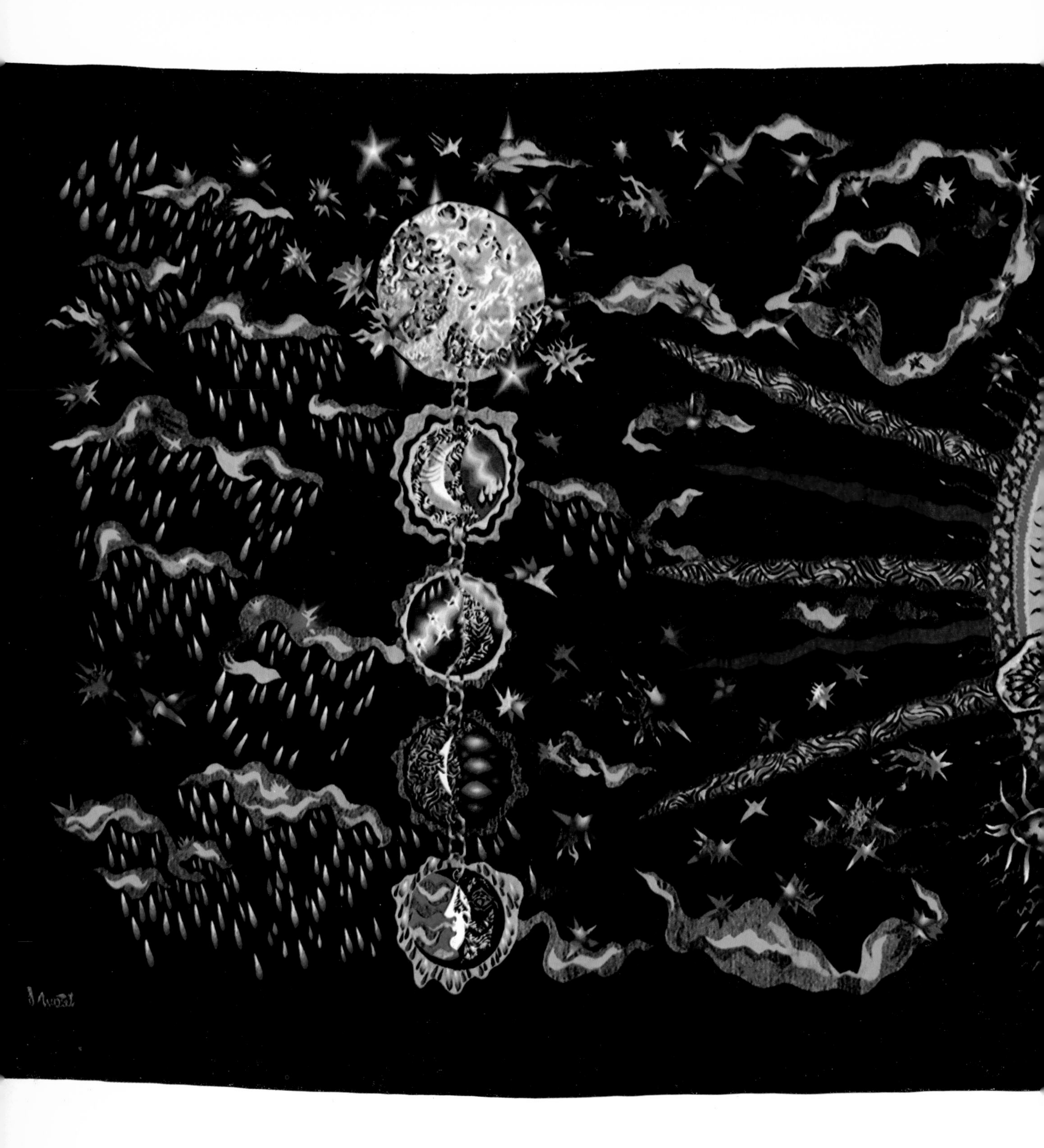

The Song of the World
ORNAMENTOS SAGRADOS (HOLY ORNAMENTS)
Tapestry by Jean Lurçat.
4.40 × 10.50 m. Photo Bloncourt.

other colored wool. By resorting to the play of oppositions and the refined mingling of these two values, producing an almost limitless variety of half white and half black, he created important mural compositions of great unity. As early as 1947 his tapestry cartoons introduced a new technique, known as *fil à fil*, which stemmed directly from his engraving craftsmanship. His tapestries are often larger and inspired by his engravings. SLABS, SAND AND WATER is taken from a series of engravings which reveal the play of the sea on the beach and the rocks. His last tapestry, now being woven at the Gobelins, will form a great triptych entitled MONT-SAINT-MICHEL.

Maurice André brought to tapestry a style reduced to essentials. He wilfully limits his palette and treats his compositions in large planes by suggesting movement through a play of obliques. His PIETA (1952) is a fresh attempt to treat a religious theme. His early compositions offer harmonious tones of ochre, yellow and black; he now uses vermilion, pink and purple tones, whose values acquire great importance, placed in a kind of architectural setting of black and gray, as is evident in such tapestries as MODERN TECHNIQUES IN THE SERVICE OF MAN, THE CONQUERORS and THE MEN OF THE SKY.

From Louis-Marie Jullien's earliest tapestries to his most recent ones there is a great change, for the artist has a fine faculty of renewal. His TWELVE SONGS OR THE HYMN TO JOY, a tapestry presented in 1963, is the end result of

Mont-Saint-Michel after Henri-Georges Adam (the cartoon dates from 1965).
MONT-SAINT-MICHEL (No. 2). 4.02 × 5.65 m. Gobelins, 1965.
Paris. Mobilier national. Photo Hachette.

THE CITY OF ROUEN after Mathieu Matégot (the cartoon dates from 1964). 6.80 × 12.50 m. Felletin, workshop of Pinton.
Rouen. Nouvelle Préfecture de la Seine-Maritime. Photo Hachette.

technical researches made over a period of years. The weaving, which increases the thickness of the points in contrast with the fine ones, creates reliefs that exalt and animate the surfaces. He also uses threads of different juxtaposed tones to bring out the vibrating effect of the dyed tints which the same mixture of coloring material fails to do, "and thus those tints are not flat or choked but, on the contrary, are lively, vibrating, luminous and animated with a transparent sensation."

Mathieu Matégot began as a stage designer, but in 1939 he became interested in tapestry. For his large compositions with full modulations, Matégot merely uses a limited number of colors, but his art requires graded tones with transparent effect. As a result, he has linked his art to technical requirements and constantly works in close contact with the weaver. His cartoons are neither paintings nor numbered effects but gouache compositions carefully prepared with almost mathematical exactitude, foreseeing and utilizing every weaving resource. In addition to *aplats*, *sertis*, graded tones, *battages* and hatching methods, he utilizes the *piqué* used in the Middle Ages, mingling colored threads of different heights and colors. He thus obtains subtle gradations and certain personal iridescent effects. One of Matégot's latest tapestries, measuring 85 square meters, commissioned by the Seine-Maritime *préfecture*, is entitled THE CITY OF ROUEN. This almost scientifically balanced composition is nevertheless a poetical evocation of the great city in Normandy.

Mario Prassinos's first contact with tapestry dates from 1951. His art in this field is revealed in his pictorial researches; the many paintings on paper which he made on the Alpilles and cypress motifs describe nature by means of a highly personal style of expression. In painting his researches have led him to recreate this picture by means of "signs" at the expense of the suggestion of volume. In the field of tapestry this form of writing, so to speak, increases and becomes monumental, yet tends to the same goal to express the artist's outer world. "It seems to me," Prassinos wrote, "that one can paint the hills of Provence only after having studied every meaning. The signs that I have taken from them are for me more real than the apparent arabesque of the landscape. They are the alphabet of an experienced story." This research of the "distant innerness" led the artist to large, dramatic compositions in which the violent dark tones are in opposition to the raw white ones and to the warm yellow and orange-red tones and to the grays obtained by mixing black and white. KING LEAR, woven in 1963, is a fine example of this striking effect of forms.

Singier (his work, we might say, is as calm "as a Sung painting") is not a stranger to technical researches. He has created carefully thought out and well composed cartoons in which color triumphs.

Michel Tourlière also takes advantage of every possibility offered by the loom. Teacher, then director of the École nationale d'Aubusson since 1960, he is acquainted with every weaving process and is acutely aware of the effect that can be derived from the weaver's work. After several trials he achieved the perfection of a *piqué rythmé* with irregular bands and obtained streaking effects which were admirably suited to what he was trying to recreate, namely, wheat fields and vineyards of his native Beaune region. His very

SARABANDE after Atlan (the cartoon dates from 1962 from a painting made in 1959). 2.55 × 4.93 m. Beauvais, 1965.
Paris. Mobilier national. Photo Visages de France.

PANEL NO. 2 after Viera da Silva. 2.83 × 1.82 m. ▶
Beauvais, 1966.
Paris. Mobilier national. Photo Visages de France.

rhythmical compositions illustrate the aspects of this characteristic landscape lined with vineyards. His recent tapestries include VINEYARD COVERS, CÔTES DE BEAUNE, CÔTES D'OCTOBRE, CÔTE D'OR, VILLAGES DE VIGNES and CARTOON. His colors range from warm red to violet blue, pink and gray.

Robert Wogensky's paintings are violent and striking. Introduced to the art of tapestry by Lurçat, he has developed his figurative compositions to abstract ones, and with an astonishing luxuriance of colors has created sensitive works in which water is mingled with light, bubbles appearing as though bursting from underwater volcanoes. In this rapid glance at contemporary tapestry, we must also mention the works of young artists such as Reynold Arnoult, Borderie, Marc Petit, Longobardi, Millecamps, Schumacher, Odette Blanc, Monique Arradon, Claire Radot, Henri Brivet and Jacques Potin.

Outstanding among these are the compositions of Vasarely, whose very special art translates an idea of movement with black and white harmonies. The artist's visual researches lean toward the discovery of a mechanical and almost industrial plastic character. The pure tones, in preference to a mixture of threads, are not allied to the modeling but to the strong design. A certain number of tapestries created by Arp, Calder, Herbin, Mortensen and Kandinsky are characterized by clear outlines and pure tones.

Contemporary French tapestry is enjoying an undeniable period of prosperity. Thanks to the plain architecture of modern buildings, it has found a choice setting in which to be displayed.

Whether in national factories of France or in the private ones of Aubusson and Felletin (Tabard, Goubely, Legoueix, Picaud, Braquenié, Pinton, Lauer, and Hamont, to mention only a few names), large mural tapestries have been created to decorate important buildings. Whereas the Aubusson production is more commercial in character, the national factories assume the role of a "conservatory." They are less interested in the cost of a particular tapestry as in training and maintaining first-class weavers. In a way they are cultivating an experimental field. The year 1967 witnessed the weaving of tapestries of various styles after works by such artists as Chagall, Atlan, Viera da Silva, Derain, Miro, Sonia Delaunay, Gleb, Picasso, Nicholas de Staël, Ubac and Riopelle.

KING LEAR after Mario Prassinos (the cartoon dates from 1962). 2.95 × 5.92 m. Gobelins, 1963. Paris. Mobilier national. Photo Hachette. Rights reserved ADAGP 1967.

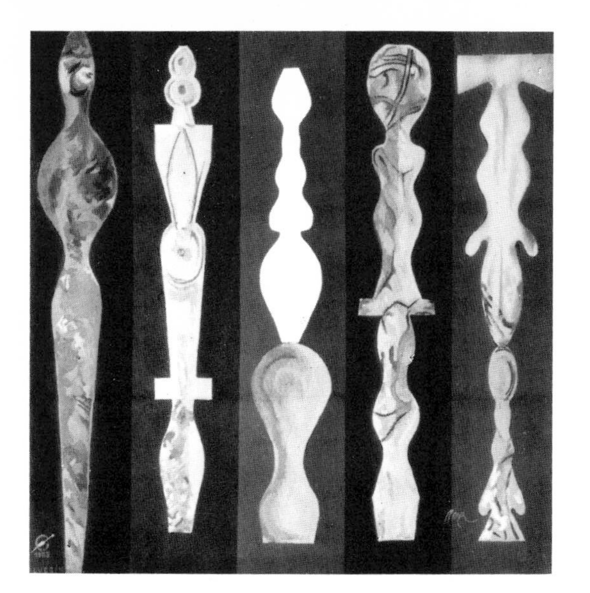

DOLLS after Jean Arp (the cartoon dates from 1963). 1.95 × 2 m. Gobelins, 1964.
Paris. Mobilier national. Photo Mobilier national. Rights reserved ADAGP 1967.

THE MEN OF THE SKY after Maurice André (the cartoon dates from 1962). 3.45 × 4.03 m. Beauvais, 1964.
Photo Visages de France. Rights reserved ADAGP 1967.

Modern tapestry outside of France

The success of the renaissance of French tapestry long supported the opinion that French tapestry and contemporary were synonymous. For the past twenty years, however, artists outside France have been inspired by her example. There is no doubt as to the dissimilarity of the works and this book can only offer a rapid glance at weaving activity throughout the world. The three international tapestry biennials, which were held at Lausanne in 1962, 1965 and 1967, measured the interest aroused by tapestry not only in Europe but in North and South America and in Japan as well. Twenty-three countries were represented in the 1965 biennial. Non-French participation in the renaissance of tapestry can be considered more than a token; painters of every nationality are turning to the possibilities offered to their art by mural tapestries and they produce cartoon designs which are woven in their own country or more often in France and Belgium where the tradition of fine weaving has been maintained for centuries. Inversely, foreign workshops were created in those countries where labor and consequently cost prices were less expensive than in France, for example at Portalegre, Portugal, and in Kashmir, India. Important artists such as Lurçat and Le Corbusier had some of their cartoon designs woven there. Finally, we often have the example of young painters fascinated by the technique of weaving who prefer to take their place before the loom and personally weave the tapestry they have dreamed of.

It is probably too soon to judge this efflorescence of new works, both representational and abstract. A leading place must be given to Belgium, which has had a long traditional association with the art of weaving. The efforts made at Malines, Brussels and Tournai have resulted in a new art. It was not until the year 1945 that a group of Tournai cartoon painters who called themselves "Forces murales," formed by Louis Deltour, Edmond Dubrunfaut and Roger Somville, sought to renew monumental Belgian tapestry by basing their art on technical principles which called for extreme simplicity, such as limited tones, heavier warp threads and numbered design. This creation of the "Centre de rénovation de la tapisserie" at Tournai, in 1947, coincided

with the important exhibition of French tapestry which was held at the Palais des Beaux-Arts of Brussels. From 1947 to 1951 the Tournai collective workshop wove more than 500 square meters of tapestry. Although it discontinued activity in 1951, it nevertheless remained the promoter of new Belgian tapestry. As a result of its impulse, painters of various tendencies turned to the art of weaving. Although Belgian painting turned toward the abstract, the renovators of Belgian tapestry chose the representational. Artists such as Dubrunfaut, Somville and Van Vlasselaer sought their inspiration in the realm of reality, and their works illustrate man in his world and in his basic occupations. Other outstanding artists who created tapestries are Mary Damblermont, Liliane Badin, Jean van Noten, and Michel Seuphor.

It is difficult to characterize the development of tapestry in Germany during recent years. Many artists such as Fritz Arend, Ida Kerkovous, Johanna Schützworlf, Woty Werber, Elsa Mögelin and Irma Goecke, head of the Nürnberger Gobelin-Manufaktur, wove their own cartoons. This same tend-

CARTOON after Michel Tourlière (the cartoon dates from 1964). 2.25 × 3.35 m. Aubusson, workshop of Goubely Gatien.
Dijon. Musée. Photo Hachette. Rights reserved ADAGP 1967.

KALOTA I after Vasarely. 2.36 × 2.22 m. Aubusson, workshop of Tabard.
Paris. Galerie Denise René. Photo Galerie Denise René.

The Twelve Songs or The Hymn to Joy ▶ after Louis-Marie Jullien (the cartoon dates from 1963).
THE SONG OF LOVE. 1.98 × 1.48 m. Aubusson, workshop of Legoueix.
Paris. La Demeure. Photo P.-L. Buer. Rights reserved ADAGP 1967.

ency is found in Austria, where such young artists as Edda Seidl-Reiter, Fritz Riedl and Marra Plachky work without cartoons and follow their own fancies. Switzerland has only a handful of small workshops. Certain artists such as Denise Voëta, Claude Loewer and Hans Stocker have their cartoons woven outside their country, whereas others like Elisabeth Giauque weave their own.

In Great Britain the Edinburgh Tapestry Studios, founded in 1910, continue their activity under the name of the Dovecote Studios. Hans Tisdall, Archie Brennan and Helen Maureen Hodge have their cartoons woven there, whereas Graham Sutherland turned to Felletin to execute his enormous tapestry (23.80 × 11.60 m.) which since 1962 has decorated the choir of Saint Michael's Cathedral of Coventry.

The countries of northern Europe also have their cartoon painters: Denmark with Jan Groth, Holland with Wilhelmina Fruyter and Herman Scholten, Sweden with Helena Barynina, Veronica Nygren, Max Walter Svanberg, Maria Triller, and finally Norway with Karen Holtsmark and Hannah Riggen.

Certain eastern countries draw greater attention: for example, Poland and Yugoslavia, which offer bold creations in which tapestry is designed in function with the material used. Since World War II a group of women who had studied at the Academy of Fine Arts—Magdalena Abakanowicz, Jolanta Owidzka, Maria Kraskiewicz, Barbara Falkowska, Sofia Butrimowicz, and Krystina Wystyna Drouet, have devoted themselves to these researches and created very personal works of outstanding interest. We must also add the tapestries by Wozciech Sadley. Artificial fibers like sisal, metal threads, jute, raffia and horsehair are often very crudely woven. The artists seek to avoid an equal and elaborate surface and the tapestry thus acquires a heavy relief. Traditional Polish weaving is the origin of this form of art far removed from the fine woven craftsmanship practiced in France and Belgium. These so called "new techniques" are fascinating for the novelty of their plastic effect.

Latin countries such as Italy, Spain and Portugal also share in such research. The Asti tapestry factory has produced interesting tapestries with their original

THE SUNKEN SKY after Robert Wogensky (the cartoon dates from 1964). 2 × 2.75 m. Aubusson, workshop of Legoueix.
Paris. La Demeure. Photo Hachette.

THE PASSAGE OF THE RED SEA. Detail. After Wozciech Sadley. 2.50 × 3.50 m. Cracow, workshop of Spoldzielnia "Wanda," 1965.
Photo Hachette. Marcel Imsand.

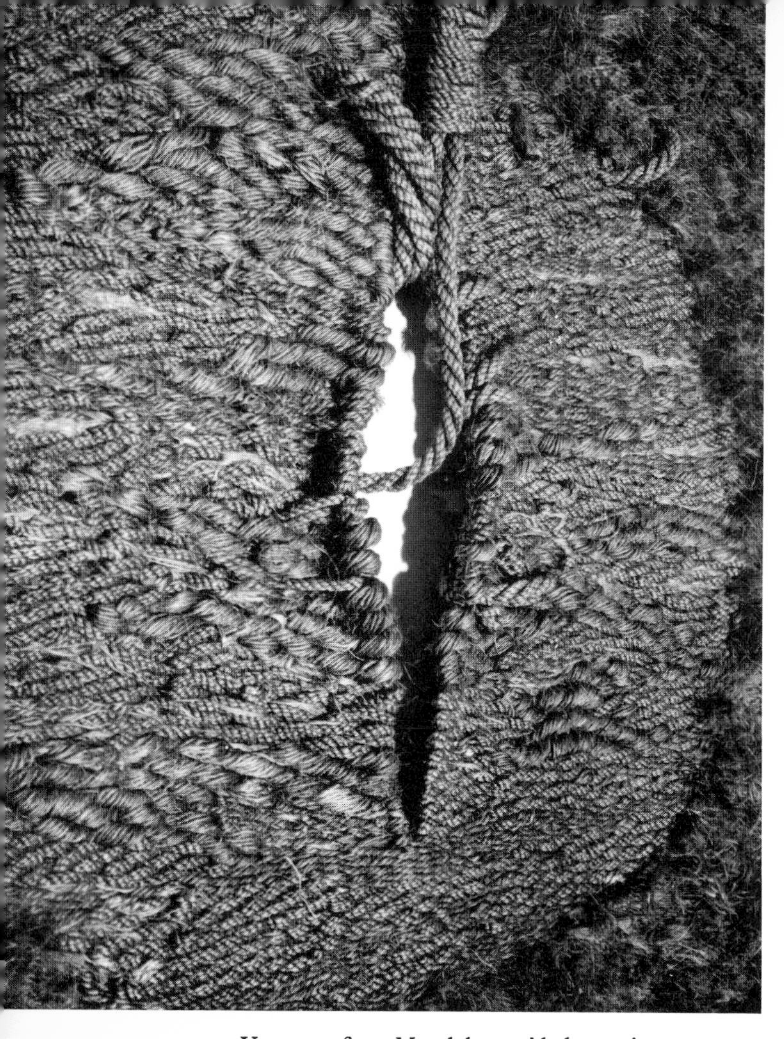

VIOLET after Magdalena Abakanowicz. 1.50 × 1 m.
Warsaw. Experimental workshop.
Photo Courtesy of the cartoon artist.

THE TWINS after Franco Muzzi. 2.61 × 1.97.
Italy, Scassa factory, Asti.
Paris. Mobilier national. Photo Hachette.

decorative effects. In Spain Josep Grau Garriga, pupil of Lurçat, developed the Catalan School of Tapestry, while Aurelia Munoz has made fresh research in a technique which combines weaving and embroidery. In Portugal the Portalegre workshop, created in 1951, worked not only on cartoons by national painters such as Guilherme Cararinha, Rogeiro Ribeiro, Amandio Silva and Eduardo Nery but also in collaboration with foreign French and Swedish artists for the most part. Finally, tapestry workshops have been created not only in Greece but also in Israel and Lebanon, where the technique of weaving has been practiced for centuries.

For inspiration American tapestry had turned to Europe. Marc Adams and Sylvia Carewe had their cartoon designs executed at Aubusson, whereas Jan Yoors, Allan Porter and Dana Romalo weave their own. Mention must also be made of Canadian cartoon designers, including Thérèse Lafrance, Paul Lacroix and Mariette Rousseau Vermette. Two attempts, quite different in spirit, were made in Brazil, that of Genaro de Carvalho at Bahia, who reproduces highly colorful tropical themes, and that of Jacques Douchez and Norberto Nicola at Sao Paulo, being closer to the new international artistic style.

In Japan the Kawashima Textile Mills have produced a number of mural tapestries in the traditional *tsuzure* technique. The creations by the painter Hiroso Murata woven with many gold threads are always of great sumptuousness.

Mutwilliges Trypticon. Detail. After Fritz Arend. 1961-1962. 2 × 5 m. Germany, woven by Fritz Arend.
Photo Hachette. Marcel Imsand.

BATHERS BENEATH THE TENT after R. Somville. 2.75 × 4.50 m. Brussels, G. Chaudoir factory, 1962.
Photo Courtesy of CITAM, Lausanne.

To end this survey of contemporary tapestry it would be interesting to mention the Harra Harraneya workshops in Egypt. During recent years the architect Wissa Wassef has made an experiment in the hope of reviving local handicrafts and of increasing the standard of living of local labor. Young Egyptians, who have settled at Harraneya, a few miles south of the Pyramids of Gizeh, are working on simple and easily managed high-warp looms; the wool used is dyed with natural colors. The great originality of this enterprise lies in the fact that these young village men, some of whom began at the age of ten and are now more than twenty, are working freely without the aid of a cartoon or a preparatory design, improvising directly on the loom and turning for inspiration within themselves and to surrounding nature. The works achieved are surprising for their fantasy, their decorative sense and their beautiful color. Thus the great tapestry tradition has been found again, as though by instinct, on the banks of the Nile.

ENTRER DANS LE BLEU after Odette Blanc.
3.94 × 1.92 m.
Lebanon, workshop of Aynab, 1965.
Photo courtesy of the cartoon artist.

HUNTER WITH A NET after Arys Mahmoud.
2.40 × 1.25 m.
Egypt, workshop of Wissa Wassef de Harraneva.
Photo Hachette.

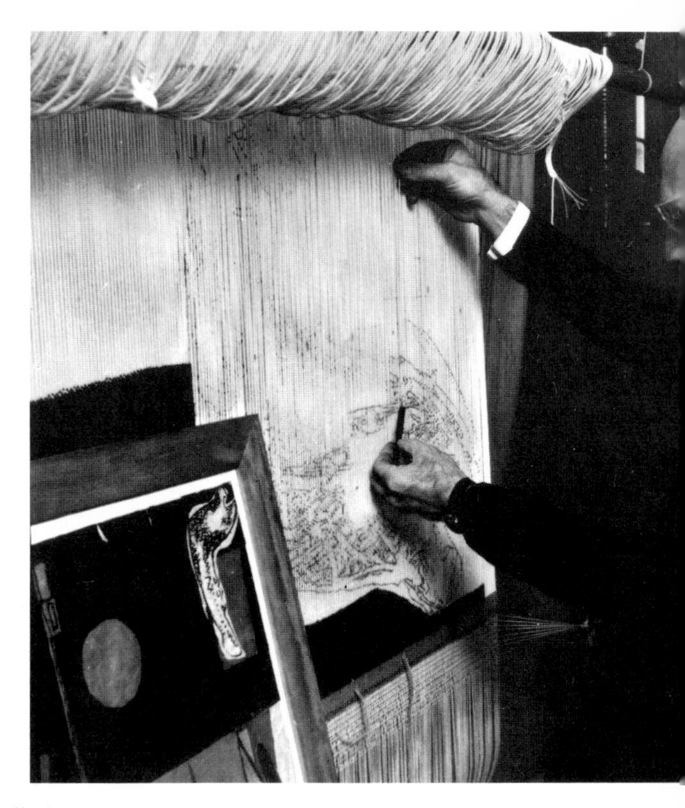

High-Warp Loom (Manufacture nationale des Gobelins).

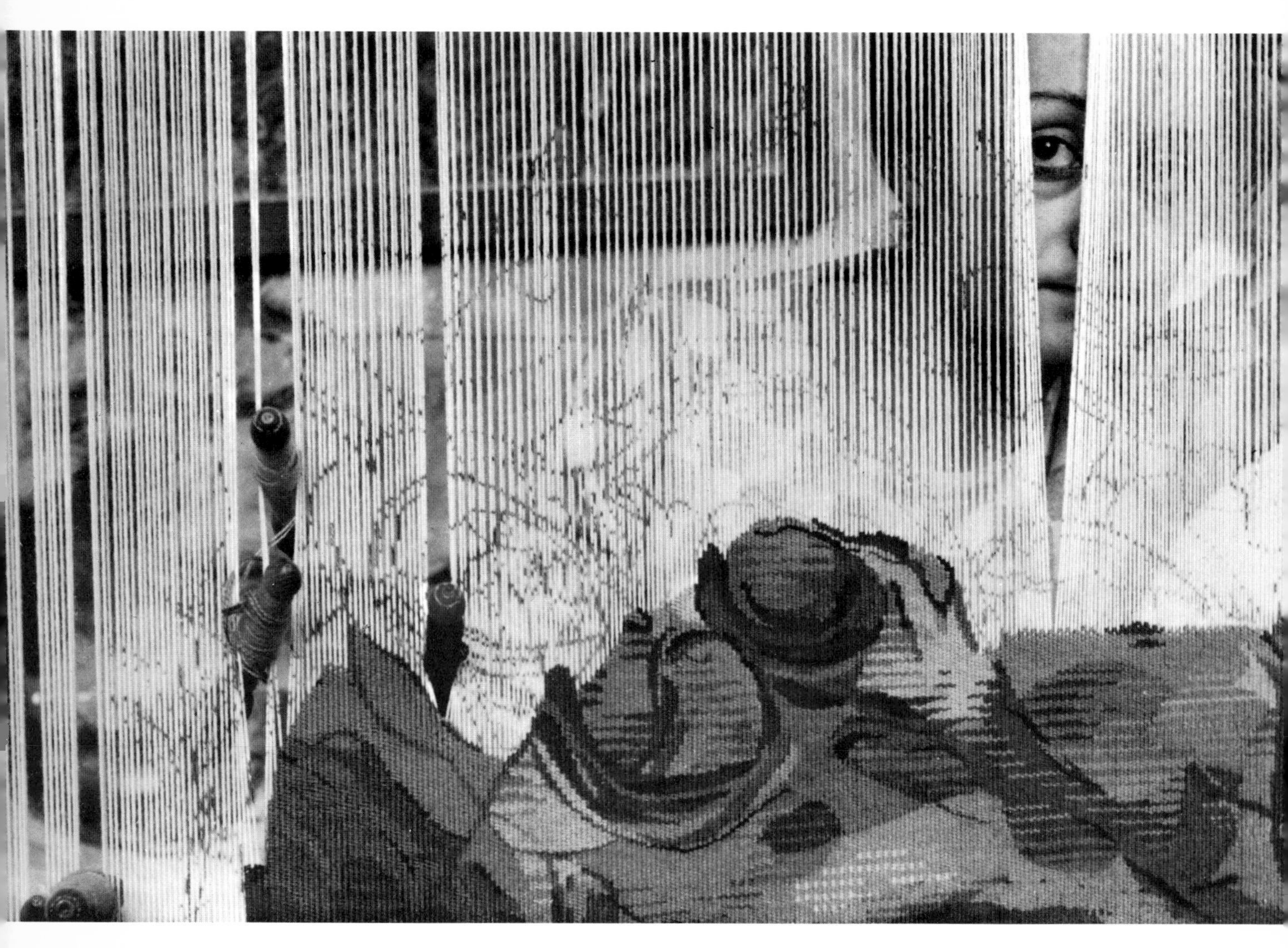

Technique

apestry is a type of woven fabric of polychrome decoration, whose weft threads do not necessarily extend from selvage to selvage but are limited to the actual decorative pattern, covering all the warp threads within the area of the design.

We will not concern ourselves here with those fabrics which are mechanically decorated with regular designs or with those which are decorated after they have been manufactured. This decoration can be achieved either by completely concealing the weft, as in stitch tapestry made on canvas (small-stitch upholstery tapestry incorrectly known as point des Gobelins*), or by covering only part of the surface as in needlework embroidery. The famous Bayeux tapestry known as* THE QUEEN MATILDA TAPESTRY *is really nothing more than an embroidered hanging.*

A tapestry is woven by hand on special looms of vertical warp (high-warp tapestry) or of horizontal warp (low-warp tapestry).

The high-warp loom (such as those used in the Gobelins factory) consists of two wooden rollers (ensouples) *arranged horizontally on the same vertical plane and supported by two uprights* (cotrets). *The warp threads are wound on and fixed to the rollers. The warp is divided into separate sheets or series, first by a string* (ficelle de croisure) *and secondly by a glass tube* (bâtons d'entre-deux). *Around each thread of the back series—from the viewpoint of the weaver seated at the loom—is passed a cotton loop, the heddle* (lice) *which is attached to the heddle rod* (perche à lices). *These heddles enable the weaver to pull the entire back series of threads to the front. The warp threads are above the weaver's head. He works seated on a movable chair and executes the tapestry in reverse. When the preparation of the warp* (ourdissage) *and of the loom is complete, the weaver uses tracing paper to transfer the outline of the design or cartoon on to the warp threads. The cartoon itself remains behind the weaver who uses small mirrors placed before him to verify the execution of his work. For the actual process of weaving, the weaver takes a bobbin* (broche) *in his right hand to form the colored weft. Then, slipping his left hand between the two series of threads, he passes the bobbin from left to right. Next, grasping the heddle rod in his left hand, he pulls the back series of threads to the front, and passes the bobbin back again between the two series from right to left. These two passages of the bobbin form what is called a* duite. *After each passage the* duites *are beaten down with the pointed end of the bobbin and then, in the case of large monochrome surfaces, with an ivory comb.*

In the low-warp technique (as practiced at the Beauvais factory) the tapestry is woven on horizontal looms. Here the jumelles *correspond to the uprights* (cotrets) *of the high-warp looms; the* ensouples *are known as rollers* (rouleaux). *The loom consists of two weaving slats: all the even threads are connected to the first and all the uneven threads to the second.*

Each slat is moved by a pedal. The weaver begins by transferring the outline of the design or cartoon, for the work reverses the composition. He places this tracing on the warp of his loom and uses it during the entire production of the work in order to follow the model. Since the tapestry is woven in reverse, the weaver uses a mirror which he has placed between the tracing and the warp to control his execution. He thus works seated, facing the light, bent over the loom. The threads are bobbined on shuttles which correspond to the spindles in the high-warp technique. The heddles are moved by pedals

formerly known as marches. *The weaver uses both hands to execute the weaving points; his left hand is constantly resting on the warp sheet and he uses his thumb to raise the number of threads corresponding to the traced drawing. With his right hand he passes the chosen shuttle into this space, then using a small needle or comb, he forces threads against the lower row of the weft. After each passage or after several rectilinear passages, the weaver uses the pedals to reverse the even and uneven series of the warp threads to execute the following passages by changing the shuttles. In former times the weaver viewed his work only piecemeal through the warp threads with the aid of his mirror. Later Jacques de Vaucanson invented the swinging loom which enabled the weaver to view his entire work during execution.*

Whether using the low-warp or high-warp technique several weavers can work simultaneously on the same loom. According to the complexity of the cartoon and the thickness of the woven texture, a Gobelins worker can weave from one to six square yards of tapestry per year.

The thickness of the warp threads will affect the thickness of the fabric or "tapestry grain" and consequently will also affect the style of the work being produced. In the Middle Ages the fabric was heavy (five threads to the centimeter in the Angers APOCALYPSE*), whereas sixteenth-century tapestry had an average of seven threads to the centimeter. The early seventeenth century was marked by diligent research and experimentation to achieve fineness of threads, and at the close of the eighteenth century certain Beauvais tapestries contained as many as ten threads to the centimeter. During the past twenty years, however, the number of threads has been reduced to four or five to the centimeter.*

The chief materials used in tapestry are, first, wool, some silk (which, unlike the situation that prevailed in the eighteenth and nineteenth centuries, was rare in the Middle Ages), and sometimes linen or metallic threads, especially gold and silver. Once the weaving is completed, the tapestry is removed from the loom and handed over to the fine-drawing workshop, where the finishing work is done, especially the sewing of the slits (relais) *where weft threads of different colors meet and are not joined by the weaver.*

Natural or synthetic dyes play a chief role in the production of wool, silk or linen tapestry which owes its essential beauty to the effect of color. Medieval weavers used from fifteen to twenty strong colors. Nine years after the Gobelins factory was purchased by Louis XIV, the number of colors was increased in 1671 to some one hundred and twenty as a result of the regulation issued by the king's Controller General of Finance, Jean-Baptiste Colbert. A century later thirty-six thousand colors were used (categorized into a thousand hues, each broken down into thirty-six different tones). Tapestry, in fact as well as in intent, became a true form of painting reproduction, for the artist insisted that the weaver adhere rigidly to the exact duplication of his color scheme and arrangement. By the middle of the nineteenth century, however—and perhaps this accounted for the decline of tapestry during the period—an attempt was made to counteract this tendency.

The genesis of every tapestry is a sketch made by the painter. Formerly known as the first drawing (petit patron), *it is now called a dummy* (maquette) *and the cartoon painter frequently reproduces it in full scale. As early as the sixteenth century the great tapestry workshops employed artists who specialized in figures, landscapes, flowers and borders. In the ensuing period, the cartoons were first executed in the distemper process, then on canvas as real oil paintings. Today the cartoon can be represented as a painting or a photograph, or it can be blocked out in numbered areas. In the latter technique, perfected by Jean Lurçat, each number inscribed on a section of a black and white drawing*

Low-Warp Loom (Manufacture de Beauvais).

Dyeing (Gobe

0
200
10
20
30
40
50
60
70
80
90
100
110

corresponds to a precise color. Although each cartoon painter has his own system, the cartoon remains the link between artist and weaver.

It is the weaver's responsibility to remain faithful to the painter's original concept, while employing techniques that do not always permit complete fidelity. Some transposition inevitably occurs since the effects achieved in weaving cannot fully parallel those of painting in every respect. To copy the drawing and indicate the modeling, the weaver can juxtapose the colors in a uniform manner or he can permit colors to "interpenetrate" or flow into one another in the direction of the weft by hatching that simulates gradation of tones.

The preceding paragraphs present only a brief general idea of how tapestries are created. The plan of this book as a historical and esthetic survey of tapestry does not permit a more detailed account of the technical processes involved. But we must not forget that tapestry is an art as well as a technique. In the creation of a tapestry, the weaver's role is as important as that of the painter's. Without complete understanding and agreement between them, no tapestry worthy of the name can be produced.

Photos Hachette

Bibliography

General works and works relating to tapestry collections

ACKERMANN (P.) : Tapestry, the Mirror of Civilisation, Oxford, 1933.
ARTS TEXTILES : 6 vol., Ghent, 1953-1966.
BALDASS (L. VON) : Die Wiener Gobelinsammlung, 3 vol., Vienna, 1920.
BARBIER DE MONTAULT (X.) : Inventaire descriptif des tapisseries de haute lisse conservées à Rome, Arras, 1879.
BARELLI (E. S.) : L'Arazzo in Europa, Novere, 1963.
BERGER (O.) : Die europäische Wandteppichwirkerei, Augsburg, 1930.
BIRYUKOVA (N. Y.) : The Leningrad Hermitage Gothic and Renaissance Tapestries, Prague, 1965. — Western European Tapestries in the Hermitage, in Burlington Magazine, vol. CVII, August 1965.
BLAZKOWA (J.) : Wandteppiche aus tschechoslowakischem Sammlungen, Prague, 1957.
BÖTTIGER (J.) : Svenska Statens Samling af Wälda Tapeter (collection of Swedish State), 4 vol., Stockholm, 1895-1896. 16th- and 17th-century figure tapestries in private Swedish collections, Stockholm, 1928.
BOYER DE SAINTE-SUZANNE : Notes d'un Curieux sur les tapisseries tissées de haute ou basse lisse, 1876-1879.
CANTON (SANCHEZ P.) : Tapices de la Casa del Rey, Madrid, 1919.
CRICK-KUNTZIGER (M.) : Musées royaux d'Art et d'Histoire, catalogues des tapisseries, Brussels, 1956.
DEMOTTE : La Tapisserie gothique, Paris, 1922-1924.
DESTRÉE (J.) and VAN DE VEN (P.) : Musées royaux du Cinquantenaire, Les Tapisseries, Brussels, 1910.
DEVILLE (J.) : Recueil de statuts et de documents relatifs à la corporation des tapissiers de 1258 à 1875, Paris, 1875.
DIGBY (G. W.) : European Tapestries and Carpets in The Concise Encyclopædia of Antiques, vol. II, London, 1955.
DUBON (D.) : Tapestries from the Samuel H. Kress Collection at the Philadelphia Museum of Art. The History of Constantine the Great designed by Peter Paul Rubens and Pietro da Cortona, New York, 1964.
ERKELENS (A. M.) : Wandtapijten I. Late goteiken-Vroege Renaissance, Rijksmuseum, Amsterdam, 1962.
ESTELLA (E.) : Museo de tapices del Cabildo Metropolitano, Saragossa, 1948.
FLORISOONE (M.), HOFFMEISTER (A.), TABARD (F.) and VERLET (P.) : Le Grand Livre de la Tapisserie (Préface de Lurçat), Lausanne, 1965.
GÖBEL (H.) : Wandteppiche, 6 vol., Leipzig, 1923-1924.
GOLDSMITH (P. J.) : The Museum's Collection of Renaissance Tapestries, in Bulletin of the Metropolitan Museum of Art, 1947-1948.
GUIFFREY (J.) : Histoire de la Tapisserie depuis le Moyen Age jusqu'à nos jours, Tours, 1886. — Bibliographie critique de la tapisserie dans les différents pays de l'Europe depuis ses origines jusqu'à nos jours, Société des études historiques, 1904.
GUIFFREY (J.), MÜNTZ (E.), and PINCHART (A.) : Histoire générale de la Tapisserie, 3 vol., Paris, 1878-1884.
GUIMBAUD (L.) : La Tapisserie de haute et basse lisse, Paris 1962.
HAVARD (H.) : La Tapisserie, Paris, 1893.
HEINZ (D.) : Europäische Wandteppiche : I. Von den Angängen der Bildwirkerei bis zum Ende des XV Jahrhunderts, Brunswick, 1963.
HUNTER (G. L.) : Tapestries. Their Origin, History and Renaissance, New York, London, Toronto, 1912.
— Victoria and Albert Museum Catalogue of Tapestries, London, 1924.
— The Practical Book of Tapestries, London, Philadelphia, 1925.
JANNEAU (G.) : Evolution de la Tapisserie, Paris, 1947.
JANNEAU (G.), VERLET (P.), YVER (G.), WEIGERT (R. A.), FONTAINE (G.), and NICLAUSSE (J.) : La Tapisserie, Paris, 1942.
JARRY (M.) : Unknown Tapestries at the Mobilier National, in Burlington Magazine, January, 1966.
JUBINAL (A.) : Les Anciennes Tapisseries historiées ou Collections des Monuments les plus remarquables de ce genre qui soient restés du Moyen Age à partir du XIe au XVIe siècle inclusivement, 2 vol., Paris, 1818-1830.
KENDRICK (A. F.) : Victoria and Albert Museum, London, Dept. of Textiles, Catalogue of Tapestries, London, 1924.
MALE (E.) : L'Art religieux à la fin du Moyen Age en France. Etude sur l'iconographie du Moyen Age, Paris, 1908.
MARILLIER (H. C.) : The Tapestries at Hampton Court Palace, London, 1931.
MIGEON (G.) : Les Arts du Tissu, Paris, 1929.
MÜNTZ (E.) : La Tapisserie, Paris.
NICLAUSSE (J.) : Tapisseries et Tapis de la Ville de Paris, Paris, 1949.
PLANES (E.) : La Tapisserie gothique. Catalogue des pièces exposées au musée de la Manufacture des Gobelins, Paris, 1928.
PLOURIN (M. L.) : Historia del Tapiz en Occidente, Barcelona, 1955.
PUYVELDE (L. VAN) : Projets de Rubens et de Van Dyck pour les tapissiers, in Gazette des Beaux-Arts, March, 1961.
QUELLE (O.) : Der spanisch-portugiesische Kulturkreis auf Wiener Gobelins, Leipzig, 1940.

ROSSI (G. B.) : L'Arte dell' arazzo, Milan, 1907.
RORIMER (J. J.), and FORSYTH (W.) : The Medieval Galleries, in Bulletin of the Metropolitan Museum of Art, 1953-1954.
RORIMER (J. J.) : Medieval Tapestries. A Picture Book, New York, 1949.
SAVARY DES BRUSLONS (J.) : Dictionnaire universel de Commerce, d'Histoire naturelle et des Arts et Métiers, 5 vol., 1759-1765.
SCHMITZ (H.) : Bildteppiche, Berlin, 1919. Die Wiener Gobelinsammlung, Vienna, 1922.
SEVENSMA (W. S.) : Tapestries, London, 1965.
SPITZMÜLLER (A.) : Kunst aus Osterreich. Tapisserien, Bad Vöslau, 1956.
THOMAS (W. G.) : A History of Tapestry, London, 1930.
TORRALBA SORIANO (F.) : Los Tapices de Zaragoza, Saragossa, 1953.
VALENCIA (J. DE) : Tapices de la Corona de España, Madrid, 1903.
VIALE (M. and V.) : Arazzi e tappeti antichi, Turin, 1952.
VIATTE (G.) : Les Tapisseries du XVIe siècle, in L'Œil, no. 131, November, 1965.

Catalogues of recent exhibitions

Première Biennale internationale de la Tapisserie. Lausanne, 1962. Musée cantonal des Beaux-Arts.
Exposition internationale de Tapisserie contemporaine. Château de Culan, 1963.
Vienne à Versailles. Les grandes collections autrichiennes au Château de Versailles, 1964.
Cent chefs-d'œuvre du musée des Arts décoratifs, Paris, 1964.
Les Trésors des Églises de France. Musée des Arts décoratifs, Paris, 1965.
Deuxième Biennale internationale de la Tapisserie. Lausanne, 1965.
Le XVIe siècle européen. Tapisserie. Paris, Mobilier national, 1965-1966.
Tapisseries françaises et flamandes du XVIe siècle. Musée d'Arras, 1966.
Lorraine-Autriche. Chefs-d'œuvre du Kunsthistorisches Museum de Vienne. Musée de Lunéville, 1966.
Tapisseries du Moyen Age à nos jours. Strasbourg, ancienne Douane, 1966.

Works specially relating to tapestries mentioned and reproduced in this book

German and Swiss tapestry

APPUHN (H.) : Der Karls-Teppich in Halberstadt, in Aachener Kunstblätter, vol. 24/25, 1962-1963.
BASSERMANN-JORDAN (E.) : Die dekorative Malerei der Renaissance am Bayerischen Hof, Munich, 1900.
BURCKHARDT (R. F.) : Wandehang mit Liebesgarten in Basel um 1460-1470 gewirkt, in Jahresberichte des Historischen Museum zu Basel, 1921.
BURCKHARDT (R. F.) : Gewirkte Bildteppiche des XV and XVI Jahrhundert im Historischen Museum zu Basel, Leipzig, 1923.
GÖBEL (H.) : Die Geschichte Otto von Wittelsbachs, in Panthéon V, 1930.
GYSIN (F.) : Tapisseries suisses de l'Époque gothique, Basle, 1947.
HERMES (E.) : Der Dom zu Halberstadt. Seine Geschichte und seine Schätze, Halberstadt, 1896.
KURTH (G.) : Die deutsche Bildteppiche des Mittelalters, 3 vol., Vienna, 1926.
LANZ (J.) : Tapisseries gothiques, Lausanne.
LEGEN (F. VON DER), and SPANIER (A.) : Die altdeutschen Wandteppiche im Regensburger Rathaus, Ratisbon, 1910.
LUITPOLD VON BAYERN : Die fränkische Bildwirkerei, Munich, 1926.
MAYER (M.) : Geschichte der wandteppichfabriken des Wittelsbachischen Fürstenhauses, Munich-Leipzig, 1892.
MÜNCHENER GOBELIN MANUFAKTUR : Munich, 1948.
REINATE (J.) : Deutsche Textilkunst, Berlin, 1942. Deutsche Textilkunst, Krefeld, 1954.
WILCKENS (L.) : Nürnberger Wirkteppiche des Mittelalters, in Bilderhefte des germanischen Nationalmuseums, Nuremberg, 1965.
WYSZ (R. L.) : Bildteppiche des XV und XVI Jahrhunderts, Berne, 1955.

English tapestry

BARNARD (E.) and WACE (A.) : The Sheldon Tapestry Weavers and Their Work, Oxford, 1928.
KENDRICK (A. F.) : The Hatfield Tapestries of the Seasons. Walpole Society, Annual volume 11/89, 1913.
MARILLIER (H. C.) : English Tapestries of the eighteenth Century, London, 1930.
THOMSON (W. G.) : Tapestry Weaving in England, in The Art Journal, 1911-1912, English Tapestry, in Apollo, I, 1925.
VICTORIA AND ALBERT MUSEUM : Handbook of English Sixteenth-Century Tapestries (Tapestry Portfolio III), 1915.

Chinese tapestry

CAMMAN, SCHUYLER : Notes on the Origin of Chinese K'o-ssu, in Artibus-Asiæ, vol. XI, Ascona, 1948.
CAMMAN, SCHUYLER : Chinese Influence in Colonial Peruvian Tapestries, in Textile Museum Journal, I, no. 3, December 1964.
DUBOSC (J.-P.) : Contribution à l'étude des tapisseries de l'époque Song, in Artibus-Asiæ, vol. XI, Ascona, 1948.
FERGUSON : Survey of Chinese Art, Shanghai, 1939.
FRY (R.), RACKHAM (B.) and HENDRICK (A. F.) : Chinese Art, London, 1935.
GOLDSCHMIDT : Arts de la Chine, IV, Soieries, Tapis..., Fribourg, 1965.
HENRY (C.-A.) : Tapisseries et Soieries japonaises, 1941.
MAILEY (J.) : A Feng Huang in a Rock Garden, in Bulletin of the Metropolitan Museum of Art, Summer 1961.
PRIEST (A.) and SIMMONS (P.) : Chinese Textiles

(Metropolitan Museum of Art, New York), 1931.
SIMMONS (P.) : An Exhibition of Chinese Textiles, in Bulletin of the Metropolitan Museum of Art, June 1939.
SIMONS (P.) : An Interim Report on Ancient Textile Collections in Japan, in Bulletin de liaison CIETA, January 1962.
SMITH (HOWELL) : Brief Guide to the Chinese Woven Fabrics (Victoria and Albert Museum).
SOAME (JENYNE R.) : French version of D. LION.
SULLIVAN : Introduction to the History of Chinese Art.
TSUAN-TSO YINT HUA : Tapisseries et Broderies des dynasties Song, Yuan, Ming et Ch'ing du Musée National de Moukden, Tokyo, 1935.
VAN LE COQ : Chotscho, Berlin, 1913.
VUILLEUMIER (B.) : Tissus et Tapisseries de la Chine ancienne, in Revue de l'Art, 1936.
VUILLEUMER (B.) : Symbolism of Chinese Imperial Robes, London, 1939.
VUILLEUMER (B.) : History of the Technique of K'o-ssu.

Exhibition catalogues

Tapisseries et Tapis de la Chine du XIIe au XIXe siècle, Musée des Gobelins, Paris, 1936.
Illustrated Catalogue of the Chinese Government Exhibits for the International Exhibition of Chinese Art, London, 1936.
Catalogue de l'Exposition d'art chinois, Venice, 1954.
Catalogue of Chinese art treasure loaned from the Chinese.
National Palaces Museum and the Chinese National Central Museum, Washington, 1961-1962.
Catalogue Kayan Book, No. II, Textile in the Shosoin, 1964.

Coptic tapestry

BECKWITH (J.) : Koptische Textilien, in Ciba Rundschau, No. 145, 13/1959.
DU BOURGUET (P.) : La Technique des étoffes coptes en rapport avec leur datation, in Bulletin du CIETA, January 1966. Les Etoffes coptes du Musée du Louvre, Paris, 1966.
BRAULIK (A.) : Altägyptische Gewebe, 1900.
DIMAND (M.) : Coptic and Egypto-Arabic Textiles, in Bulletin of the Metropolitan Museum of Art, XVI, New York, 1931.
DIMAND (M.) : Die Ornamentik der ägyptischen Wollwirkereien, Leipzig, 1924.
GEIGER (A.) and THOMAS (E. B.) The Viminacium Gold Tapestry (Meddelenden Fran Lunds, Universitets Historiska Museum), 1964-1965.
GERSPACH (E.) : Les Tapisseries coptes, Paris, 1890.
PFISTER (R.) : Tissus coptes au Musée du Louvre, Paris, 1932.
RONCHAUD (L. DE) : La Tapisserie dans l'Antiquité, Paris, 1894.
WACE (ALAN J. B.) : Preliminary Historical Study. A Late Roman Tapestry from Egypt, Workshop (Textile Museum, Washington, No. 9), May 1954.
WULFF (O.) and VOLBACH (W.) : Spätantike und koptische Stoffe aus ägyptischen-Grafbunden, Berlin, 1926.

Exhibition catalogue

L'Art copte, Petit Palais, Paris, 1964.

Spanish tapestry

BOTTINEAU (Y.) : L'Art de cour dans l'Espagne de Philippe V (1700-1746), Bordeaux, 1962.
CRUZADA (V. D. G.) : Los tapices de Goya, Madrid, 1870.
DUGUE-TRAPIER (E.) : A Sketch by Francisco Bayeu y Subias for a Tapestry-Cartoon, in The Art Quarterly, XXVI, No. 3, Autumn 1963.

Flemish and Brussels tapestry

ALFASSA (P.) : Les Tapisseries des Chasses de Maximilien, in Gazette des Beaux-Arts, 1920.
BERTAUX (E.) : Les Tapisseries flamandes de Saragosse, in Gazette des Beaux-Arts, 1909.
BRUNARD (A.) : Les deux fragments de la tapisserie de la légende de Notre-Dame du Sablon au Musée communal de Bruxelles, in Bulletin des Musées de Belgique, 1962-1963.
CARLBERG (M.) and PAUWELS (H.) : Découverte de la marque du tapissier de l'Histoire de Jacob, in Bulletin des Musées royaux d'Art et d'Histoire, 33e année, Brussels, 1961.
CETTO (A. M.) : Der Berner Trajan und Herkenbald Teppich, Berne, 1966.
COLLOQUE INTERNATIONAL : Les Tapisseries flamandes aux XVIIe et XVIIIe siècles, Brussels, 1959.
CRICK-KUNTZIGER (M.) : Tapisserie de l'Histoire de Vertumne et Pomone, in Bulletin des Musées royaux d'Art et d'Histoire, Brussels, 1929.
CRICK-KUNTZIGER (M.) : Un Fragment inédit de la Bataille de Roncevaux, in Bulletin des Musées royaux d'Art et d'Histoire, Brussels, 1931.
CRICK-KUNTZIGER (M.) : La Tenture de la légende de Notre-Dame du Sablon, Antwerp, 1942.
CRICK-KUNTZIGER (M.) : Bernard van Orley et le décor mural en tapisserie (Société royale d'archéologie de Belgique), 1943.
CRICK-KUNTZIGER (M.) : Les Tapisseries de l'Hôtel de Ville de Bruxelles, Antwerp, 1944.
CRICK-KUNTZIGER (M.) : Une ancienne tapisserie de la suite bruxelloise de Tristan et Iseut, in Mescellanea Leo van Puyvelde, 1949.
CRICK-KUNTZIGER (M.) : Notes sur la tenture de l'Histoire de Jacob d'après Bernard van Orley, in Bulletin des Musées royaux d'Art et d'Histoire, Brussels, 1951.
CRICK-KUNTZIGER (M.) : La Tenture de l'Histoire de Jacob, d'après Bernard van Orley, Antwerp, 1954.
DENE (V.) : Tapisseries flamandes (Museum of Arts of the Rumanian Socialist Republic), Bucharest, 1966.
DENUCE (J.) : Les Tapisseries anversoises, Antwerp, 1936.
DESTRÉE (J.) : La Tonte des moutons, in Bulletin des Musées royaux d'Art et d'Histoire, Brussels, 1908.
DESTRÉE (J.) : Verdure. Tapisserie flamande du

XVIe siècle, in Bulletin des Musées royaux d'Art et d'Histoire, Brussels, 1942.
DIEZ (E.) : Ein Karton der "Giuochi di Putti" für Leo X, in Jahrbuch der Preussischen Kunst Sammlungen, 31, 1910.
DIGBY (W.) : The Restoration of the Devonshire Hunting Tapestries, in Victoria and Albert Museum Bulletin, July, 1966.
DUVERGER (J.) : Brüsselsche Legwerkers uit de XV de en XVI de eeuw, Gentsche Bijdragen, tot de Kunstgeschiedenis, 1934.
DUVERGER (J.) : Brussel als Kunstcentrum in de XIV de en XV de eeuw, Antwerp-Ghent, 1935.
DUVERGER (J.) : Tapijtkunst te Oudenaarde, Oudenaardse Schatten van Kunst en Geschiedenis, 1952.
DUVERGER (J.) : Jan de Haze en de Bourgondische-Wapentapitten Bern, in Artes Textiles, VI, Ghent, 1965.
EHRMANN (J.) : Caron et les tapisseries de Florence, in la Revue des Arts, 1952.
ERKELENS (A. M. L.) : Raphaeleske grotesken op Brusselse Wandtapijtseries, in Bulletin van Het Rijksmuseum, No. 4, 1962.
GEBAROWICS (M.) and MARKOWSKI (T.) : Arrasy Zygmunta (La collection de tapisseries du roi Sigismund Auguste), in Rocznik Krakowski, vol. 29, Cracow, 1937.
GILBERT (P.) : Les Tapisseries de la Victoire des Vertus, Brussels, 1964.
GILBERT (P.) : Les nouveaux panneaux de la tenture de Notre-Dame du Sablon aux Musées royaux d'Art et d'Histoire et au Musée communal de Bruxelles, in Bulletin des Musées de Belgique, 1962-1963.
HULLEBROECK (A.) : Histoire de la tapisserie à Audenarde du XVe au XVIIIe siècle, Renaix, 1938.
HULST, R. A. D' : Tapisseries flamandes, Brussels. 1960
JARRY, M. : New Testament Tapestries in St. John Malte's Triumphs after Rubens, in The Burlington Magazine, April 1960.
LE MAIRE (O.) : Les Portraits de François de Tassis dans les tapisseries de la légende de Notre-Dame du Sablon à Bruxelles, in Revue belge d'archéologie et d'histoire de l'art, 23, 1954.
LORIQUET (C.) : Tapisseries de la cathédrale de Reims, Paris, 1882.
MAROT (P.) : La Condamnation de Banquet, in Mémoires de la Société nationale des Antiquaires de France, séries 9, 3, 1954.
MAROT (P.) : La Condamnation de Banquet. La moralité et les tapisseries, in Mémoires de la Société des Antiquaires de France, 1955.
MORELOWSKI (M.) : Der Krakauer Schwanenritterteppich, in Jahrbuch der K. K. Zentral Kommission, VI, 1912.
MÜNTZ (E.) : Les Tapisseries de Raphaël au Vatican et dans les principaux musées de l'Europe, Paris, 1897.
POPE-HENNESSY (J.) : The Raphael Cartoons, Victoria and Albert Museum, London, 1950.
RORIMER (J. J.) : The Glorification of Charles VIII, in Bulletin of the Metropolitan Museum of Art, 1953-1954.
SANTOR (M.) : Les Tapisseries de Reims, Rheims, 1912.
SCHNEEBALG-PERELMAN : Les Sources de l'histoire de la tapisserie bruxelloise et la tapisserie en tant que source, in Annales de la Société royale d'archéologie de Bruxelles, IV, 1966.
SCHNEEBALG-PERELMAN : Le Retouchage dans la tapisserie bruxelloise ou les origines de l'édit impérial de 1544, in Annales de la Société royale d'archéologie de Bruxelles, L, 1961.
SCHNEIDER (A.) : Bemerkungen zu einigen niederlandischen Wirkteppichen des Bayerischen Nationalmuseums, in Münchener Jahrbuch der Bildenden Kunst, N. F., I, 1924.
SCHOUTHEETE DE TERVARENT, DE : Les Tapisseries de la Rédemption de Bruxelles, in Bulletin de l'Académie royale de Belgique, Classe des Beaux-Arts, XLVIII, 1966.
SOIL DE MORIANE (E.-J.) : Les Tapisseries de Tournai, 1892.
STEINMANN (E.) : Die Anordnung der Teppiche Raffaels in der Sixtinischen Kapelle, in Jahrbuch der Presussischen Kunstsammlungen, XXIII, 1902.
THOMAS (B.) : Die Wiener Tapisserien mit der Taten des Dom João de Castro in Indien und weitere Portugalensia in Wien, in Alte und Moderne Kunst, No. 83, 1965.
TOWNSEND (G.) : The Martyrdom of Saint Paul. A Fifteenth-Century Tapestry, in Bulletin of the Museum of Fine Arts, XXXVI, Boston, 1938.
VASQUEZ DE PRADO (V.) : Tapisseries et tableaux flamands en Espagne au XVIe siècle, in Annales (Economies, Sociétés, Civilisations), Paris, 1955.
WAUTERS (A. J.) : Tapisseries bruxelloises, Brussels, 1878.
WAUTERS (A. J.) : Jean van Roome, dit Jean de Bruxelles, Brussels, 1904.
WEESE (A.) : Die Cäsar-Teppiche im Historischen Museum zu Bern, Berne, 1911.
WYSS (R.) : Die Cäsarteppiche und ihr ikonographisches Verhältnis zur Illustration der "Faits des Romains" im 14 und 15 Jahrhundert, in Jahrbuch des Bernischen Historischen Museums in Bern, 1955-1956.
WYSS (R. L.) : Die Cäsarteppiche, Berne, 1957.
YATES (F.) : The Valois Tapestries, in Studies of the Warburg Institute, XXIII, London, 1959.

Exhibition Catalogues

Catalogue of the exhibition of Flemish tapestries of Spain, Ghent, 1959.

Catalogue of the exhibition of Trésors d'art d'Enghien, Enghien, 1964.

French tapestry

ACKERMAN (P.) : The Lady and the Unicorn, in The Burlington Magazine, LXVI, 1935.
AJALBERT (J.) : Beauvais. La Manufacture nationale de tapisseries, Paris, 1927.
ANTOINE (M.) : Les Manufactures de tapisseries des ducs de Lorraine au XVIIIe siècle, Nancy, 1965.
BACRI (J.) : La Tenture de la Vie de la Vierge de Notre-Dame de Beaune et son cartonnier Pierre Spicre, peintre bourguignon du XVe siècle, in Bulletin des musées de France, 1933.
BADIN (J.) : La Manufacture de tapisserie de Beauvais, Paris, 1909.

BASCHET (J.) : Tapisseries de France, Paris, 1947.
BAZIN (G.), LURÇAT (J.), PICART LE DOUX (J.), SAINT-SAENS (M.), DEGAND (L.), and TABARD (F.) : Muraille et laine, Paris, 1946.
CASSOU (J.), DAMAIN (M.) and MOUTARD-ULDRY (R.) : La Tapisserie française et les peintres cartonniers, Paris, 1957.
CRICK-KUNTZIGER (M.) : Un chef-d'œuvre inconnu du maître de la Dame à la Licorne, in Revue belge d'archéologie et d'histoire de l'art, XXIII, 1954.
DARCEL (A.) : Histoire et Description de la Manufacture nationale des Gobelins, Paris.
DAUTERMANN (C. C.), PARKER (J.) and STANDEN (APPLETON E.) : Decorative Art from the Samuel H. Kress Collection at the Metropolitan Museum of Art, New York, 1964.
DAYRAS (M.) : Les Tapisseries du presbytère d'Anglards-de-Salers, in Cahiers de la tapisserie, April, 1961.
DAYRAS (M.) : La Tapisserie marchoise aux XVe et XVIe siècles, in Mémoires de la Société nationale archéologique de la Creuse, XXXV, 1963.
DELESALLE (H.) : Les Tapisseries des Jeux russiens, in Bulletin de la Société de l'histoire de l'art français, 1941-1944.
DELESALLE (H.) : Tapisseries exposées à Beauvais pour le troisième centenaire de la manufacture royale (1664-1964), in Revue du Louvre et des musées de France, Nos. 4-5, 1965.
DENE (V.) : Tapiserii Franceze. Secolele XVII-XVIII, (Museum of Arts of the Rumanian Socialist Republic), Bucharest, 1964.
DESCŒURS (J.), and DODINET (R.) : Les Tapisseries d'Anglards-de-Salers (Cantal), XVIe siècle, in Revue de la Haute Auvergne, XXXVIII, 1962.
DIMIER (L.) : La Tenture de la Galerie de Fontainebleau à Vienne, in Gazette des Beaux-Arts, XVI, 1927.
DUMONTHIER (E.), : Les Tapisseries d'ameublement de la manufacture royale de Beauvais, Paris, 1921.
EHRMANN (J.) : Antoine Caron, peintre à la cour des Valois (1521-1599), Geneva, 1955. — Tapisserie et tableau inédits dans la série de la reine Artémise, in Bulletin de la Société de l'histoire de l'art français, 1964.
FELS (F.) : Les Vieilles Tapisseries françaises, 1924.
FENAILLE (M.) : Etat général des tapisseries de la manufacture des Gobelins, depuis son origine jusqu'à nos jours (1600-1900), 6 vol., Paris, 1903-1923.
FOUGÈRE (V.) : Tapisseries de notre temps, Paris, 1968.
FREEMAN (M.) : A New Room for the Unicorn Tapestries, in Bulletin of the Metropolitan Museum of Art, 1949.
GEFFROY (G.) : Les Gobelins, Paris.
GRANCSAY (S.) : Knights in Armor, in Bulletin of the Metropolitan Museum of Art, 1947-1948.
GUIFFREY (J.) : Nicolas Bataille, tapissier parisien du XIVe siècle, auteur de la tapisserie de l'Apocalypse d'Angers, in Mémoires de la Société d'Histoire de Paris et de l'Ile-de-France, X, 1877.
GUIFFREY (J.) : Histoire de la Tapisserie en France, Paris, 1878-1885.
GUIFFREY (J.) : Les Manufactures parisiennes de tapisseries au XVIIe siècle, Paris, 1892.
JANNEAU (G.), FONTAINE (G.), NICLAUSSE (J.) and VERLET (P.) : La Tapisserie française, Paris, 1947.
JARRY (M.) : The "Tenture des Indes" in the Palace of the Grand Master of the Order of Malta, in The Burlington Magazine, September 1958.
JARRY (M.) : « Les Indes, série triomphale de l'exotisme, » in Connaissance des Arts, May 1959.
JARRY (M.) : La Tenture des Rinceaux, in l'Œil, September 1963.
JARRY (M.) : Les Gobelins in the Early Twentieth Century, in Apollo, March 1967.
LACROCQ (L.) : Chronique des tapisseries anciennes d'Aubusson et de Felletin, in Bulletin Soc. archéol. histor. limousin, 1911-1927.
LANCKORONSKA (M.) : Wandteppiche für eine Fürstin. Die historische Persönlichkeit der « Dame mit dem Einhorn, » Frankfurt, 1965.
LEJARD (A.) : Les Tapisseries de l'Apocalypse de la cathédrale d'Angers, accompagnées du texte de Saint-Jean, Paris, 1942.
LEJARD (A.) : French Tapestry, London, 1946.
LESTOCQUOY (J.) : Origine et décadence de la tapisserie d'Arras, in Revue belge d'archéologie et d'histoire de l'art, 1940.
LURÇAT (J.) : Les Tapisseries du Chant du Monde, Annecy, 1963.
LURÇAT (J.) and KOZAKIEWICZ (J.) : L'Apoclaypse d'Angers, Angers, 1955.
MARGERIN : Les Tapisseries de verdure, de leur origine au milieu du XVIe siècle dans les ateliers d'Arras, de Tournai et d'Audenarde, in Bulletin des musées de France, 1932.
MARQUET DE VASSELOT (J.-J.) : Les Tapisseries dites « La Dame à la Licorne, » Paris, 1949.
MARQUET DE VASSELOT (J.-J.) : and WEIGERT (R.-A.) Bibliographie de la tapisserie, des tapis et de la broderie en France, Paris, 1935.
MARTIN (P.) : La Tapisserie royale des « Cerfs-volants, » in Bulletin monumental, CV, 1947.
MESSELET (J.) and WEIGERT (R.-A.) : Cinq siècles de tapisseries d'Aubusson, Paris, 1925.
MONTAGU (J.) : The Tapestries of Maincy and the Origin of the Gobelins, in Apollo, No. 7, September 1962.
NICLAUSSE (J.) : Chasses nouvelles de Monsieur Oudry, in Gazette des Beaux-Arts, May-June 1957.
NICLAUSSE (J.) and JANNEAU (G.) : Le Musée des Gobelins, Paris, 1938.
NICLAUSSE (J.) and JANNEAU (G.) : Le Musée des Gobelins. De la tapisserie décor à la tapisserie peinture. Paris, 1939.
PERATHON (C.) : Histoire d'Aubusson : le vicomté, la ville, les tapisseries, la maison d'Aubusson, Limoges, 1886.
PLANCHENAULT (R.) : Les Tapisseries d'Angers, Paris, 1955.
PLANCHENAULT (R.) : L'Apocalypse d'Angers, Paris, 1966.
RORIMER (J. J.) : The Unicorn Tapestries at the Cloisters, New York, 1946.
RORIMER (J. J.) : The Unicorn Tapestries Were Made for Anne of Brittany, in Bulletin of the Metropolitan Museum of Art, 1942.
RORIMER (J. J.) and FREEMAN (M.) : The Nine Heroes Tapestries at the Cloisters, New York, 1953.
ROSE (G.) : The Apocalypse Tapestries from Angers, in The Burlington Magazine, LXXXIX, 1947.

SALET (F.) : La Tapisserie française du Moyen Age à nos jours, Paris, 1946.
SOUCHAL (G) : Etudes sur la tapisserie parisienne. Règlements et technique des tapissiers sarrazinois, hauts lissiers et nostres (vers 1260 - vers 1350), in Bibliothèque de l'Ecole des Chartes, CXXIII, January-June 1965.
STANDEN (E. A.) : The Tapestries. Croome Court, in Bulletin of the Metropolitan Museum of Art, November 1959.
VERLET (P.) and SALET (F.) : The Lady and the Unicorn, Paris, 1961.
WEIGERT, (R.-A.) : Cinq siècles de tapisseries d'Aubusson, Paris, 1935.
WEIGERT (R.-A.) : Musée des Gobelins. Les belles tentures de la manufacture royale des Gobelins (1662-1792), Paris, 1937.
WEIGERT (R.-A.) : La Tapisserie française, Paris, 1956.
WEIGERT (R.-A.) : Les Commencements de la manufacture royale de Beauvais (1664-1705), in Gazette des Beaux-Arts, LXIV, December 1964.
WEIGERT (R.-A.) : La Tapisserie et le Tapis en France, Paris, 1964.

Catalogues of important exhibitions

La Tapisserie française du Moyen Age à nos jours, Paris, 1946.
La Tapisserie française du Moyen Age à nos jours, Brussels, 1947.
Chefs-d'œuvre des tapisseries de Beauvais du XVIIe siècle à nos jours, Arras, 1961.
Charles Le Brun. Musée des Gobelins, Paris, 1962.
Les Gobelins (1662-1962). Trois siècles de tapisserie française, Château de Coppet, 1962.
Les Tapisseries d'Aubusson et de Felletin, Arras, 1963.
Trois siècles de tapisseries de Beauvais, Beauvais, 1964.
Les Gobelins. Trois siècles de tapisseries, Mobilier national, Paris, 1966.
Chefs-d'œuvre de la tapisserie parisienne (1597-1662), Orangerie de Versailles, 1967.

Dutch tapestry

YSSELSTEYN (G. T. VAN) : Geschiedenis der Tapijtweverijan in de Noordelijke Nederland, Leyden, 1936.

Italian tapestry

GEISENHEIMER (H.) : Gli arazzi nella sala dei Dugento a Firenze, in Bollettino d'Arte, 1909.
SALMI (M.) : Il tesoro del Duomo di Milano, in Dedalo V, 1924-1925.
VIALE AND FERRERO (M.) : Arazzi italiani del cinquecento, Milan, 1963.
VIALE AND FERRERO (M.) : Arazzi italiani, Milan, 1951.
VIALE AND FERRERO (M.) : Mostra del Barroco Piemontese, 1963, II, Arazzi.

Norwegian tapestry

DEDEKAM (H.) : Baldisholtaeppet, Oslo, 1918.
DEDEKAM (H.) : Kunstindustri Museet i Oslo fenti aar, Oslo, 1926.
KIELLAND-THOR (B.) : Norsk Billednev (1550-1800), 2 vol., Oslo, 1953.

Peruvian tapestry

HARCOURT (Q. D.) : Les Textiles anciens du Pérou et leurs techniques, Paris, 1934.
JONES (J.) : Art of Empire. The Inca of Peru (The Museum of Primitive Art), New York, 1964.
MEANS-AINSWORTHY : A Study of Peruvian Textiles, Boston, 1932.

Catalogue :

Les tapisseries de l'ancien Pérou des origines au XVIIe siècle, Musée des Gobelins, 1935.

Polish tapestry

GRABOWSKI (J.), MARKIEWICZ and PLUTYNSKA (E.) : Tissus polonais, Warsaw, 1959.
MANKOWSKI (T.) : Tissus et Broderies polonaises des XVIe-XVIIIe siècles, Breslau, 1954.
PAGACZEWSKI (J.) : La Tapisserie en Pologne, Cracow, 1929.

Catalogue of tapestries reproduced

Color plates

Praying Figures and Cross (fragment). Coptic, 11th century. 10-11
Square with Nereids. Coptic, 6th century. 14
The Angers Apocalypse. Important personage beneath a canopy. 31
The Angers Apocalypse. The prostitute. St. Michael and the Dragon. The woman and the serpent. 33
The Angers Apocalypse. The Angel carries St. John away into the wilderness (detail). 37
The Capture of Jerusalem. Arras or Tournai (?), mid-14th century. 66-67
The Dance of the Wild Men and Women (detail). Tournai (?), second half of the 15th century. 92
The Legend of Our Lady of Le Sablon. The arrival in Brussels of the miraculous statuette. Brussels, about 1516-1518. 114-115
The Story of Perseus. Banks of the Loire or Flanders (?), late 15th century. 118-119
The Winged Stags. France, about 1430-1450. 122-123
The Triumphs of Petrarch. The Triumph of Love. France or Flanders, early 16th century. 126-127
The Planets. Mercury. Brussels, last third of the 16th century. 154-155
The Labors of Hercules. Hercules and one of Diomedes' stallions. Audenarde, second half of the 16th century. 163
The Story of Furious Roland (detail). Brussels or Delft, 1602. 196
Ensemble. 197
The Story of Artemisia. The Colossus of Rhodes. Paris, first half of the 17th century. 200-201
Rinceaux. The Peacock or Air. Paris, about 1650-1660. 205
The Story of the King. The King visiting the Gobelins factory. 1673-1680. 216
The Ancient Indies. The dappled horse or the Indian on horseback. Gobelins, 1689. 217
Les Ports de Mer (detail). Beauvais, end of the 17th century. 220-221
The Turkish Costume. The sultana ordering works from the odalisques. Gobelins, 1781-1784. 238
Second Chinese Set. Fishing. Beauvais, 1758. 242-243
The Story of Telemachus. The young hero dines with Calypso. Brussels, about 1725. 258-259
The Song of the World. Ornamentos Sagrados. 318-319
Rouen. Felletin. 322
King Lear. Gobelins, 1963. 326-327
Cartoon. Aubusson. 330-331
The Sunken Sky. Aubusson. 334
The Passage of the Red Sea (detail). Cracow, 1965. 335
Mutwilliges Trypticon (detail). Germany. 337
Hunter with a Net. Egypt. 341

Monochrome illustrations

Fish (fragment). Coptic, 2nd or 3rd century. 12
Medallion with Horsemen. Coptic, 5th-6th century. 13
Peruvian Tapestry (fragment). End of the Chimu period (900-1400). 16
Peruvian Tapestry (fragment). 17
Peruvian Tapestry (fragment). End of the Chimu period (900-1400). 17
Tapestry Braid or K'o-ssu (detail). China, about the 9th century. 18
K'o-ssu (fragment). China, Southern Sung period (1127-1279). 18
The Saint Gereon Tapestry (detail). Cologne, late 11th century. 20
Christ and the Apostles (detail). Lower Saxony, last quarter of the 12th century. 21
Abraham and the Archangel Michael. Lower Saxony, mid-12th century. 22-23
Charlemagne and the Philosophers. Convent of Quedlimburg, Lower Saxony, late 12th century. 24
The Months (detail of April). Norway, first half of the 12th century. 26
The Angers Apocalypse. The Revelation of St. John. 35
The Presentation in the Temple. Paris, last quarter of the 14th century. 38-39
The Nine Heroes. King Arthur. Paris, 14th century. 40-41
The Nine Heroes. David and Joshua. Paris, 14th century. 42
St. Maurice. Switzerland, first half of the 14th century. 44
Les Jeux. Alsace, last quarter of the 14th century. 46-47
Tapestries with Birds (detail). Germany, first half of the 14th century. 48
The Prophets. Franconia, late 14th century. 49
The Annunciation (detail). Arras (?), early 15th century. 52
Ensemble. 53
The Story of St. Piat and St. Eleuthère. Predication scene. Arras, 1402. 53
The Knight of the Swan. The knight Elias and his brothers. Tournai, mid-15th century. 54

The Passion. Christ bearing the Cross. The Crucifixion and Scenes from the glorious life of Christ. Arras (?), first quarter of the 15th century. 55
La Geste de Jourdain de Blaye. Arras (?), about 1390-1400. 56-57
Hunting Tapestries. Bear and beaver hunt (detail) and swan hunt. Arras or Tournai, mid-15th century. 60-61
Court Scenes (detail). Arras (?), about 1420. 62
The Story of St. Peter. The decapitation of St. Paul. Arras or Tournai (?), about 1460. 65
The Story of Strong King Clovis. Clovis attacking Ragnacaire. Assault of Soissons. Arras or Tournai (?), mid-15th century. 68-69
The Story of Strong King Clovis (detail). Face of a dead soldier. 70
The Battle of Roncevaux. Tournai, third quarter of the 15th century. 71
The Story of Caesar. The crossing of the Rubiçon and the battle against Pompey. Tournai (?), about 1465-1470. 72-73
The Justice of Trajan and Herkenbald or Archambault. Tournai, about 1460. Detail. 74-75
Herkenbald slashes his nephew's throat. 75
The Adoration of the Magi. Tournai (?), about 1440-1455. 76-77
The Seven Sacraments. Marriage (detail). Tournai, third quarter of the 15th century. 78-79
The Vengeance of the Rescuer. The imperial messenger before Pilate. Tournai, third quarter of the 15th century. 80
The Presentation of the Roses (detail). Tournai (?), about the mid-15th century. 81
Woodcutters. Tournai, third quarter of the 15th century. 82-83
The Story of Carrabara (or of the Egyptians). Sale of children. Tournai, late 15th century. 84
The Story of Carrabara (or of the Egyptians). Village fair scene. Tournai, late 15th century. 85
The Morality of Supper and Banquet. The feast given by Banquet. Tournai, early 16th century. 86-87
The Morality of Supper and Banquet (detail). Young man with his elbow on a sideboard. 88-89
Picking Oranges (detail). Tournai, late 15th century. 90
Sheep Shearing (detail). Tournai, about 1460-1475. 91
The Dance of the Wild Men and Women (ensemble). Tournai (?), second half of the 15th century. 94
Tapestry with the Arms of Charles the Bold (detail). Brussels (?), third quarter of the 15th century. 96
The Three Coronations. Northern France, third quarter of the 15th century. 98-99
The Adoration of the Magi (detail). Brussels (?), 1466-1488. 100-101
The Adoration of the Magi (ensemble). Brussels (?), 1466-1488. 102
The Life of Christ and the Virgin. Mary in the Temple. Brussels (?), early 16th century. 102
The Glorification of Christ known as the "Mazarin Tapestry." Brussels, about 1500. 105
The Mass of St. Gregory. Brussels, about 1500. 106-107
The Triumphs of Petrarch. The triumph of Fame over Death (detail). Brussels, about 1510-1520. 108-109
The Victory of the Virtues. Dance (detail). Brussels, about 1520. 110
The Story of the Redemption. The creation of the world. Brussels, about 1500-1515. 111
The Story of the Redemption. The creation of animals. Brussels, about 1500-1515. 112-113
The Lady with the Unicorn. Sight. Banks of the Loire workshop (?), late 15th century. 116
The Hunt of the Unicorn. The unicorn a prisoner (detail). France or Flanders, late 15th century. 120
The Angels Carrying the Instruments of the Passion. The angel of the whips and the column of the flagellation (detail). French workshop, after 1513. 121
The Life of Christ. The resurrected Christ appearing to Mary Magdalene. France or Flanders, 1516-1518. 124
Tapestry with Heraldic Décor (detail). France, itinerant workshop, about 1450. 125
The Lives of St. Gervais and St. Protais. The baptism of St. Gervais and St. Protais. France (?), early 16th century. 128
The Life of the Virgin. The Visitation and the Nativity. France (?), 1475-1500. 129
The Kings of Gaul. Belgius Jasius and Paris (detail). France, itinerant workshop (?), about 1530. 130-131
Eagle and Ostrich. Swiss, 15th century. 132
The Garden of Love. Basle, about 1460-1470. 134-135
The Legend of the Count of Savoy (fragment). Basle, about 1477. 134-135
The Combat of Vices and Virtues (detail). Nuremberg, about 1400. 135
The Story of Guillaume d'Orléans (detail) Germany, middle Rhineland, first quarter of the 15th century. 136
The Acts of the Apostles. The miraculous draught of fishes. Brussels, 1516-1519. 138
The Acts of the Apostles. The handing of the keys to St. Peter. Brussels,

1516-1519. 138-139
The Triumph of the Gods. The triumph of Venus. Brussels, about 1570. 140-141
The Hunts of the Emperor Maximilian. The boar's last attack (detail). Brussels, 1521-1533. 143
The Story of Jacob. Jacob receiving the blessing which Isaac meant for Esau. Brussels, second quarter of the 16th century. 144-145
The Seven Deadly Sins. Sloth (detail). Brussels, second half of the 16th century. 147
The Life and Exploits of Joao de Castro. The victory won at Goa over the King of Cambaja (detail). Brussels, late 16th century. 148
Charles V's Campaign Against the City of Tunis. The Emperor enters the harbor of Tunis with his galleys. Brussels, 1548-1554. 150-151
Vertumnus and Pomona. Vertumnus, disguised as a hay gatherer, approaches Pomona (detail). Brussels, the 16th century. 152
The Seven Virtues. Wisdom (detail). Brussels, second quarter of the 16th century. 153
The Valois. Water festivity at Fontainebleau. Brussels, about 1590. 156
Tristan and Isolde. Tristan and Morgain. Brussels, mid-16th century. 158
The Months with Grotesques. October (detail). Brussels, third quarter of the 16th century. 159
Scenes from the Book of Joshua (detail). Brussels, second quarter of the 16th century. 160-161
Jeux d'Enfants. Cupids playing in a garland of fruit. Ferrara or Mantua (?), about 1545. 164
The Story of Moses. The bronze serpent. Ferrara or Mantua, about 1545. 165
The Story of Joseph. Joseph sold by his brothers. Florence, 1549. 166-167
The Banquet. Florence, second half of the 16th century. 168-169
Tapestry of the Gallery of Fontainebleau. Danaë (detail). Fontainebleau, 1540-1550. 173
Tapestry of the Gallery of Fontainebleau. The death of Adonis. Fontainebleau, 1540-1550. 174-175
St. Walburga and Her Nuns. Eichstätt, first third of the 16th century. 177
Allegory of the Reformation (detail). Torgau, about 1550. 178
Throne Tapestry of Frederick II, King of Denmark. Elsinore, Denmark, 1585. 179
The Righteous Man and Christian Virtue. Nordtröndelag, Norway, about 1580. 180
The Story of the Kings of Sweden. King Sveno (detail). Kalmar, Sweden, about 1560. 181
The Kings of Denmark. King Frederick II and his son, Christian. Elsinore, Denmark, about 1584. 182-183
The Story of Decius Mus. The death of Decius. Brussels, about 1620-1625. 186-187
The New Testament. The triumph of divine love or charity. Brussels, 1700. 188
The New Testament. The triumph of the Catholic Church. Brussels, 1700. 190
Horsemanship. Execution of a pesade. Brussels, about 1650. 191
Scenes from Country Life. The manager's wife feeding the poultry (detail). Brussels, about 1635. 192
Transfer of the Relics of St. Augustine. Bruges, 1637. 194
Scenes from the Martyrdom of St. Gervais and St. Protais. The decapitation of St. Protais. Paris, Galerie du Louvre, about 1645. 198-199
The Old Testament. The daughter of Jephthah (detail). Paris, first half of the 17th century. 202
Ensemble. 203
The Life of the Virgin. The Nativity (detail). Paris, before 1657. 204
The Benediction of an Abbess. Charleville, about 1628. 206
Portière of Mars. Gobelins, late 17th century. 207
Les Enfants Jardiniers. Summer (two details). Gobelins, 1703-1704. 209-210
The Story of Alexander. The triumph of Alexander. Gobelins, 1664-1680. 212-213
The Months or the Royal Houses. Entrefenêtre : The new château of Saint-Germain. Gobelins, about 1680. 214
The Ancient Indies. The elephant or the horse Isabella. Gobelins, 1690. 218
The Conquests of the King of Sweden. The battle of Landskrona. Beauvais, 1699. 222
Grotesques. The rope dancer and the dromedary. Beauvais, about 1689. 223
Marine Triumphs. The triumph of Venus (detail). Paris and Beauvais, late 17th century. 224
Ensemble. 225
First Chinese Set. Pineapple Harvest. Beauvais, about 1725. 226
The Story of Don Quixote. Don Quixote is served by the duchess' ladies. Gobelins, 1776-1779. 228-229
The Hunts of Louis XV. The death of the stag in the Saint-Jean Pond. Gobelins, 1743-1745. 231
The Loves of the Gods. Venus at the forge of Vulcan (medallion detail). Gobelins, 1766-1771. 232-233
Russian Games. Bird hunting. Beauvais, 1771-1772. 235
The Story of Psyche. Psyche led by Zephyr into the palace of love. Beauvais, 1741. 237
The Iliad. Agamemnon refusing to return Chryseis to her father. Beauvais, second half of the 18th century. 239
The Loves of the Gods. The rape of Europa (detail). Beauvais, 1764. 244-245

Les Verdures d'Anglards-de-Salers. Combat between a lion and dogs (detail). Aubusson, second half of the 16th century. 246
The Pagoda. Aubusson, 18th century. 247
The Story of Daphnis and Chloë. Grape gathering where Daphnis and Chloë are admired. Aubusson, mid-18th century. 248
The Story of Charles V of Lorraine. The battle of Kahlenberg and the relief of Vienna (detail). Lorraine, 1724. 250-251
Portière with Turkish Trophies. Lunéville, about 1720. 252
Country Scenes. Foraging. Brussels, early 18th century. 254-255
The Story of the Duchy of Brabant. The abdication of Charles V in 1555. Brussels, 1717-1718. 257
The Months. May. Munich, 1604-1615. 261
The Story of Otto of Wittelsbach. Reception of the Greek ambassadors. Munich, 1611. 262-263
Two details. 264-265
The Story of the House of Wittelsbach. Coronation scene. Munich, 1726. 266-267
The Venetian Carnival. Harlequin's entry into Venice (detail). Würzburg 1740-1745. 268
Ensemble. 269
The Story of Constantine. The campaign against Licinius. Rome, 1635. 270-271
The Story of Constantine. Constantine fighting the lion. Rome, 1637. 272
The Four Seasons. Spring. England, 1611. 274-275
The Four Parts of the World. Asia. Florence, 1719. 277
The Acts of the Apostles. St. Peter and St. John healing the paralytic at the Temple gate. England, about 1630. 278-279
The Story of Hero and Leander. The meeting of Hero and Leander before the temple of Cythera (detail). England, 1628-1630. 280-281
The Naval Battle of Solebay. The English fleet engages in combat. England, about 1685. 282-283
The Martyrdom of St. Stanislas. Cracow, 1758. 284
Portrait of Peter the Great. Russia, about 1720. 285
The Hunts. Horses making a halt. Madrid, 1723. 287
The Story of Don Quixote. Madrid, about 1730. 288
Life in Madrid. El Cacharrero (the faïence merchant). Madrid, about 1794. 290
Peruvian Tapestry (detail). Peru, 17th century. 291
T'ung Fung Stealing the Peaches of Longevity. China, 1368-1644. 292
Phoenix in a Rock Garden (detail). China, late Ming period. 293
K'o-ssu : Feng Huang. China, 1622-1722. 294-295
K'o-ssu : The Feast of the Dragon (detail). China, Ming period. 296-297
Tsuzure : Horses. Japan, late 18th century. 298
Napoleonic Subjects. Napoleon receives the army deputies after his coronation (December 8, 1804). Gobelins, 1809. 301
Selene. Gobelins, 1877. 302
Basket of Fruit. Beauvais. 1831. 303
Poems, also Known as Apollo. Entrefenêtre : Marble vase. Gobelins, 1886-1888. 303
Angeli Laudantes. England, 1894. 304
Swans. Germany, 1896. 305
The Four Seasons. Holly or winter. Gobelins, 1910-1911. 306
Guilds. Les Brasseurs. Belgium, 1878-1879. 307
La Loge. Gobelins, 1923-1925. 308-309
The Rooster and Its Shadow. Aubusson. 310
Dawn. Aubusson. 311
The Four Elements. Water. Gobelins, 1944-1948. 312
June. Aubusson. 314
Signs of the Sky. Gobelins, 1962. 315
Polynesia. The sea. Beauvais, 1962. 316
Three Women Against a White Background. Aubusson. 317
Mont-Saint-Michel. Mont-Saint-Michel (No. 2). Gobelins, 1965. 320
Sarabande. Beauvais. 1965. 324
Panel No. 2. Beauvais, 1966. 325
Dolls. Gobelins, 1964. 328
The Men of the Sky. Beauvais, 1964. 329
Kalota I. Aubusson. 332
The Twelve Songs or the Hymn to Joy. The song of love. Aubusson. 333
Violet. Warsaw. 336
The Twins. Italy. 336
Bathers Beneath the Tent. Brussels, 1962. 338-339
Entrer dans le Bleu. Lebanon, 1965. 340

IMPRIMÉ EN FRANCE
PAR LES IMPRIMERIES DE BOBIGNY
ILLURTRATION ET SAPAO RÉUNIES
Dépôt légal n° 265 - 4e trimestre 1968.
23-81-1722-01